BETRAYED

How the Education Establishment Has Betrayed America and What You Can Do About It

Laurie H. Rogers

ROWMAN & LITTLEFIELD EDUCATION

A division of
ROWMAN & LITTLEFIELD PUBLISHERS, INC.
Lanham • New York • Toronto • Plymouth, UK

Published by Rowman & Littlefield Education
A division of Rowman & Littlefield Publishers, Inc.
A wholly owned subsidary of
The Rowman & Littlefield Publishing Group, Inc.
4501 Forbes Boulevard, Suite 200, Lanham, Maryland 20706
http://www.rowmaneducation.com

Estover Road, Plymouth PL6 7PY, United Kingdom

British Library Cataloguing in Publication Information Available

Library of Congress Cataloging-in-Publication Data

Rogers, Laurie H., 1961–
  Betrayed : how the education establishment has betrayed America and what you can do about it / Laurie H. Rogers.
    p. cm.
  Includes bibliographical references.
  ISBN 978-1-61048-044-4 (cloth : alk. paper) — ISBN 978-1-61048-045-1 (pbk. : alk. paper) — ISBN 978-1-61048-046-8 (electronic)
  1. Public schools—United States. 2. School improvement programs—United States. I. Title.
  LA217.2.R65 2010
  370.973—dc22

                                                                   2010042133

∞™ The paper used in this publication meets the minimum requirements of American National Standard for Information Sciences—Permanence of Paper for Printed Library Materials, ANSI/NISO Z39.48-1992.

Printed in the United States of America.

CONTENTS

PREFACE: WHY YOU SHOULD READ THIS BOOK vii

THANK YOU ix

1 BETRAYED 1

2 SOMETHING'S WRONG WITH PUBLIC
EDUCATION 5
 Where Are We As a Nation? 10
 Why You Should Care about the Math Problem 15

3 THE SQUARE OF EFFECTIVE LEARNING,
METT-TC, AND THE OODA LOOP 23
 METT-TC 27
 The OODA Loop 30

4 CORNER 1: THE TEACHER'S ABILITY
TO TEACH 33
 Teacher Training 33
 Master's of Education Degree 37
 Substitute Teachers and Student Teachers 39

5 CORNER 2: THE CURRICULUM 41
 Math As the Canary in the Coal Mine 41
 Reform Math in the Classroom 49

The Math Debates and the Big, Fat Lies   61
The NCTM, the NSF, and the Department
   of Education   76
Learning Standards   85
How Reform Curricula Are Adopted   89
Beware of the Delphi Technique   92
How to Influence a Curriculum Adoption Committee   96

6   **CORNER 3: THE LEARNING
ENVIRONMENT**   **105**
How Standardized Testing Affects Learning   107
Social Promotion   112
Equity versus Excellence   115
Inclusion versus Differentiated Instruction   120

7   **CORNER 4: THE STUDENT'S ABILITY
TO LEARN**   **129**
Turnabout Is Fair Play   132
Remediation and Tutoring   133

8   **ADMINISTRATIVE ACCOUNTABILITY**   **141**
Insubordination versus Coercion   142
School Boards: Checks and Balances   144
The Proof of Success Depends on Your Definition
   of "Success"   149

9   **DEALING WITH DIVERSIONARY ISSUES**   **175**
Divert Our Attention to Class Size   176
Divert Our Attention to Standardized Testing   182
Divert Our Attention to Money   192
Divert Our Attention to Technology   204
Divert Our Attention to No Child Left Behind   211
Divert Our Attention to National Standards,
   Tests, and Curricula   218

10   CONSEQUENCES TO THE STUDENTS
     AND THE NATION   227
     Why Parents Don't Speak Up   230
     Why Teachers Don't Speak Up   235

11   WHAT CAN BE DONE?   241
     Laurie Rogers's Wish List   242
     Asking Questions of Administrators   251

APPENDIX: ACRONYMS AND TERMS   257

REFERENCES   261

ABOUT THE AUTHOR   283

PREFACE:
WHY YOU SHOULD
READ THIS BOOK

If you have just picked up this book, you're wondering if you should read it. You should. The children and the country need your help.

Because of a failing public-education system, American children are at serious risk. Their situation puts the country at risk. These are not outrageous, excessive, or uninformed statements. The children are not being properly educated, and where they go, the country goes. Americans take their standard of living for granted, but this standard is not assured. Even if your children are homeschooled or privately schooled, the country's future will affect them.

Despite the estimated $658 billion spent on just one year of K–12 education, the system still fails our students. Many aren't learning sufficient arithmetic, algebra, grammar, spelling, civics, or history. They aren't being readied to take over the country. They aren't being prepared academically to begin college, start their own company, or begin a trade. About 30 percent drop out of high school. Of those who apply to attend college, up to 90 percent require extensive remediation.

Many administrators blame this on teachers, students, parents, legislation, money, or society. They rarely appear to accept blame themselves. Yet, ultimately, it is their responsibility. They and school board members make decisions, create budgets, buy curricula, accept federal taxpayer money (and the strings that go with it), set policy, and hire and fire. Whether they accept it or not, central-office administrators and school board members are where the buck stops.

This book is *not* a slam against teachers. Teachers have a tough job. Unless they rise up and take back their classrooms from those who have stolen them, it's only going to get tougher.

Teachers are now in the crosshairs, at substantial risk of being removed for "insubordination" or "ineffectiveness." As a rule, this author does not care for anonymous sources; however, you will find anonymous sources throughout the book. The fear in the Spokane Public Schools district, this author's base of operations, is widespread among teachers. Asked about this fear in 2008, the district superintendent said she wasn't surprised, and she began talking about good teachers and bad teachers. This author felt compelled to grant anonymity to those who asked.

This book does not discuss the unions. That discussion belongs in a different book. The investigation and discussion of union money, goals, lobbying, and leadership require more time and attention than this volume can provide. People have argued that teachers unions are the problem with public education, but teachers unions are not there to have an impact on the classroom. In theory, unions exist to represent the employment concerns of their members. The decision making in public schools does not—with respect to student learning—rest with unions.

In 2006, this author was just a parent, perplexed by the K–12 math program in Spokane, Washington. Asking questions of board directors led nowhere. Reporter instincts thus piqued, she interviewed a dozen people; pored over books, reports, and data; poked into dusty corners of the Internet; attended more school board meetings than she cares to recall (actually, just one would have been plenty); communicated with concerned parents and math advocates; enrolled in a remedial college math class; and spent several long months on a math curriculum adoption committee.

Not everyone can expend this kind of effort, but public education needs you. The children and the country need your help. You don't have to spend years getting up to speed. Read this book, and then please do what you can to take back the classroom from those who have stolen it.

THANK YOU

First, foremost and always: To Warren and Heather—the lights of my life and the rocks on which I stand. I couldn't have finished this without your love, faith, patience and support.

Many wonderful people contributed. My eloquent daughter is quoted throughout, at different stages of her schooling. She is not the only student quoted, however, and in an effort to protect all of the students, I have identified none of them.

Several people provided suggestions on drafts of this book. My husband can probably recite all seven hundred versions of it in his sleep. Thank you to Laura Brandt, parent and co-founder of Where's the Math?, and to professional engineer Dick Padrick, who went above and beyond multiple times for someone he's never even met. Thank you also to Ted Nutting, Breann Treffry, Heather Rogers, and several other teachers, advocates, professionals, and parents who provided thoughtful comment. (No reader is to blame for errors I accidentally left in.)

Several administrators agreed to taped interviews: Dr. Nancy Stowell, superintendent; Dr. Brian Benzel, former superintendent; Karin Short, associate superintendent of Teaching and Learning Services; Christine Querna, former board director; Debbie Oakley, former elementary curriculum coordinator; Rick Biggerstaff, secondary mathematics coordinator; and Dr. Jeff Bierman, board director. Almost without fail, central office staff members in Spokane Public Schools were helpful and professional, and I'm thanking them without naming them, which I'm sure will be a relief to them.

Several teachers and professionals met with me or exchanged e-mails. Thank you all for your kindness, including Dr. Sandra Stotsky, University of Arkansas; Dr. John Hattie, University of Auckland; Dr. David Klein, California State University, Northridge; Dr. David Geary, University of Missouri; Dr. Tom McKenzie, Gonzaga University; Dr. Shannon Overbay, Gonzaga; Dr. Lyle Cochran, Whitworth University; Jim Brady, Spokane Falls Community College; Andrew Holguin, businessman and philanthropist, and many others.

Thank you to Tom Koerner of Rowman & Littlefield Education for giving me a chance, and to the Rowman & Littlefield editors and production staff, who made this book a much more polished product.

I'm specially acknowledging the advocates, parents, and professionals who participate in the Where's the Math? Yahoo group. They're a constant source of new information, diverse perspective, and collegiality. Thank you to Jimmy Kilpatrick, Education News, for giving me an opportunity to be heard, and to Aaron Arnold, Preferred Transcription, for your generous nature and good work. Susan Wilson, public disclosure officer for Washington's Office of Superintendent of Public Instruction, responded promptly and professionally to all requests.

Except where otherwise noted, "administrator" refers to education decision makers and policy setters, and "education advocate" refers to people who work for more traditional approaches to education, especially relative to math instruction.

The fact that any of those listed here were willing to assist me or to share their views with me should not be construed to mean that they support some or all of my views, or that I speak for them. In fact, a few didn't agree with me at all (which helped me learn as well). I thank them all for their time, their willingness to participate, and for helping to bring light to the shadows.

1

BETRAYED

In a nutshell, here's what you should know about public education in America: Many things are right, but the wrong things vastly outweigh the right things. Fixing the wrong things can seem impossible, but don't despair. "Seems impossible" is not "impossible." This book details specific areas of policy failure—from ideology to administrative procedure. It also offers proven strategies for change—how to improve education; how to advocate for it; how to help the children, your community, and your country. Know this for sure: The situation is bad, but you aren't alone, and you aren't helpless.

Public education is a right idea that's being executed in a wrong fashion. This is not the fault of students, parents, or teachers. It's the fault of central-office administrators, colleges of education, government types, school board members, various businesses and associations, and lawmakers—all of whom collectively built, and zealously guard, this failing system. There are good decision makers in public education, but their numbers are too few, and their efforts are hampered and lessened by the weight of the others.

Decades of egotistic, opportunistic, politically motivated, and generally uninformed or misinformed decision making have left public education reformed and transformed half to death. Most parents don't grasp the full depth of the destruction, and they're given almost no voice in repairing the damage. That's because public education is a bureaucracy—a stubborn, close-minded, arrogant monolith that's almost impossible to budge. Advocating for effective change is a thankless task with few successes. The burnout rate for parent and teacher advocates is somewhere in the area of "dropping like flies."

Tip your hat to those who persist in buzzing and beating at the window, believing that some day, they'll find a way in. Some do get in.

Parents and teachers mustn't wait to be given these opportunities, however. Most would wait forever. Advocating for effective change is tough but necessary. The children trust in us to make the system work for them. It's their future on the line. It doesn't help them when we sit obediently on the sidelines, expecting things to magically turn out, or when we don't speak the truth about failing policy. Everyone's nervous about making waves, but someone must. Although teachers must advocate very carefully, their voice is vital.

This book describes how the country is being betrayed by an ego-inflated wall of well-paid administrators, bureaucrats, professors in colleges of education, politicians, and businesspeople, whose concern for children's academic skills takes a perennial backseat to their own interests. Curricula are weak, learning environments are distracting, students aren't ready for the material, and teachers are prevented from doing what they need to do.

This book offers ways to stand up and advocate for the children. The situation is dire. Barring intervention, your children—or children you know—are at substantial risk of requiring extensive remediation, dropping out, or growing up thinking they're incapable of learning.

It isn't disrespectful to want something better for children and teachers. It isn't a cheap shot to publicize what leaders say and do when we aren't looking or to point it out when they refuse to come clean. Advocates are optimistic, persistent, and dedicated. They care about the children's long-term welfare. They're also patriots. Our broken education system puts this country's stability in jeopardy. Debate is a good and healthy thing, and democracy rests easily on it. Advocates are willing to fight for the children and their country.

It's cynical and negative to just give up—to accept a rotten situation out of apathy, ignorance, self-interest, fear, or denial. If not us, then who? If not now, then when? It's good to be hopeful, and this is a book full of hope. But, as Gen. Gordon Sullivan wrote in his 1996 book *Hope Is Not a Method*, the solution requires more from us. If we are to change anything in public education, we need a method.

Teachers and parents don't have to accept the excuses we get from administrators—like this one: "That was just a lower class of students." From that, we're supposed to believe that the problem was a student failure, not a school failure. If we say, "When the children weren't taught . . . " administrators interject, "When the children didn't learn . . . " This isn't a subtle difference. Once you know how students are expected to learn—by teaching themselves—you understand the seismic gap between "failed to teach" and "failed to learn."

Here's another excuse: "We have so many low-income families." The message is that those students won't do as well. This insidious message carries statistical backing—many children from lower-income families *don't* do as well on tests. But statistics aren't children. Trends aren't a given. Low test scores shouldn't be an expected and accepted consequence of an economic condition. As an eighth grader said, "Starving kids in Africa can grow up to be doctors."

Over and over, however, test scores are blamed on teachers, students, and parents. It's happened so often that the phrase "struggling students" is now irritating. Students "struggle" to learn mostly because the education establishment refuses to acknowledge or act on the truth.

The children are being betrayed. At a time when they're most ready to learn, administrators and other decision makers condemn them to poorly supported policies, curricula, and methods of instruction—then turn around and blame the failure on them, their families, and their teachers. It's true that some children arrive with a poor attitude. Some parents could be more involved. Some societal trends are unhelpful. Some families don't take education seriously. Some teachers aren't as effective as they should be.

But K-12 instruction has been tinkered with and experimented on until it's practically impossible for public schools to work well for even the most dedicated teachers and families. Naturally, administrators steadfastly refuse to accept blame. They'd also rather, if you don't mind, that you left it at that and then left them alone, closing the door softly on your way out.

Don't leave it at that. Don't leave them alone. And if you're going to close the door on your way out, slam it.

2

SOMETHING'S WRONG WITH PUBLIC EDUCATION

"If an unfriendly foreign power had attempted to impose on America the mediocre educational performance that exists today, we might well have viewed it as an act of war. As it stands, we have allowed this to happen to ourselves. We have even squandered the gains in student achievement made in the wake of the Sputnik challenge. Moreover, we have dismantled essential support systems which helped make those gains possible. We have, in effect, been committing an act of unthinking, unilateral educational disarmament."

—*A Nation at Risk: The Imperative for Educational Reform*, 1983

American public education has not improved since *A Nation at Risk* was published in 1983. If anything, it has deteriorated further. If the situation in 1983 was comparable to an act of war, what is it comparable to today?

Let's begin with a discussion of what's right about American public education.

This country has the intention of educating everybody—all types of learners and children from families of all income levels. It wants to teach all ethnicities, whether they grew up speaking English, Spanish, Russian, or Canadian, eh. Everybody gets in, including populations once insensitively labeled. People aren't legally denied an education because of race, gender, disability, religious affiliation, or socioeconomic status. This is noteworthy and admirable in a world where these attitudes aren't universally held.

In addition, the learning content isn't set by gender. Girls aren't expected to take shorthand, typing, and home economics, regardless of their interests or skills; boys aren't automatically expected to engage in sports and "shop."

Many administrators in America work hard to improve the system. We can appreciate the dedication that went into their efforts, even if we think most of them have gone off in a wayward direction. Most working members in the field of education truly care. This group is filled with compassionate, hard-working teachers, principals, and school staff who spend their days working on behalf of students and parents.

American families also care about education. Many parents volunteer. Most children do their best every day. Collectively, this effort assists the system, helps with learning, and replenishes the nation.

Now, let's talk about what's wrong with American public education.

Across the country, a particular philosophy has a stranglehold on K–12 education. It's been sewn into the fabric of teacher education, promulgated as the answer to all concerns, and forced into schools and classrooms and down the throats of principals, teachers, parents, and children. This philosophy says it encourages other ways of thinking, and yet for years it has been closed to contrary views. It values self-esteem over achievement, group effort over individual success, and equal outcomes for all (regardless of how mediocre) over individual outcomes that include brilliance by some.

In American education, it's customary and acceptable to say that children naturally "struggle" with math or reading, don't understand science, or just aren't that good in school. Before students ever have a chance to think it, education decision makers have thought it, said it, accepted it, and incorporated it into their programs, watering them down so they aren't so hard. In today's public school system, everyone must learn the same things in the same way with the same packaged curriculum, and they must all get to the same place at the same time so they can all take the same tests on the same day.

Academic gifts are cherished in theory, yet often actively discouraged in practice. Superior talents of any sort are frequently not given room to shine. Ironically, this system that is built almost entirely on the concept of self-esteem is actually the antithesis of self-esteem, having produced an entire generation of children who can't cope with basic academic tasks. It's also the antithesis of excellence, competitiveness, and innovation.

Many public school students can't do basic mathematical, scientific, or literary activities that are reasonable for their age. In elementary school, they don't progress from addition to multiplication. In middle school, they can't multiply in vertical formats, do long division, or convert fractions into decimals. They don't read at grade level. They come out of high school not ready for college and also lacking sufficient knowledge in the untested subjects, such as civics, history, economics, debate, foreign languages, social studies, art, music, health and fitness, geography, and communication.

In 2010, this author was startled to learn that middle school students in Spokane, Washington, didn't seem to know grammar. An informal survey showed that no one could define an adverb, a conjunction, or a past participle. No one could conjugate a verb or point out a preposition. No one could demarcate a sentence, identifying the subject and the predicate. Asked when grammar was taught in Spokane Public Schools, Associate Superintendent Karin Short said it was "taught in all grades" and "embedded in the language arts curriculum."

But students said they didn't get specific instruction in grammar. Language arts classes were filled with group projects, they said. Grammar was supposed to be "intuitive."

According to A. Habash's 2008 Education Trust report, "Counting on Graduation: An Agenda for State Leadership," the United States is the "only industrialized country in the world in which today's young people are less likely than their parents to have completed high school."

Of those who do graduate from high school, however, a substantial majority must take remedial classes if they move on to college, vocational school, or the military. As a consequence, an increasing number of parents perceive public schools to be inadequate for their children. Some choose to supplement the program; others leave, sending their children to private schools, alternative schools, or private tutors. Some teach their children at home. Oddly, despite the exodus, education decision makers have a really hard time saying anything is wrong. Give us more time, they say. Give us more money. Give us a break.

Some of the most egregious problems in public education had their origin in federally sponsored activities that took place decades ago. Other problems are being created now, particularly in mathematics. Because mathematics is a straightforward subject that should be easy to teach and test, this book focuses on the math-education problem.

This is not to blithely dismiss other weaknesses in the typical K–12 curriculum. College English professors know that K–12 students aren't learning proper grammar. Political science professors know they aren't learning enough civics. History professors know they aren't learning enough history. Those subjects are mentioned in later chapters, but the math problem is crystal clear, and serves as a solid framework for demonstrating how public education has gone seriously awry.

School districts nationwide have adopted "reform" approaches to mathematics. These approaches downplay (or avoid) "traditional" procedures, equations, practice, and memorization. The teacher is supposed to guide, not teach. Reform depends on constructivism (also known as "inquiry" or "discovery learning"), where students work in groups and on their own to "construct" or "discover" their own knowledge and methods for solving problems. Reform math focuses less on accuracy, efficiency, and achievement than on student-constructed strategies.

Reform comes under many names: "problem based," "standards based," "inquiry based," "discovery based," "student centered," "NSF funded," and so forth. This book mentions three non-reform textbook series: *Saxon Math*, particularly the older editions; *Holt Mathematics*, a hybrid (or "balanced") series; and *Singapore Math*. As of this writing, this author considers all others named within to be "reform," to greater or lesser degrees.

The folks selling, promoting, or supporting reform math include curriculum developers; publishers; federal, state, and local governments; and other organizations that have a vested interest in seeing reform adopted nationwide. Developers and publishers have practical and financial government support as they sell their products. Meanwhile, many state and central-office administrators work hard to justify, explain, and deny the public's negative experiences with these products and approaches.

- Even as students fail to learn basic math skills (evidenced by dismal scores on state, national, and international standardized tests and evaluations), the administrators deny that children aren't getting what they need from public schools.
- Even as families disappear from public schools and the numbers of privately educated and homeschooled students increase, administrators deny that families are disgruntled by the failed programs and are voting with their feet.
- Even as dropout and remediation rates show that students are not academically proficient, administrators issue reams of carefully selected numbers as "proof" that they are.
- Even as engineers, giants of industry, and mathematicians speak out against reform math—and even as standards and curricula are reviewed and replaced—administrators deny that reform math is flawed, and they continue to waste taxpayer dollars on it.
- Stop by your local community college or university and find out the percentage of recent high school graduates who require remedial (or "refresher") math courses before enrolling in college-level math classes. The remedial courses will take extra time and money to teach information that should already have been learned.

This national catastrophe is unlikely to improve any time soon. The education establishment is insular, the issues are major, and the ideology is ingrained in the system. Ego, money, and social-engineering agendas all have roles to play. In all of the administrator-produced data and supposed "best-practices" materials floating around, there is very little truth. There are, however, hundreds of billions of taxpayer dollars being spent and made.

American taxpayers spend too much on public education and achieve too little. It's a frustrating story, but don't fret. The story can have a different ending. All it takes is you.

WHERE ARE WE AS A NATION?

"Our approach is working for students. According to NAEP, more reading progress was made by 9-year-olds from 1999 to 2004 than in the previous 28 years combined. Math scores have reached record highs across the board. History scores improved in all three grade levels tested—fourth, eighth and 12th. And the number of students taking an Advanced Placement exam in high school has risen 39 percent since 2000."

—Former U.S. secretary of education Margaret Spellings, in a 2007 *Washington Post* op-ed

The above quotation from former U.S. secretary of education Margaret Spellings (2007c) paints a rosy picture of a grim situation. It ignores the country's generally poor math and science knowledge, dropping pass rates on Advanced Placement exams, weak on-time graduation rates, high remediation rates in college, and high dropout rates.

Statistics are thrown at parents and teachers every year, and most of them tell us things are getting better, scores are going up, and students are achieving. As students fail the tests, drop out of school, or test into remedial courses, what are we to believe? That it's just our child, our class, our district, or just us with a problem? Many administrators say, "This is the first time I've ever heard this." Don't believe it.

In the fall of 2008, frustrated by an inability to get through to administrators in Spokane, this author began writing an online blog called Betrayed. The e-mail list grew by word of mouth to include people from all across the country, as well as from Australia, New Zealand, England, and Canada. It's helpful to band together. Advocates have to know enough about the issues to stand tall in the face of the well-rehearsed excuses and massaged statistics. Despite what we're consistently told, things are not okay, we are not the problem, we are not alone in our concerns, and we are not the first to speak up.

Comparison of High School Transcripts and the National Assessment of Educational Progress

In 2007, the U.S. Department of Education (ED) found that high school students were taking more high school credits and college-preparatory classes and obtaining higher average GPAs than in years past. And yet, the ED found, those improvements did not translate into commensurate successes on a national test.

Researchers compared two reports: one on twenty-six thousand high school transcripts from 2005 and another on data from the 2005 National Assessment of Educational Progress (NAEP), a standardized test given to twenty-one thousand twelfth graders. The results conflicted. The transcript study found that students had 360 more hours of instruction in 2005 than in 1990; classes were supposedly at a higher level in 2005 than in 1990; and students received "significantly" better grades in 2005 than in 1990. And yet, according to the 2005 NAEP, twelfth-grade students were having trouble achieving "proficiency" in reading and math (Shettle et al. 2007).

NAEP scores fall into one of three categories. "Basic skill" constitutes "partial mastery of the knowledge and skills that are fundamental for proficient work at a given grade." "Proficient skill" indicates "solid academic performance," that students have shown competency over "challenging" material. "Advanced skill" constitutes "superior performance."

On the 2005 twelfth-grade NAEP,

- overall twelfth-grade reading scores dropped since 1992 for all groups except the top achievers in the ninetieth percentile;
- in reading, 27 percent scored below "basic," and just 35 percent scored at or above "proficient";
- in reading, 43 percent of white students scored at or above "proficient," compared with just 20 percent of Hispanic students and 16 percent of black students;
- in math, 39 percent scored below "basic," and just 23 percent scored at or above "proficient";
- in math, 29 percent of white students scored at or above "proficient," compared with just 8 percent of Hispanic students and 6 percent of black students (Grigg, Donahue, and Dion 2007).

This should be a major alarm bell. People in education should look at these results and say, "What we're doing must not be working." The ED said further study was needed to determine why the data conflicted, but only so many things could have happened:

- The NAEP grading was unfair.
- The NAEP material was confusing or inappropriately difficult.
- The high school grades were vastly inflated.
- The high school courses were based on weak content.
- The people who did the comparison didn't do it properly.

These reports are part of a pattern. A different ED report ("Mapping Washington's Educational Progress 2008" n.d.) compared results of state testing against the 2007 NAEP. Again, there was a significant disparity between state reports and NAEP data.

In March 2008, the National Mathematics Advisory Panel issued "Foundations for Success: The Final Report of the National Mathematics Advisory Panel." Created in 2006 by a presidential order, the panel was to take the country's temperature with respect to mathematics education. The report said, in part, that students need more emphasis on fractions, algebra, and math facts and that America is falling behind internationally: "International and domestic comparisons show that American students have not been succeeding in the mathematical part of their education at anything like a level expected of an international leader. Particularly disturbing is the consistency of findings that American students achieve in mathematics at a mediocre level by comparison to peers worldwide."

It's strange that American students tend to rank lower than students in smaller, more challenged countries. With our resources, Americans should be at the top, or near the top, of any international comparison. And yet, they often score closer to the bottom of the field.

The first thing to understand is that many reports on international studies are "norm referenced." Students are compared against other students, not against a standard of knowledge. While helpful, such comparisons don't tell us what students know. It's hardly a feather in our cap to rank high if no one is doing well. Second, international studies are large and well supported, but they don't include all, or even most, of our students. Third, we don't have clear data on the participants' background. How many were taught in private, military, or charter schools? How many were tutored, taught at home, or educated outside of their country of residence?

Although these international studies provide an imperfect picture of American public education, they nevertheless have something important to tell us. America's tendency to rank lower in international studies is the result of a serious problem.

The Program for International Student Assessment

The Organization for Economic Cooperation and Development's (OECD) Program for International Student Assessment (PISA) tests fifteen-year-olds in reading, mathematics, and science literacy. Conducted every three years, each study assesses all three subjects—but one each time in depth. (The results of the 2009 PISA will be released in December 2010.)

In 2006, the PISA's emphasis was primarily on science. In science, the United States was twenty-ninth out of fifty-seven countries, scoring an average of 489 (on a scale of 0 to 1,000), just above the Slovak Republic's 488 and well below Finland's top score of 563 (Lemke et al. 2004). America's average of 489 was lower than the PISA average score of 500. In mathematics, it was worse. America was thirty-fifth out of fifty-seven countries, scoring an average of 474, just above Croatia's 467 and well below Chinese Taipei's top score of 549. America's 474 was below the PISA average of 498.

The Trends in Mathematics and Science Study

The Trends in Mathematics and Science Study (TIMSS) tests fourth and eighth graders every four years in math and science. Figure 2.1 shows some results from the 2007 TIMSS.

Looking at the rankings, one might say, "Hey, that's not too bad." A press release from the ED suggested that things must be getting

Grade	Subject	U.S. Ranking Compared to Other Participants/Countries	Average U.S. Score	Top-Scoring Locales
4th	Math	11th of 36	529	Hong Kong: 607
4th	Science	8th of 36	539	Singapore: 587
8th	Math	9th of 48	508	Chinese Taipei: 598
8th	Science	11th of 48	520	Singapore: 567

Figure 2.1. Comparison of 2007 U.S. TIMSS scores.

Notes: Score Range = 0–1000. Data collection for the TIMSS 2011 survey begins in Fall 2010. *Source:* Data extracted from TIMSS & PIRLS International Study Center, http://www.timss.org

better ("American Students Show Steady Progress in Math" 2008). But that release spoke only of rankings and didn't discuss ability. So let's do that.

The TIMSS uses a four-point scale. In descending order, the scale begins with "advanced," then "high," "intermediate," and "low." In fourth-grade math, "advanced" skill is defined in this way:

> Students can apply their understanding and knowledge in a variety of relatively complex situations and explain their reasoning. They can apply proportional reasoning in a variety of contexts. They demonstrate a developing understanding of fractions and decimals. They can select appropriate information to solve multistep word problems. They can formulate or select a rule for a relationship. Students can apply geometric knowledge of a range of two- and three-dimensional shapes in a variety of situations. They can organize, interpret, and represent data to solve problems. (Gonzales et al. 2008)

We want our students to be able to do all of that. They should have it nailed, too, considering America's decades-long commitment to conceptual understanding and problem solving in mathematics. But our students do not have it nailed.

In math, 60 percent of American fourth graders and 69 percent of American eighth graders could not achieve better than the "intermediate" level.

Meanwhile, nearly half of eighth graders in Taiwan, Korea, and Singapore scored at the "advanced" level of math in 2007. In contrast, just 10 percent of American fourth graders and 6 percent of American eighth graders achieved "advanced" skill.

In science, 53 percent of American fourth graders and 62 percent of our eighth graders could not achieve better than the "intermediate" level.

Meanwhile, 36 percent of fourth graders in Singapore and 32 percent of their eighth graders achieved "advanced" skill in science. In contrast, just 15 percent of American fourth graders and 10 percent of our eighth graders achieved "advanced" skill.

Some people say it's okay for America to fall behind internationally. This is a big country, with a large, diverse population. Many students take tests in a language that isn't their native language. Additionally, some countries encourage lower-performing students to move into a trade or vocational school, whereas America's policy is to provide a basic, standardized education to all children (thus opening up the testing process to a broader group).

Others say those "reasons" are just excuses. Every child deserves the best education possible, and America is better positioned than most to provide it. International studies are instructive because they tell us that our education system is weaker than the ones in other countries and that our graduates compete with people who are better prepared.

American graduates—and this country—will continue to pay for a flawed vision that's perpetuated by colleges of education, researchers, businesses, the federal government, states, and local education systems. That vision will haunt the hallways in schools and businesses for generations. For most of these children, what's been done to them has been done forever. It's a tragedy, but more than that, it's a betrayal.

WHY YOU SHOULD CARE ABOUT THE MATH PROBLEM

"Math education isn't just about a school subject. It's fundamentally about the chances that real people all across this country will have in life. And it's about the well-being and safety of the nation."

—Dr. Larry R. Faulkner, chair of the National Mathematics Advisory Panel, in a *Washington Post* article (Glod 2008)

An ongoing debate in education is over the math skills needed to graduate. Advocates know that career choice largely determines which skills are "necessary" and that not all graduates need calculus. What we don't know is who does need it. No one—not even students themselves—can accurately predict career paths or college attendance. Therefore, all students need strong basic math skills, and to give them maximum flexibility, divergences in math courses should come late in their education.

But these discussions are often one-sided, pursued by advocates. Administrators seem to prefer the comfort of vagueness and generalities, speaking glowingly of things like conceptual understanding, real-world application, and twenty-first-century skills (whatever those are).

When advocates say high school graduates are ill prepared for college math, we're told, "Not everyone will go to college." This is technically true but not an answer to our concern.

When advocates say the country's long-term welfare depends on students gaining skills that are largely taught in college, we're told, "Many good careers don't require a college degree." Again, true but not a sufficient answer.

When advocates point to careers that require college, we're told that some students don't want advanced math classes. Again, true. Some don't. But those who do face a nearly insurmountable challenge. Many try those classes and fail. Others don't try.

All students should be on the same college math track for as long as possible. At some point in high school, they should be allowed to take alternate tracks, but all students require arithmetic skills, number sense, standard algorithms, algebra, and geometry. These skills should be ingrained and automatic. The world doesn't have the time or inclination to wait for graduates to "discover" their own methods. Dr. Shannon Overbay, associate professor at Gonzaga University, said the entire K–12 math curriculum prepares students for future careers:

> These basic skills are the foundation upon which advanced work in logic and philosophy, science, law, mathematics, engineering, business, and many other areas is based. . . . I have received many e-mails from professors in philosophy, chemistry, law, biology, economics, business, and engineering who have become increasingly concerned with the lack of

student proficiency in algebra and their inability to construct a logical proof or derive a basic mathematical formula.

The fewer math skills graduates have, the fewer career options they have. Without sufficient math, career paths tumble out of reach: statistician, electrician, plumber, carpenter, engineer, draftsman, surgeon, and so many others. N. R. Augustine's 2007 National Academy of Sciences report "Is America Falling Off the Flat Earth?" provides an enlightening (and alarming) look at how America has largely ceded its place in growth and production to other countries.

A few decision makers realize that if students are to really learn algebra, it must be introduced earlier than high school. Efforts to do that, however, aren't wholly successful—largely because students head into those algebra classes without necessary arithmetic skills. In a press release for his report "The Misplaced Math Student: Lost in Eighth-Grade Algebra," Dr. Tom Loveless of the Brookings Institution put it this way: "The 'democratization of algebra' sounds like a worthy goal—it certainly stems from good intentions"; however, "when a large number of students who don't even know basic arithmetic are placed in classes with students several grade levels ahead of them, the result is false democratization. That's bad for the misplaced students, and it's bad for their well-prepared classmates too" ("New Study Shows" 2008).

The building blocks for algebra must be laid in elementary school and built up carefully and steadily. Algebra isn't just a process; it's a way of thinking. According to Dr. Lyle Cochran, chair of the math and computer science department at Whitworth University, "Algebra is the backbone of everything we do in freshman calculus courses on up in college." It's "the language of science," he added.

Besides the issue of getting into college, math skills play a role in success at college. In 1999, Clifford Adelman, senior research analyst at the U.S. Department of Education, studied potential influences on success in obtaining bachelor's degrees at four-year colleges. He found that high school graduates who took math beyond Algebra II were likely to earn a degree at twice the rate of other graduates. No other high school subject had "such an obvious and powerful relationship to ultimate completion of degrees as the highest level of mathematics [that] one studies in high school," he said.

And yet, some administrators and instructors don't connect college math with K–12 math. In 2009, about half of the students in a remedial algebra class at a local college melted away before the end of the semester. Asked about the dropouts, an instructor there refused to criticize K–12 instruction, instead blaming students for not wanting to learn. No support was given for the comment. The students were in the class, intending to learn. The fact that they couldn't handle the remedial class might not have been their fault; yet, they were blamed.

The Trades

Administrators say not every student wants to go to college, and that's true. Some want to begin a trade. They'll need math skills there too. People entering the trades should be able to add, subtract, multiply, and divide with whole numbers, fractions, and decimals—and they should know how to convert between fractions, percents, and decimals. Several trades professionals interviewed for this book commented that new applicants seem to lack necessary arithmetic skills.

Eventually, workers need aspects of algebra, geometry, and trigonometry. Calculators are used in the trades, but it's important to first know the underlying math. Otherwise, workers won't know if their calculation is correct or even close. One trades professional, who wishes to remain anonymous, said many new applicants come in questioning their academic ability, but most are actually capable learners who just need a different approach. They were "treated differently in the education system and so they end up living down to that level of expectation," he said.

There is a shortage of skilled craftspeople in every trade, all across the country, the professional said. "We've stopped shop classes in many of the high schools, they don't have them anymore like they used to, and so there's no exposure to those options." The average age of skilled craftsmen is currently between forty-eight and fifty years old, he said. Over the next decade, those experienced workers will start retiring, and "there aren't people in the pipeline to pick up the slack and take their place."

Business

Shortages are hitting business as well. It isn't necessarily a shortage of qualified applicants; it's a shortage of qualified American applicants. In particular, companies are desperately searching for employees with math skills.

In its flyer "Math & Science Matter: The World Is Waiting," advocacy group College & Work Ready Agenda said, "The number of jobs requiring technical training is growing 5 times faster than other occupations." And yet in 2005, the group said, twenty-six thousand Washington State employers couldn't find sufficient numbers of applicants with enough math skills to fill even entry-level positions ("Math & Science Matter" n.d.). In 2006, twelve members of the College & Work Ready Agenda wrote a letter to state legislators asking for early-learning programs, improved math and science education, more degree fields, and better support for public research universities:

> Math and science are the foundation of the innovation economy, however, our state's requirements for instruction and achievement in these areas are not adequate to prepare today's students for college and work. Research indicates that all students need to leave high school having learned content through at least Algebra II and, to succeed in college, to have taken math in their senior year of high school. And yet, a large percentage of Washington's high school juniors have been unable to demonstrate competency of even pre-Algebra skills. . . . This glaring disconnect requires a bold response. (Brunell et al. 2006)

America faces a shortfall in homegrown scientists and engineers. Insufficient numbers of American college graduates will be on hand to replace the ones about to retire.

In 2006, the Commission on Professionals in Science and Technology (CPST) said that, from 1966 to 2006, there was "a significant decrease in the proportion of doctorates earned by U.S. citizens and permanent residents in STEM [science, technology, engineering, and mathematics] fields" ("A Forty Year Analysis" 2006). In 1966, the CPST said, Americans earned 83.5 percent of "all STEM doctorates awarded" in the United States; by 2004, it was just 59.8 percent.

The slide in doctorates appears likely to continue. Between 2001 and 2006, CPST said, "enrollments in bachelor's programs in computer science dropped 40 percent" ("Policymakers Urged to Take a Closer Look" 2007).

Bill Gates, cofounder of Microsoft, has been vocal about the country's desperate need for scientists and engineers, even testifying before Congress about his difficulty in filling highly skilled positions. Companies like Microsoft, Google, and Verizon, as well as defense and aeronautics companies, compete for American college graduates who are technologically capable and mathematically inclined. Through his foundation, Gates has donated to reform-minded education programs and is among business professionals who have pushed for more relaxed immigration policies so they can hire more freely from other countries.

For defense and aeronautics, the shortages of scientists, mathematicians, and engineers are especially acute. Many employees must obtain security clearances; often, government policy is to hire Americans. Foreign nationals can be hired in some positions, but the process is cumbersome, and there is always the risk they'll have other allegiances. In an October 2008 speech, Defense Secretary Robert Gates blamed a "brain drain" for the "bleak" outlook he has for the security of America's nuclear weapons.

Desperate, some companies and professional organizations visit the schools to incite interest and build future employees. It isn't difficult to get young students to picture themselves as scientists, architects, carpenters, and engineers. They have a natural enjoyment of math and science—indeed, the subjects are built for them. STEM fields and the trades are logical and reasonable, and they allow for curiosity, experimentation, and cool results. Children appreciate problems that result in clear answers. They like to work with their hands and think creatively. They don't want to work in groups to recreate thousands of years of mathematics.

Awakening their interest in math and science isn't the problem. Getting K–12 schools to teach the subjects properly is a problem. Because so many districts refuse to do it, the problem then becomes retaining the children's interest. Despite the allegedly "fun" nature of discovery, it's off-putting to children. The approach isn't logical, clear, or efficient, and its inherent assumption is an insult. "Real math is too hard for you," it whispers. "You won't understand it."

Even if some children do enjoy constant discovery and group work, in the end, they aren't learning enough mathematics. Take a look at any old math textbook and compare the knowledge that was expected seventy to one hundred years ago against the knowledge that's expected now. Despite the adoration reformers profess for "21st Century" knowledge, technology, and toys, they have sent America into a mathematical Dark Ages.

On February 9, 2008, Bruce Williams, managing principal of Geo-Engineers and chair of the K–12 Committee for Greater Spokane Inc., spoke at a public forum attended by the district and state superintendents. He issued a call to the community, asking for high-quality K–12 math and science instruction:

> We want to be competitive both locally and internationally, and we need problem solvers. . . . As an employer, I'm looking for engineers and scientists, and quite frankly there aren't that many around in undergraduate or graduate school that are available for employment. . . . I go into college campuses and I'd say anywhere from a quarter to half of the students in the engineering programs are foreign born, with those students fully intending to leave the U.S. after receiving their degree to practice in their home country. The competition for those qualified students that plan to be available for employment in the U.S. market is very fierce.

Williams said some high school students shared with him their concern about competing against people from other states and countries. Those students felt they were not challenged in STEM-related classes and believed students from other states and countries were better prepared for college science and engineering course work.

With increasing "wait lists" at universities and booming numbers of foreign applicants who have money and skills, the students are wise to be concerned. Shall we do the math? More foreign students + enough tuition money + better math and science skills = a tough road ahead for American students. This isn't just a problem for the students. It's a threat to the nation.

The executive summary of the 2008 National Mathematics Advisory Panel report says, "Much of the commentary on mathematics and science in the United States focuses on national economic competitiveness and the economic well-being of citizens and enterprises. There is reason enough for concern about these matters, but it is yet more fundamental to recognize that the safety of the nation and the quality of life—not just the prosperity of the nation—are at issue."

Our children's future is on the line, and their future is the country's future.

3

THE SQUARE OF EFFECTIVE LEARNING, METT-TC, AND THE OODA LOOP

In America, enough local, state, and federal taxpayer money is spent each year on education to nearly fund private educations for every child. According to appendix 3 of the U.S. Department of Education's "FY 2011 Budget Summary," the total projected expenditure in 2009–2010 for elementary and secondary education from all sources is $664 billion. This is $28 billion more than the U.S. Department of Defense spent in 2009 ("Department of Defense Funding Highlights" n.d.). And still, state and district administrators claim to need truckloads more just to keep the doors open. That's because they keep wasting money on diversionary issues.

Diversionary issues suck up time, money, and resources, while giving little or nothing back in terms of student learning. In chapter 9, we'll look at six of them:

1. Class size
2. Standardized testing
3. Money
4. Technology
5. The No Child Left Behind Act
6. National standards, tests, and curricula

There are others, but keep these six in mind as you read through the next sections on issues that *are* relevant to students' academic learning. The constant diversion away from what's relevant to the classroom is why teachers and parents rarely see improvements in the classroom.

Taxpayers dutifully vote for bonds and levies for "our kiddos," and we watch as record numbers of federal taxpayer dollars go to education. We aren't told where all of the money goes, but billions pay for things that are extraneous to student academics—software, calculators, laptops, SMART Boards, conferences, studies, panels, committees, standardized testing, administrative travel, constant "professional development," building improvements, social programs, area directors, instructional coaches, central-office administrators and assistants, and old and new federal requirements—to name just a few.

(We aren't generally asked to fund administrative pay raises, yet frequently—even amid budget cuts—they somehow manage to sneak their way in there too.)

Many districts have a problem with ineffective learning environments and poor curricula, yet their administrators stubbornly refuse to publicly criticize the learning environment or curriculum. Spokane, the second-largest school district in Washington State, has deteriorating pass rates on state math tests and outrageously high remediation rates in math in college—and yet, to hear central-office administrators talk, the constant curricula changes are because of changes in the state standards, not because they chose badly.

If we had a few dollars for every proposal for "fixing" education that ignored the problem of weak curricula, we could rein in the national debt. It's as if they're in a cult.

"It's about the curriculum," advocates say.

"We really need education to be fully funded," they say.

"It's the curriculum," advocates say.

"Most of our district families are lower income."

"It's the curriculum, curriculum, curriculum!"

"If the state would stop messing with the standards. If the kids didn't have so many challenges. If we had better teachers. If parents were more involved."

At a February 2010 town hall meeting put on by a state representative, Spokane's superintendent blamed the district's nearly 30 percent dropout rate on changes in the state learning standards. Others at the meeting blamed parents, social issues, and funding. A few attendees tried to talk about the curriculum issue, but those efforts were snuffed out.

A February 25 *Spokesman-Review* article reported that the Spokane school board had appointed an advisory group to determine how to improve middle school and hopefully reduce the dropout rate (Lawrence-Turner 2010c). A community member said the whole community bore responsibility for the dropout rate. No one said anything about curriculum.

Getting anyone to criticize the curriculum is like trying to force together the north poles of two magnets. But curriculum directly affects what happens in the classroom. It's one of the four elements that make up the Square of Effective Learning.

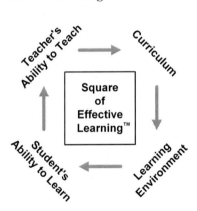

This author developed the concept of the Square of Effective Learning to illustrate a "square" of factors having a direct and consistent impact on how well students absorb information or learn a skill. It holds true for all students, whether they're in kindergarten, college, professional athletics, or basic training. Other factors play a role—sometimes a major role—but these four are immediate, dramatic, and critical to the learning process.

The four corners of the Square are as follows:

1. Teacher's ability and motivation to teach: How well trained is the teacher in content and teaching methodology? Is the teaching approach effective? How capable is the teacher? How interested?
2. Quality and effectiveness of the curriculum: How well does the material cover the subject? Is the material designed for the capabilities of the target group?
3. Effectiveness of the learning environment: How much opportunity is there to learn and practice the material? How much distraction is there?
4. Student's ability and motivation to learn: How well prepared is the student for the material? How capable is the student? How interested?

When a student learns, these four factors have worked for that student. The process is simple: The effective teacher teaches the motivated student with the effective curriculum in the focused and effective learning environment. Efforts to improve learning must necessarily have a positive impact on one of these factors. If they don't, they'll only line someone's wallet or fluff someone's ego. Compare these four factors with places where taxpayer money typically goes.

Building improvements, for example, might indirectly affect the learning process by making the staff happier or more comfortable or by bringing in or retaining people, but they aren't required for classroom learning. Calculators? Not required. SMART Boards? Not required. Conferences and new data systems? Not required.

Administrators continually blame parents for a supposed lack of participation, but parent participation is only helpful, not required. Parents can be absent, in jail, dead, abusive, drunk, or addicted to drugs—and students can still learn. It happens every day all over the world.

Effective curricula and an effective learning environment, however, are requirements. Students and teachers can be as prepared as they like, but if these two corners of the Square are inadequate, students won't learn what they need to learn.

Other countries lacking America's substantial resources and infra-structure somehow manage to provide solid educations to their citizenry. They might have self-inflicted distractions and complications—different ones from America's—yet they are managing to focus on the four areas that are critical to learning: teacher, curriculum, environment, and student.

When American union leaders, legislators, administrators, and policy wonks talk about how to "fix" public education, take a moment to map their proposals against the Square of Effective Learning. Typically, what they want is extraneous to the Square.

METT-TC

It's instructive to look at how other large organizations manage themselves. The U.S. military, for example, conducts complex, dangerous, and precise operations involving large numbers of diverse people. Its success is measured—not in effort—but in accomplishment. When the mission doesn't go as planned, troops can die. The military therefore tries to avoid the "gray area" (where things are murky) and "mission creep" (where additional duties are layered onto the original mission).

There are six critical considerations in conducting a military mission, summed up by the acronym "METT-TC," articulated in the Army Research Laboratory's *Cognitive Representations of Battlespace Complexity: Six Fundamental Variables of Combat* (Cook et al. 2000). The acronym can help frame the discussion of K–12 public education. It stands for the following:

1. Mission: the who, what, when, where, and why of the primary task
2. Enemy: the capabilities and likely courses of action of the opposition or threat, along with the impacts of their troops, positions, morale, reserves, and tactics
3. Troops and support: troop quantity, combat experience, level of training and morale, availability of quality support (beans, bullets, boots, cooks, doctors, etc.)

4. Terrain and weather: the impact of the terrain and weather on the capabilities of both friendly and enemy capabilities to shoot, move, and communicate
5. Time available: all aspects of time management, including co-ordination and planning, preparation and reconnaissance, and completion of specific actions
6. Civil considerations: all other factors not noted above that could affect the mission, including politics, economics, area stability, media, cultures and subcultures, power groups, ethics and mor-als, allies, partners and neutrals, nongovernmental organizations, refugees, humanitarian assistance, rules of engagement regard-ing civilians. (Legal considerations also can be added here.)

Our most pressing problem in public education is that students aren't learning what they *need to* learn. The second most pressing problem is that students aren't learning what they *could* learn. The solutions to those problems must entail things that directly affect the Square of Effective Learning. Applying the six critical considerations noted above, we can see right away where public education goes awry.

Mission: Many administrators have lost sight of their mission, their primary task, which is to educate the children in academics to a point where they can move on to successful postsecondary lives. We know administrators are failing in this because of the high dropout rates and college remediation rates around the country. Not only have they lost sight of their mission, but a bunch are quick to argue whether academ-ics is the mission.

"Not everyone needs to go to college," they say. "Not everyone will or should go to college." Granted. These statements are technically true, even if they're being used as excuses. We also hear, "Not everyone needs algebra." "Students don't need arithmetic skills—they have calculators." "They don't need to know how to spell—they have spell checkers." "They don't need to remember facts—they have the Internet."

These statements are shortsighted and incorrect. Skills build on skills. Ignoring the need for basic skills when teaching academics is like ignor-ing the need for a foundation when building a house. Additionally, basic skills are required for college, careers, and life. These truths are immaterial to people who believe that the point of education is to teach values, work together for a common cause, build social skills, and create nice people. But it's the parents' job to raise the children. If schools are to be effective, they must focus on their mission and stay out of ours.

Even as they fail to focus on their primary mission, school districts operate day cares, food programs, self-esteem programs, diversity-awareness programs, field trips, parties, fund-raisers, assemblies, and other nonacademic activities. In early 2010, Washington Senate Bill 6696 "encouraged" schools to make room for food banks, clothing banks, and dental care. It's good to have social services for children in need, but hosting them in public schools is "mission creep." It drains time and resources away from schools' primary mission.

If that weren't bad enough, public education has become its own "gray area." Classroom curricula deliberately deemphasize the memorization of math facts, practicing of skills, and right answers. This is supposed to foster improved self-esteem, but the students are not fooled. A critical piece of the learning process is knowing when one has been successful. Uncertainty breeds worry, resistance, and lowered self-esteem.

Enemy: In public education, the "enemy" is ignorance, reflected and perpetuated in an undereducated populace. This enemy is a danger to the children's future and to the well-being of the country. Unfortunately, the enemy has collaborators—people who are motivated not by the mission but instead by social agendas, self-interest, ego, and politics.

Troops and support: Despite the billions spent annually on teacher "supports" (computers, calculators, supplementary materials, coaches, and aides), the best teacher supports are good curricula, a distraction-free classroom, and strong content knowledge. Many teachers have acknowledged the weakness of their college education programs: heavy in psychology and teaching methodology ("pedagogy") and weak in academic content. New teachers, therefore, head into their classrooms insufficiently prepared.

When they get to the classroom, "professional development" for teachers continues to focus on pedagogy, not on subject content. Thus, teachers are filled to the brim with educational theory on how to "guide" the students but are often woefully unprepared in content. It's a betrayal of their trust and professionalism. (For more, see chapter 4, "Corner 1: The Teacher's Ability to Teach"). Teachers also are prevented from developing their own curricula. What they're given, therefore, must be top quality. But in the sections on curriculum, you'll see that it isn't—and why.

Terrain and weather: Administrators tend to blame poor academic results on "social problems," education's version of "terrain and weather." It's a way to distract the public. No administrator can fix poverty, drug abuse, poor parenting, excessive television watching, video game playing, lack of exercise, poor nutrition, medical problems, and student attitudes. Therefore, if administrators can convince the public to blame social issues for weak academic outcomes, they can shrug their shoulders and be excused from responsibility.

Administrators obviously must consider social issues while fulfilling their mission, but they've allowed and encouraged social issues to become both the excuse and the mission. Ironically, if they focused on their primary mission—academics—their success could serve to mitigate some of the social problems. ("Give me a fish" versus "teach me to fish.") It happens just like that, every day, around the world.

Time available: Schools only have six hours a day, 180 days a year, for twelve or thirteen years to teach students the academics they need in order to move on to a successful postsecondary life. Schools fritter away a great deal of this precious time on activities unrelated to academics. Every distraction adds up, and the time that's left is insufficient.

Civil considerations: Administrators spend an enormous amount of time and effort on budgets, legal issues, and politics. While these areas are important, they're ancillary to the primary mission. Focusing on them will not improve actual student outcomes.

School administrators would hear all of the above from teachers and parents if they actually engaged in a proper feedback loop with their publics.

THE OODA LOOP

Every organization must evaluate itself and determine where it needs to modify behavior. In the U.S. military, this is often known as the OODA Loop.

The following explanation of the OODA Loop is simplistic and lightly drawn so as to provide a framework for understanding the decision-making process in public education. For a deeper understanding of Col. John Boyd's fascinating military model, please refer to the more nuanced explanation found in books about Colonel Boyd, such as Robert Coram's *Boyd: The Fighter Pilot Who Changed the Art of War* (2004).

Colonel Boyd, a U.S. Air Force fighter pilot, hypothesized that organisms go through a constant process of interaction with and evaluation of their environments, allowing the organisms, in part, to adapt their behavior to changing circumstances—and thus survive. Colonel Boyd suggested four overlapping processes:

1. Observation: collection of data and information through the senses
2. Orientation: analysis of input to form an up-to-date perspective
3. Decision: determination of a course of action based on this new perspective
4. Action: physical action that is based on the decision

Orientation is a critical aspect of the OODA Loop because it encompasses culture, personal experience, genetics, prior knowledge and beliefs, and the ability to assess information and data. These factors filter information obtained through observation, thus shaping decision making and action. Who we are determines what we think and want to do.

Relative to the best course of action being taken in education, however, this author believes the critical piece is observation. Done properly, observation results in a constant reassessment of one's orientation and the modification of one's understanding. Sometimes it's a slight tweak; other times it's a completely new point of view. In education, this is the piece that frequently gets neglected in everyone's haste to get over to orientation, the piece that feels most important to us as individuals.

In public education, the loop tends to get stuck in ODA-ODA-ODA, with lots of orienting, decision making, and action but insufficient amounts of honest, open, and unbiased observation. When all incoming data point to the need for a new framework, many education administrators simply reject this data and cling to the old one.

It's easier to ignore contrary data, which is why so many administrators don't welcome feedback from the most important "stakeholders"—teachers, parents, and students. Without this input from the folks at the "pointy end of the spear," however, administrators tend to muddle around in herds of similarly minded people, tossing increasingly whacky ideas at the problems, unable and unwilling to see the necessary destination, much less head for it.

Open, honest feedback is critical. Administrators shouldn't try to control or contain it. They should welcome feedback at any and all points in the process. Teachers, parents, and students must be the observation and the honest feedback that a strong education system requires. Don't blindly trust administrators to do what's right for you. Speak up. Tell them what you need, and don't accept platitudes. Make them hear you.

The rest of this book has been structured around the Square of Effective Learning. The first corner of that square is "the teacher's ability to teach."

4

CORNER 1:
THE TEACHER'S
ABILITY TO TEACH

The first corner of the Square of Effective Learning is the teacher. Administrators say, "The textbook doesn't matter; it's all about the teaching." (They usually say this when people are criticizing the textbook—or the lack of one.) Textbooks matter, but teachers also matter—to what students learn, how well they learn it, and whether they enjoy learning it.

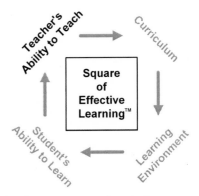

Besides being educators, teachers are substitute parents for six hours a day—no less so for older students than for younger ones. Our children are in their care.

But teachers get it from all sides. They have a difficult job, and each grade has its challenges. It's a hard-knock life. Their job is complicated by the lack of core content in many teacher-education programs. It's a shame because research and common sense tell us that teachers who know subject content are better able to teach it to others.

TEACHER TRAINING

There's a strong correlation between teachers' knowledge and student success. You might say, "Well, of course," but this point is argued in the education community. In fact, the idea that teachers should even teach is argued in the education community. Administrators say, "We want teachers to be the guide on the side, not the sage on the stage." Advocates say, "Teachers should *teach*," and some administrators reply, "You just don't understand."

A degree in education is not the same as a degree in subject content. The first is more about how to teach a subject. The second is *about* a subject. Many college education programs focus too much on how to teach and not enough on what to teach. Consequently, new teachers often graduate with insufficient training in subject content.

In 2010, a local student teacher told her second-grade class that President Abraham Lincoln fought and died in the Civil War. A seven-year-old corrected her. A local middle school math teacher did an Internet search for the slope-intercept formula (in front of his class) because he wasn't sure about it. Many teachers have serious knowledge gaps like these in grammar, civics, history, science, and mathematics. Perhaps the situation is intentional. Follow along over thirteen years of warnings:

1997: In a press release for its 1997 study *Different Drummers: How Teachers of Teachers View Public Education*, Public Agenda found that, of nine hundred professors of education, 86 percent believed it's more important for aspiring teachers to "struggle with the process of finding the right answers than knowing the right answer" ("Professors of Education" 1997). Fifty-seven percent thought that children who used calculators from the beginning would have better problem-solving skills. Just 55 percent would require high school graduates to demonstrate proficiency in "spelling, grammar, and punctuation." Sixty percent wanted "less emphasis on memorization" in the classroom.

2005: Dr. Sandra Stotsky is a professor of Education Reform and holds the Twenty-first Century Chair in Teacher Quality at the University of Arkansas. She's on the Common Core Validation Committee and was a member of the 2008 National Mathematics Advisory Panel. In 2005, she wrote that schools of education are "a major part of the problem," not the solution, and that they're responsible for three critical issues facing public schools:

- Teachers, especially those in K–8, haven't gained an adequate academic background in the subjects they're supposed to teach.
- Colleges and universities aren't providing public schools with sufficient numbers of "academically qualified teachers" for core secondary school subjects.
- "Education schools do not train prospective teachers how to teach."

"Instead," Dr. Stotsky wrote, "they arm new teachers with a host of pseudo-teaching strategies like small group work, and with the philosophy that students should 'construct their own knowledge' and are more capable of shaping their own intellectual growth than teachers if they are sufficiently motivated by 'inquiry.'" Meanwhile, Dr. Stotsky said, schools of education often disparage scientifically based evidence as "positivistic and irrelevant," rejecting scientific research that supports systematic and explicit instruction in reading, practicing skills, and providing "highly structured teaching" for at-risk children.

"They thus mistrain those who are preparing to teach in costly licensure programs," she said, "and continue to mistrain them in even more costly professional development programs."

2008: In a 2008 report for the National Council on Teacher Quality titled "No Common Denominator: The Preparation of Elementary Teachers in Mathematics by America's Education Schools," J. Greenberg and K. Walsh found that teachers were ill prepared to teach math, having received insufficient math instruction in college. The problem becomes a "treadmill," the report said. "We fail to teach mathematics well, and our weak students become the next generation of adults, some of whom become the teachers who produce the next crop of weak students."

In 2008, the National Mathematics Advisory Panel said that teacher-education programs should focus more on traditional aspects of math such as whole numbers, fractions, geometry, measurement, and algebra. Besides knowing the math for their own grade, teachers also must understand the "connections" to concepts taught before and after that level.

Dr. David Geary is Curators' Professor and Thomas Jefferson Professor at the University of Missouri and was chair of the panel's subcommittee on learning processes. In his closing remarks to the panel, he addressed the issue of teacher education:

> On reflection I must conclude that the necessity of these panels arises because of a failure of schools of education in this country, and many professors in these institutions, to do what the country has asked of them: Produce quality educators for our children, and train them with sound, proven, educational practices that are scientifically research-based. . . . Schools of Education must take the lead on developing and scientifically testing educational interventions, and we need to hold them accountable for the success or failure of their work.

2010: In April 2010, researchers at Michigan State University released "Breaking the Cycle: An International Comparison of U.S. Mathematics Teacher Preparation" (Babcock et al. 2010).

This study of thirty-three hundred future math teachers is an extension of an international study in sixteen countries. In the study, the math knowledge of American students in education programs placed far below the knowledge of future teachers in high-achieving countries like Singapore and Taiwan. In other countries, an average of 80 to 100 percent of future middle school math teachers took advanced math courses such as linear algebra and calculus, whereas in America, just 50 to 60 percent did. America's overall grade in this study of future math teachers was a C.

"U.S. future teachers are getting weak training mathematically," the report said, "and are just not prepared to teach the demanding mathematics curriculum we need especially for middle schools if we hope to compete internationally."

Public education is based on low expectations—for students and teachers. It's why administrators barely bat an eye when parents are concerned about a 50 percent pass rate on a test that's based on low-level content and that requires just 56 percent to pass. It's why many administrators don't require teachers (or staff) to have strong backgrounds in academic content.

Teachers are being betrayed. They can't know something they weren't taught. They weren't taught it because it wasn't required, and it wasn't required because certain college decision makers don't believe it's necessary.

MASTER'S OF EDUCATION DEGREE

Frequently, teachers receive additional pay for master's degrees. Some teachers believe their master's degree helped them in the classroom; others say it didn't. But not all master's degrees are created equal. Dr. Marguerite Roza concluded in her 2007 report "Frozen Assets" that master's degrees in math or science are beneficial for math and science teachers but that other master's degrees (such as education) seem to yield little benefit to student learning.

Dr. Sandra Stotsky also is critical of the typical master's of education degree, calling it "an academically impoverished set of courses touting a body of 'professional' knowledge that has little, if any, support from credible research."

In 2007, the Washington State Institute for Public Policy concluded, based on a statistical summary of research articles, that there was no "consistent relationship between teachers with graduate degrees and increased student outcomes as measured by test scores" (Aos, Miller, and Pennucci 2007).

The hard work that goes into earning a master's degree should be respected, but if the point of paying extra for a master's degree is to encourage teachers to gain more knowledge in order to better help the students, then the knowledge must be pertinent. A Spokane math teacher said he isn't proud of his master's degree in education. Asked why, he said, "Because education degrees are . . . they're nothing. When I was getting my math degree, I took one class per semester and that was a ton of work. When I got my education degree, [the university] had no limit on how many credits you could take . . . for the flat rate of tuition. I took twenty credits in an eight-week summer quarter, and I got a 4.0. Come on. I took twenty credits the next summer and got a 4.0."

Why would universities and colleges support weak education programs? Consider the time and billions of taxpayer dollars spent annually on "professional development" and coaching. If teachers still require this training after graduating from college, then something was lacking in their education. Or perhaps the training and coaching are bogus. An elementary school teacher said the "professional development" she gets is just indoctrination. It never offers her more academic content, she said, and it rarely offers a new way to teach. Taxpayers pay for this constant training and coaching, as do the students, who are repeatedly left behind with substitutes.

University presidents should be embarrassed if their colleges of education turn out teachers who require all of this training. District superintendents should be embarrassed if they keep hiring unprepared teachers. And teachers should be angry if they paid for an education that was inadequate. This isn't an argument to fire a bunch of teachers. Follow the thought to its logical conclusion: Something is awry. It's surprising that teachers haven't filed a class-action lawsuit against schools of education.

Meanwhile, new teachers graduate, stuffed full of a heady mixture of reform philosophy and "student-centered" coaching styles. Can we expect professors of education to step back and say, "Maybe we were wrong"? They taught reform, promoted it, fought for it, received grants for it, and published on it. How long until they admit, or even see, their error?

While we're "waiting for Godot" on that, regular folks can press for more content in education programs. They can ask legislators to ensure that incentive programs for master's degrees focus on core subject content. Prospective teachers can deliberately supplement their education with core subject content. Parents can find out if decision makers have degrees in core subject content and determine if they know what they're talking about.

Teacher-education programs aren't the only weakness in Corner 1 of the Square of Effective Learning, however. Frequently, the teachers aren't even in the classroom.

SUBSTITUTE TEACHERS AND STUDENT TEACHERS

Teacher absenteeism is a problem in K–12 schools, according to Roza's 2007 study. In addition to personal days, teachers are away for mandatory professional-development days, teacher collaboration, and student-teacher days.

In some districts, teachers also are away for special assignments. In Spokane in mid-2010, there were 23.1 full-time equivalent TOSAs, or teachers on special assignment—almost all of them working as assistants for principals and administrators. But when teachers are absent, classrooms must still go on. The children are there, and someone must teach them.

Substitutes are educated, talented, and caring, but they don't know the routine, the syllabus, or the students. Roza's study notes that teacher absences are costly for school districts and also can put students behind. When teachers return to their classrooms, they often have to reteach the material and restore order. Teaching time is thus lost twice.

Student teachers, on the other hand, are university students who passed a required set of classes and are sent to a school to learn "on the job." At some point, they take over the class. Many handle the transition well, but others, especially those in complicated classes, are less effective. Valuable teaching time is lost if student teachers struggle to maintain control. As an eighth grader said, "While they're learning 'on the job,' we're losing our opportunity to learn."

Students need every available minute of hands-on, competent teaching. They benefit from consistency, from having experienced, well-qualified teachers all of the time. This system that relies so heavily on substitutes and student teachers isn't helpful to students, efficient for teachers, economic for taxpayers, or logical. Teachers supposedly need constant "professional development," yet classes are handed off to people who don't have it. Given a challenging class, a weak curriculum, an ineffective learning environment, and an absent teacher—honestly, what do administrators think is going to happen?

The entire point of the classroom is the learning. Parents and teachers must monitor the classroom. If it isn't working, something must change. If students aren't paying attention, if their attitudes are deteriorating, if they aren't coming to class, if the work isn't getting done, then all necessary steps must be taken to get them back on track.

Don't accept this: "The professional development is a necessary support for our teachers." No, it isn't. Speak up and tell them it's interfering with learning. Don't accept this: "The student teacher has to learn, so we've got to wait it out." No, we don't. Say something, even if it's to offer your help. Don't accept this: "We can't control which substitute we get." You have influence. Voice your concerns. Don't accept this: "It's only one day." These are precious learning opportunities that are gone forever.

Student learning is the mission and thus the priority. There should be limits on district and state-initiated teacher absences.

An elementary school teacher suggested assigning full-time substitutes to each school so they could learn routines, help out, tutor, or "team teach" and so that everyone would know each other. This idea has potential. If you like the idea, plan carefully before presenting it, and don't say anything until you've worked out the details. Once bureaucrats say no, it's often no for good.

5

CORNER 2:
THE CURRICULUM

MATH AS THE CANARY IN THE COAL MINE

There are several things wrong with the typical public school curriculum, but this chapter focuses on mathematics. Math is an inherently black-and-white subject. The basics are easy to teach to children—easy to learn and easy to grade. That's why math is the "canary in the coal mine"—a glaring indicator of just how dangerously wrong things are in public education.

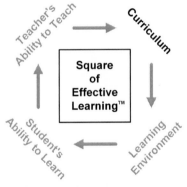

As you read this chapter, you'll understand why so many administrators would rather talk about money, social issues, buildings, legislation, staffing, budgets . . . anything other than mathematics. You'll also see why parents and teachers must make them do it.

Across the country, "reform math" has taken over the classroom. Reform comes under different names: "inquiry based," "standards based," "discovery," "student centered," "constructivist," or "problem centered." It's all "reform." Current reform curricula include TERC's *Investigations in Number, Data, and Space*; *Connected Mathematics Project*; *Core-Plus Mathematics Project*; *Everyday Mathematics*; the *Discovering* series; and others.

Typically, reform curricula are based on "NCTM *Standards*" that were written in 1989 (and clarified in 2000 and 2006) by the National Council of Teachers of Mathematics (NCTM). Many of those involved in writing the NCTM Standards documents also were involved in developing reform math curricula. (See "The NCTM, the NSF, and the Department of Education" below.)

Reform math encourages group discussion, estimation, group projects ("explorations" or "investigations"), supposed "real-world" applications, lots of writing about math, the use of calculators and other technologies (instead of proficiency with paper-and-pencil computation), and constructivism ("discovery" or "inquiry"), where students develop ("discover") their own methods for solving problems. Teachers are supposed to be "coaches" (rather than teachers), but an eighth grader said the term "coach" is a misnomer: "Coaches do tell you how to do things," she noted.

Standard algorithms have been replaced by "student-discovered" methods and by other nonstandard, less efficient methods. In reform, there are few rules, definitions, explanations, examples, summaries, or opportunities for students to practice to fluency. Probability and statistics are emphasized. Deemphasized are memorization, arithmetic, algebra, and direct instruction (also known as "teaching by telling," with the teacher as the expert).

Parents find they can't help with reform homework, partly because textbooks often aren't available, partly because of the group work and student "discovery," and partly because math concepts are presented erratically and in a disconnected manner. The concepts flit around like butterflies, touching down briefly before flying off again.

Reform proponents believe that "traditional" math lacks conceptual understanding and that children get bored with "rote memorization." Reform, they say, provides deep thinking and "context," closes achievement gaps, and makes math more fun and accessible. Supposedly, constructivism helps teachers better engage and motivate the students.

Those who prefer more traditional approaches, however, argue that reform math and constructivism are inefficient and confusing, as well as lacking sufficient mathematical content. They say reform curricula don't properly present multiplication, long division, fractions, algebra, or exponents—much less close achievement gaps. Students can appear to do well yet not have the basic mathematical skills they need. Consequently, they graduate from high school—if they graduate from high school—completely unprepared for postsecondary math.

Reformers point to classrooms where students do "math" by coloring, counting bird chirps, or crawling around on the floor, and they say, "We didn't change what we teach. We changed how we teach it." It isn't true. Reform math completely changed what's being taught.

Dr. Lee V. Stiff, a former NCTM president, discussed in his 2001 article "Status and the Status Quo—the Politics of Education" what he sees as a "political view" of math:

> The political view of traditional mathematics tends to compartmentalize number concepts, algebra, geometry, and measurement in ways that promote rote learning of the content. Students are left on their own to make sense of the disjointed collection of information and relationships. Often it is assumed that there is something inadequate about the students themselves if they are unsuccessful. Consequently, the status of the students is demeaned. No value is seen in changing the content and how it is presented. Of course, many students are able to make sense of the mathematics when it is organized in a traditional framework. The best of these students are seen as special and talented. Hence, the point of view that mathematics can be understood only by the few is widely accepted.

Dr. Stiff's argument contains a straw man fallacy. He builds up a false and unattractive picture of a traditional classroom (other than where he acknowledges its effectiveness), and then he criticizes his caricature. As you ask questions of administrators, you'll hear variations on this straw man fallacy over and over. You'll hear, "You just want traditional math because it's what you had as a child." Or "the old methods didn't work." You'll hear about twenty-first-century math, today's math, or the math of tomorrow. But they aren't talking about math. They're talking about how they want to teach math. The way they want to teach it is to remove a great deal of actual math from the process.

Over thousands of years, bright and curious adults developed efficient methods for solving complex mathematical problems. Innovations continue, but basic math looks about the same as it did when Albert Einstein developed the theory of relativity, when René Descartes explained analytic geometry, when Sir Isaac Newton described the laws of motion, and when Galileo faced down the Roman Inquisition. Traditional algorithms have stood the test of time.

Dr. Tom McKenzie, chair of Gonzaga University's Department of Mathematics, wrote in 2006, "Traditional math is a rock upon which the foundations of modern physics, biology, and economics are being built."

Unfortunately, the traditional rock was replaced by reform sand, and the house is crumbling.

In Spokane, the longer students are in reform math classes, the more trouble they have. State test scores for math are highest in grade four; then they go down, down, down until they bottom out in tenth grade. (A middle school student confided fretfully to a parent, "It's like I'm getting dumber!") Fourth grade isn't where the math problem begins; it's where the math problem becomes apparent.

N. R. Augustine's 2007 National Academy of Sciences report "Is America Falling Off the Flat Earth?" says that students who come to dislike math and science often have decided this by fourth grade. A retired high-tech executive commented on this unfortunate decision: "This is like amputating one of their organs before they have even realized they need it."

One must consider the possibility that the students' decision about mathematics is directly connected to how mathematics is currently being taught.

Parents and advocates have reported that middle school students need a calculator to subtract single-digit numbers, don't know basic addition and subtraction, can't add fractions, can't do long division, and don't know how to calculate the area of a rectangle.

In Spokane, a fourth-grade teacher said the curriculum *Investigations in Number, Data, and Space* hadn't allowed her to teach multiplication. A high school math teacher said many honors math students can't consistently multiply and divide. A parent said her daughter passed honors calculus, yet tested into remedial math in college. Dr. Jeff Bierman, a Spokane school board director, acknowledged in a 2009 public meeting that he and his wife supplement the district's reform math curricula with materials at home. Some math teachers have tutored outside of their classrooms, using more traditional methods to try to help a few students.

In 2008, just 45.9 percent of Spokane's tenth graders passed the state standardized math test. In 2009, it was 42.3 percent. In 2010, it was 38.9 percent. That's terrible, awful, a complete district failure, especially when you know that the tenth-grade test was based on lower-level content and required a score of just 56.9 percent to pass. In 2009, several students at Spokane Falls Community College (SFCC) told this author they had to take remedial math classes more than once. They couldn't understand how they could receive an A in high school honors math, yet require remediation.

In 2008–2009, according to data from Spokane Community Colleges, which includes Spokane Falls Community College and Spokane Community College (SCC),

- of all recent high school graduates enrolling in these two colleges, 90.5 percent took remedial math classes. Most tested into elementary algebra or below.
- 45.8 percent of those 1,820 remedial students withdrew early from their remedial math classes or failed to achieve a 2.0 or better. The rates hold true over five years.
- narrowing the data to just recent graduates from six high schools in Spokane Public Schools, four high schools had a math remediation rate (averaged over the two campuses) of more than 90 percent. At the more technically oriented SCC campus, four high schools had a math remediation rate of 100 percent (CCS Institutional Research 2010a, 2010b).

Granted, these numbers provide an imperfect picture. About 28.3 percent of Spokane's graduating class of 2008 are included—those who self-identified as Spokane Public Schools graduates and who enrolled in remedial math classes at SCC or SFCC within a year of graduation. Not included are graduates who left the area or who went to a four-year college. However, also not included are students who didn't want to go to college, who dropped out prior to graduation, or who tested into remedial math and decided it was too much to do.

Spokane is a microcosm of a national problem. In Pennsylvania, Quakertown Community School District directors voted in 2007 to return to a more traditional high school math program. A 2007 *Morning Call* article said the change was motivated by high school graduates who said their K–12 math experience left them unprepared for post-secondary life (Rizzo 2007). In Dublin, Ohio, reform curricula were blamed for problems that sixth, seventh, and eighth graders had with division, a *Columbus Dispatch* article reported. On a 2007 test, just 29 percent of three thousand students could correctly divide 651 by 14. At least half missed four of the eleven test questions (Sebastian 2007).

Border to border and coast to coast, similar battles have been waged. You'd think such widespread resistance would win the day, but reform math is still here. Many administrators continue to support it, regardless of the evidence against it. Parents and teachers say they've voiced concerns about reform math, only to be told, "This is the first time I've ever heard this" or "You're the only one who's ever complained." What do we believe? Do the administrators have amnesia or short-term memory loss? Do they not care enough to retain what they're told?

Indeed, the clash over reform math mirrors the one over "whole language" instruction in reading. Advocates who fought on behalf of phonics had much success, but their struggle continues to this day—not because of any failure on their part but because they battle a nearly immoveable force, the education bureaucracy.

What Is Traditional Math?

Education administrators will say without proof that "traditional" math didn't work. What do they mean by "didn't work"? Are they saying it didn't work for anyone? (Weird. How did all of these buildings, roads, and machines get here?)

Most American schools haven't had classically traditional math in decades. This doesn't prevent administrators from continuing to blame it for students' difficulties in math (as Spokane's elementary curriculum coordinator did at a school board meeting in May 2009).

Dr. David Klein, mathematics professor at California State University, Northridge, wrote in 2007 that the "seeds" of current reform approaches were planted in the 1980s but that the debate between traditional (or classical) instruction and reform (or progressive) instruction can be traced back to John Jacques Rousseau and even Plato.

Different "reform" movements in education include progressivism, the Activity Movement, the Life Adjustment Movement, outcome-based education, New Math, and the Open Education Movement. Who knows what classically traditional math looks like?

According to Dr. Shannon Overbay, associate professor at Gonzaga University, traditional math is "the development of integers, real numbers, complex numbers, properties of equality, graphs, algebra, geometry, trigonometry, functions, etc., in a logical fashion in which ideas are built upon and practiced." A 1999 joint report of the Education Connection of Texas and the Texas Public Policy Foundation referred to traditional math as "classical math":

> Students are expected to learn the specific facts and skills that comprise the established body of math knowledge and skills developed by mathematicians through centuries of western civilization. Teachers are responsible for directing and correcting learning. "Classical" math is taught as a specifically organized sequence of building math language, symbols, and manipulations. "Classical" instruction is based on the premise that learning complex math is predicated on mastery of basic components. When repeated practice enables the use of basic skills to become automatic, learning can be most effectively focused on developing abstract and sophisticated problem-solving. (Patterson 1999)

Perhaps the term "traditional math" is obsolete. Reform math has been haunting the hallways for so long, it's now a "tradition." When this book uses the term "traditional math," however, it's referring to a "classical" approach to mathematics and not to a particular program that might have been used when any of us were children.

Method of Instruction

Direct instruction generally entails teacher-led lectures, with feedback and discussions. There also can be individual and group practice, along with special projects, but the emphasis is on activity that is teacher directed.

Constructivism (or "discovery," "student-centered," or "inquiry"), on the other hand, asks students to develop their own methods. The teacher is a "facilitator"—a "guide on the side," not an instructor. Thus, students are guided away from standard algorithms and terminology that the rest of the world knows and uses, and toward the "discovery" of terminology and methods that are confusing, inefficient, often inexact, and even incorrect.

Dr. Lee Stiff said in his 2001 article "Constructivist Mathematics and Unicorns" that there are two kinds of constructivism.

Social constructivism "maintains that students can better build their knowledge when it is embedded in a social context. . . . Students help one another create richer meanings for new mathematical content." With social constructivism, Dr. Stiff says, "mathematics should be taught emphasizing problem solving," and "students should be encouraged to create their own strategies for solving problem situations."

Radical constructivism, on the other hand, contends "that knowledge cannot be provided in some final form from parent to child or from teacher to student but must be actively assembled in the mind by each learner in his or her own way."

But students are children. They can't assemble thousands of years of mathematics. In its article "What Is Changing in Math Education," anti-reform advocacy group Mathematically Correct provides an amusing take on constructivist teaching: "This notion holds that students will learn math better if they are left to discover the rules and methods of mathematics for themselves, rather than being taught by teachers or textbooks. This is not unlike the Socratic method, minus Socrates."

For years, these debates over how to teach math have been uniquely North American in nature. On other continents, a traditional (or classical) approach has been the norm. In a 1997 Boston College press release, researchers for the Third International Mathematics and Science Study (TIMSS) said the most common approaches internationally were direct teaching or individual work with instructor assistance ("Largest International Study" 1997). In math and science, small group work was seldom used, and the textbook was the main resource.

Ominously, there are indications that reform math is working its way into other countries. The upside is that, as skills in those countries begin to slide, America will look better in comparison. The downsides are (1) the world will be worse off mathematically, and (2) reformers will probably look at America's improved relative standing and say, "See? Reform works."

REFORM MATH IN THE CLASSROOM

"We don't need to 'increase spending by $200 million to hire more and better teachers and improve math and science teaching statewide.' Children can't do math because they aren't being taught the basics of mathematics."

—George Brown, Cheney, WA, in a
February 9, 2007 *Spokesman-Review* op-ed

Supposedly, reform math and constructivism are better at helping children learn, enjoy, and understand mathematics. Some say reform is better for "struggling" students; others say it's best for the gifted. To argue these statements is to pretend that a dirty mop will clean better on a different floor. Tutors see that most students are stymied by reform curricula (especially when delivered via discovery learning). Reform goes around its elbow to get to its ear. It doesn't teach enough mathematics. Just look around you, at any real measure.

After years of reform math classes, students rely on their calculators and their classmates. They lack the procedural fluency, basic arithmetic skills, and number sense required for problem solving. They count on their fingers and add instead of multiplying. They're perplexed by long division. The division of fractions is a mystery. These are capable students. The Square of Effective Learning is simple. If someone had taught these students how to multiply and divide, they would have learned it.

Reject administrators' constant refrain that "math is so hard" or that "math might not be their best subject." All over the world, students enjoy and excel in math. Americans don't have a "math-is-too-hard" gene.

They're just stuck in classes where they're expected to be mini-adults and mathematicians. They have to "discover" complex mathematical procedures and work constantly in groups, trying to teach each other thousands of years of math. In reality, most of them could develop solid math skills. The sole reason they haven't is because they aren't taught enough math. Here's what many students learn in reform classes.

Multiplication

Rather than learning how to multiply, students learn "tricks" to solve multiplication problems. For example, they might find multiples of nine by holding up their fingers and putting down the finger that represents the number other than nine. The remaining fingers display the answer. For example, with 9×4, students put down the fourth finger. On one side of the down finger there are three fingers, and on the other side, there are six. Hence, the answer is 36. All of this comes at the expense of knowing that $9 \times 4 = 36$. People who complain that students "are counting on their fingers" should know that students have been taught to do it that way.

Another "trick" is to group and add. Instead of multiplying the standard way (figure 5.1), children learn to group: "Twelve plus twelve is twenty-four. If I add twenty-four plus twenty-four, I get forty-eight. Another twelve plus twelve is twenty-four, and I need two of those to get another forty-eight. When I add the two forty-eights, I get ninety-six." Students' ability to keep track of these groups is impressive, but this is adding, not multiplying. "Group and add" isn't helpful with larger numbers or algebra.

$$
\begin{array}{r}
12 \\
\times\, 8 \\
\hline
96
\end{array}
$$

Figure 5.1. Traditional Vertical Multiplication

An elementary school teacher said another reform method is to teach only doubles, as in 2×2, 3×3, 4×4—because students can add up or subtract down from there.

Then there is the lattice method. To multiply 927×836, students draw a diagram (see figure 5.2, left): "927" is written across the top; "836" is written along the right side. Each digit from the top and right sides is multiplied in the grid (9×8, then 2×8, then 7×8), and each answer is placed in the corresponding box (with "tens" in each upper triangle and "ones" in each lower triangle). Diagonals are added (starting from the bottom right of the square), carrying tens to the left and up the left side. The answer is in the numbers along the outer left and bottom edges:

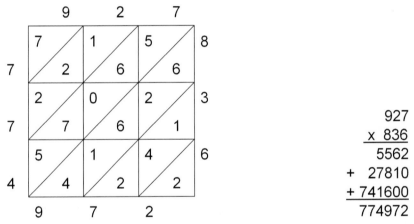

Figure 5.2. **Lattice Method (or Diagonal) Multiplication (left); Traditional Vertical Multiplication (right)**

It takes time and skill to draw the figure, line up everything, do the multiplication, carry, and add. Imagine for a moment how many hours of class time it must take to "guide" young students into using the lattice method. What students need, but aren't taught or allowed to practice, is the more efficient traditional method (figure 5.2, right).

Division

The traditional method of dividing (long division) looks like figure 5.3 (left). In reform curricula, however, students inch their way to the answer, and they learn to multiply and add rather than actually divide. Using the cluster method, as in figure 5.3 (right), students work out multiples and then add the multiples.

I want to divide 306 by 6.

I know that   6 x 10 = 60

That means that   6 x 20 = 120 (60 x 2)

And therefore that   6 x 40 = 240 (120 x 2)

If I add one more "60," I get 6 x 50 = 300

I need to add one more 6 to get to 306.

If I add the last two multiples of 6, I get 51.

Therefore, 306 divided by 6 equals 51.

```
      51
   _____
6 / 306
   −30
   ____
    06
   − 6
   ____
     0
```

Figure 5.3.   Traditional Long Division (left); Reform math "Cluster Division" method (right)

The cluster method is not "dividing." It isn't efficient with larger numbers.

Using the partial quotients method, as in figure 5.4, students again multiply their way to the answer. They add the multipliers of six (ten, twenty, twenty, and one), and get 51.

Missing from the cluster and partial quotient methods are (1) efficiency, (2) decimals, and (3) the idea that "division" means to break up a whole into equal parts. The more efficient standard method in figure 5.3 (left) (needed for understanding, as well as for algebra and calculus) is neither taught nor practiced. Given the partial quotients method for early instruction, many students who are tutored outside of the reform classroom seem to have a difficult time transitioning to the more efficient long division.

An elementary school teacher said that when she showed her students the traditional method of doing long division, they were excited. "Show me, show me," they said, exclaiming at how easy it is. But reformers would not appreciate this enthusiasm. "Well, of course they want it to be easy,"

```
6 / 306
  −  60    6 x 10
   _____
   246
  − 120    6 x 20
   _____
   126
  − 120    6 x 20
   _____
     6
  −   6    6 x 1
   _____
     0
```

Figure 5.4.   Division: Partial Quotients

they would say. Reformers expect students to struggle. In a reformer's mind, if the learning is efficient, the lesson has failed.

Area

By fourth grade, students should be calculating the area of rectangles by multiplying the length by the width ($A = lw$): 4 in. × 6 in. = 24 sq. in. Some classes now use $A = bh$, as in area equals base times height. But reform curricula repeatedly direct students to draw rectangles, fill them with squares and then count, as in figure 5.5:

6 inches

1	2	3	4	5	6
7	8	9	10	11	12
13	14	15	16	17	18
19	20	21	22	23	24

4 inches

Figure 5.5.   Calculation of Area by Counting Units

Doing this once or twice might be worthwhile, but it's counterproductive to do it repeatedly. Imagine solving problems like 12 in. × 8 in. It's easy to miss squares or count them twice. Students make mistakes out of inattention or boredom. Drawing their own squares, they lose the sense that squares must be the same size. Many don't gain deeper understanding by repeating this method. Instead, it can muddy any understanding they already had.

Percentages

A local sixth grader was to find percentages, such as "Find 27 percent of eighty." She wasn't taught the quick and efficient standard algorithm ($27/100 × 80 = 21.6$). She was taught to begin with calculations she knew and then multiply her way to the answer in increments. Figure 5.6 shows the methodology she was taught.

The student might gain understanding this way, but it isn't the
most efficient method. She should
have been taught the most efficient
method first and then been allowed
to practice it. But reform math remains inefficient and ineffective. A
tutor showed the student the standard algorithm, but the student had

100% of 80 =	80
0% of 80 =	0
50% of 80 =	40
25% of 80 =	20
If 1% of 80 =	.8
Then 2% of 80 =	1.6
So 20 + 1.6 =	21.6
So 27% of 80 =	21.6

Figure 5.6. A Reform Math Approach to Calculating Percentage

not been given sufficient early instruction in multiplication, division,
and fractions. Additionally, her homework problems were complex,
requiring decimals.

On another day, this student was to "discover" the slope-intercept
formula from two points. On that day, she cried, staring at her
homework. On another day, she was to develop pie charts from raw
data. She didn't know how to use the data to come up with percentages or how to properly use a protractor. This was not her fault.
She's a capable student, and if she'd been taught these things, she
would know them. She articulated the problem she was having with
"discovery" learning: "You can't search for things if you don't know
what they are."

The Law of Primacy

Students who can do the impressive mental gymnastics required in
"alternate" methods are capable of learning traditional arithmetic. And
they must learn it because the alternate methods don't hold up well.
Multiplying 72,347 × 6,893 is an enormous trial if children are using
their fingers, drawing squares and triangles, or adding 72,347 nearly
seven thousand times. (For a discussion of calculators, see chapter 9
"Dealing With Diversionary Issues.")

Unfortunately, in reform math, these "alternate strategies" are
presented first, and they tend to stick. In many cases, there isn't any
follow-up with traditional methods, but even if there is, the law of
primacy (as articulated in the 1974 Air Force manual *Principles and*

Techniques of Instruction) says that people tend to draw on the skills they learned first. Therefore, they should learn the most efficient ways first: "Primacy, the state of being first, often creates a strong, almost unshakeable, impression. For the instructor, this means that what he teaches must be correct the first time. For the student, it means that his learning must be correct. Unteaching is more difficult than teaching. . . . The student's first experience should be positive and functional in preparation for what follows."

We want students to learn math processes properly the first time—in the most efficient, most effective, and most precise way possible. But reformers don't want that.

Asked about this, a local principal explained that, years ago, children didn't have a "different strategy" for solving problems. Now they do, he said. But saying that "adding is a different strategy for multiplication" is like saying that "walking is a different strategy for driving." You wouldn't pay someone to teach you to walk when you're supposed to learn to drive. You could walk, but it's slow and inefficient. What if you had to walk across the state? You'd be walking for a long time, and all of the students from Singapore would pass you, waving and smiling as they headed off to jobs you couldn't get because you didn't know how to drive.

Meant well or not, the "different strategy" explanation is idiotic. Sorry, but it is what it is. The number of students who can't learn arithmetic is very small. The different strategies are inefficient and won't help the students advance. With reform math and discovery, all students

- must slow down, thereby being shortchanged in what they could learn;
- must learn inefficient methodologies that won't work for them later;
- must learn inefficient methods first, thereby gaining them as the primary skill;
- are given insufficient opportunity to absorb basic math skills or to excel;
- are forced to try to rediscover thousands of years of math.

A high school teacher described a ninth-grade class that used *Core-Plus Mathematics*: "When I go into a 9th-grade math class and they're making things out of [molding clay] and pipe cleaners and soda straws and gumdrops, and I'm thinking to myself, okay, how does that kid get from those kinds of things, which may be good for some kids, how do they get from that to calculus? How do you get there? You can't do it. . . . The stuff that they use for those math classes, it looks like an elementary classroom."

Sometimes it seems as if the education establishment is determined to treat the entire student body as if it's a special education class. This is not to disparage special education classes—just to note that only special education students need them.

"Drill and Kill" and the Spiral Technique

In reform math, children don't practice skills to mastery. Practicing of skills is labeled "drill and kill," derided as an old-school philosophy that "hinders" critical thinking skills and conceptual understanding. It's a strange, flippant way to dismiss a logical process for learning. Practice is how anyone learns a skill. Removing practice from the learning process is like saying, "We'll just remove this gravity."

Everyone practices—tennis and football players, soldiers, plumbers, and pianists. At Carnegie Hall in New York City, this famous phrase is printed on gift items: "How do you get to Carnegie Hall? Practice, practice, practice." Imagine if we told doctors they had to figure out medicine on their own, in fits and starts, by trial and error and by asking their colleagues. Imagine if we expected them to save lives when they hadn't had a chance to practice basic skills. Practice is necessary. It isn't good or bad—it's what must be done.

But in reform math classes, students are introduced to concepts and told to play around with them for a while ("discovering"), and then they're swept off to the next concept before they have the last one down. Later, the curriculum is supposed to "spiral" back and review concepts, but it's too late. The students have forgotten them. Plus, the concepts return with new presentations. Not having truly grasped the original concepts, students are confounded by the twists.

This esoteric, conceptual approach to math, with a constant struggle to understand the process, isn't a logical approach for children. Children are concrete thinkers who appreciate concrete ideas. They want instructions, guidance, and things that make sense. It's ironic that proponents of reform math criticize traditionalists for supposedly not knowing how to teach math to children. Constructivism seems completely oppositional to how children learn best.

In its March 2008 report, the National Mathematics Advisory Panel (NMAP) reintroduced the notion of practicing the basics: "Practice allows students to achieve automaticity of basic skills—the fast, accurate, and effortless processing of content information—which frees up working memory for more complex aspects of problem solving."

Complicated Word Problems

Besides being generally inadequate, reform math curricula are excessively long-winded and complicated. They teach concepts by using supposedly "real-world" situations that often are way beyond the common experience of most students. To teach elapsed time, for example, the district materials presented fourth graders with a problem similar to this one:

> Becky gets on a plane at LaGuardia Airport, New York, at 7 a.m., and lands in Salt Lake City at noon. She gets off the plane and has a layover in Salt Lake City. She sits for an hour eating lunch, which consists of milk and a ham sandwich. At 3:15 p.m., she gets on another airplane, landing at Seattle's SeaTac airport at 4:30 p.m. How much time was Becky on an airplane during the entire day?

This flood of superfluous information is too much for students who are still learning about elapsed time. After reading through his problem, one boy sighed and said, "I don't like ham sandwiches." He had nothing else to say. It's senseless to expect students to "discover" how to solve complicated word problems using arithmetic they haven't even been taught. The students get frustrated. Why not just teach them the skills?

Form over Function

Reform math curricula often require words or pictures in order to get maximum points on answers. It's insufficient to just "know" the answer, as children do when they've memorized standard algorithms. While students should be expected to show proof of their thinking through visible mathematical calculations, it isn't helpful when the process never goes there, when it remains stuck with drawings, paragraphs of writing, or less efficient methodologies.

Students often are asked to show more than one way to arrive at an answer (like turning left, left, and left in order to make a simple right turn). Then they must explain why they turned left, left, and left, and they have to draw pictures or boxes as part of their answer.

This writing, in a math class, is pointless repetition (as opposed to the repetition students should be doing, which is practicing mathematical skills). The students become bored and frustrated. There's little opportunity to excel. A well-known phrase for this kind of work is "form over function." It means to engage in activities whether or not they're useful. How much math could children learn if they weren't so busy drawing boxes and writing redundant explanations?

If the mission is to learn math, the writing is a distraction. If students know the math but are less capable with reading and/or writing, they can lose points even if their math is correct. If students lose points over the writing, it muddies teacher and parent understanding of what the students don't know in math. If students just know the answer, or if they calculate it using standard algorithms, they must still come up with the answer in a way that's more "acceptable" to the district. A local fifth grader lost points on a test when she used a standard algorithm for multiplication. Her answer wasn't written horizontally, so she lost points for a correct answer.

In 2006, a fourth-grade class in a neighborhood school was piloting *Investigations in Number, Data, and Space,* along with supplementary materials. Student homework often was incorrect or unclear or asked questions that had no good answer.

A sample of one type of question is illustrated in figure 5.7. Students were to find the perimeter of a polygon that was built

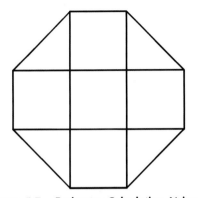

Figure 5.7. Perimeter Calculation Using a Polygon

using squares and triangles. Students were to come up with an answer of "eight units." All straight edges and diagonals were supposedly the same length, but this is mathematically impossible. The hypotenuse (the diagonal) of a right-angle triangle will always be longer than its other two sides. The perimeter was incorrectly determined.

Second graders were taught to use a "hundred chart" to solve subtraction problems. (Hundred charts are numbered from one to one hundred. Children add and subtract by starting with one number and counting forward or backward to the other.) To get full points, they must explain their thinking, so a student wrote, "I used the hundred chart." The teacher told him he had to say how he used the chart—for every problem. The student said he used the chart the way he was supposed to. The teacher helped him come up with a more "acceptable" explanation, and he painstakingly wrote it down for every problem.

Reform "math" problems for older students have included writing down ideas for why the number of manatees in Florida decreased, working in groups to determine the relationship between bird chirps and cricket calls (it turns out there isn't one), comparing the number of steps in a mile against the time it takes to walk it, and timing a partner writing the alphabet.

No Continuity, No Context, No Textbook

Traditional textbooks have tables of content and indices. They provide context and continuity from one concept to another. Students can look back and review concepts or look ahead to see what's coming. In a traditional textbook, it's all there. Many reform classes, however, depend on papers copied from a "master" that presents concepts to be learned at that time. Each paper is an island of information, with no connection to anything else.

Teachers keep folders of these papers, but most students don't. Math paperwork thus fills up desks and winds up buried in backpacks. If students need to review a previous concept, or parents need to refresh their memories in order to help their children, these papers are of no help. There is no way to look back or ahead, no way to see how it all fits together.

Some reform classes have books or booklets. Often, however, new concepts are introduced with an application, no explanation, and inadequate follow-up. This author began a list of new concepts in the *Connected Mathematics 2* curriculum. Over three booklets, the list of unexplained or poorly explained concepts was several pages long.

A bright seventh grader who had been perplexed by the *Connected Mathematics Project* (CMP) curriculum was tutored with a traditional approach. He talked about all the different ways his CMP class had taught him to do problems. But now, he said, using the traditional algorithm, he had one way that worked. A sixth grader who was pulled out of a CMP class and homeschooled was able to cover, in six months, the textbooks for *Saxon 7/6, Singapore Math 5a, 5b, 6a,* and *6b,* and half of *Saxon Algebra 1/2.* She wasn't pushed, but these textbooks were clear, and no one wasted her time.

Mathematics could be the easiest subject in school. It's a straightforward, provable, concrete task. It's perfectly designed for children, who tend to be straightforward, concrete thinkers. Children should love math, and initially they do. But that love is beaten right out of them. Math has been turned into an exercise in literacy and futility (and perhaps senility). Only people who do too much self-involved thinking could come up with an approach that aims to teach mathematics by not teaching it.

No wonder Singapore consistently overwhelms America in international competitions. As Singaporeans "turn right" and zoom off to other challenges, Americans turn left, left, and left, write a soliloquy about it, and still get the answers wrong, whereupon they get partial credit.

THE MATH DEBATES AND THE BIG, FAT LIES

"The ability to compute is a basic skill, absolutely necessary to succeed in high school algebra, just as mastery of high school algebra is crucial for success in college mathematics."

—Wilfried Schmid, Harvard mathematics professor, in the
Columbia (Missouri) Daily Tribune (Heavin 2007)

For decades, math professionals have advocated against reform math, yet reform is still with us, like something sticky on our shoes. Why?

Dr. Lawrence Gray, mathematics professor at the University of Minnesota, said in 2001 that educators tended to support integrated math courses almost universally, while scientists, research mathematicians, and engineers viewed them with "widespread suspicion." At the time, he wondered, "Are scientists, engineers, and mathematicians badly misinformed about what is important in their own fields? Should their input be ignored?"

It shouldn't be. Although Dr. Gray says his experiences as a math professional have improved since then, many other science, technology, engineering, and mathematics (STEM) professionals still say they're treated with disdain, and their deep knowledge of mathematics is dismissed as irrelevant. This idea that STEM professionals know nothing about K–12 math instruction is one of the many untruths the public hears. First, let's address the concept of a lie.

When we say someone lied, we mean the person intentionally hid the truth or intentionally told an untruth. We can presume the intent of education administrators, but we don't know. We mustn't, therefore, say they are lying. Some decision makers probably don't intend to hide the truth or intentionally mislead teachers and parents. Some might be misinformed, deluded, ignorant, illogical, unintelligent, or pressured to speak wrongly. For the purposes of this book, therefore, the word "lie" refers not to the person but to the argument. The lie rests in the illogic and wrongness of the thing being stated, and this author does not extend the lie to any particular person nor to anyone's intent.

Lie 1: Mathematicians have nothing to say about K-12 mathematics.

In many administrative minds, advice from educators carries more weight than advice from mathematicians, engineers, and scientists. They see education—not math—as the important background. This belief effectively eliminates the need to listen to all learned advice from STEM professionals. If you think this is too strange to be believed, rest assured that most advocates have seen it. What kind of evidence can we bring when evidence doesn't matter? The most knowledgeable mathematician will never persuade those who refuse to listen to mathematicians.

But knowledge and expertise matter. A few definitions will help explain:

- Mathematician: a specialist or expert in mathematics. Mathematicians typically have degrees in math, frequently doctorates, and they tend to make a living by doing math, researching math, or solving problems that are mathematical in nature.
- Math professor: typically a holder of a degree (or degrees) in math, who teaches math to others in a postsecondary setting. This person might also be a mathematician.
- Math teacher: typically a teacher of math in a K-12 setting. This teacher might or might not have a math degree or even a strong math background. (Most high school math teachers have stronger math backgrounds than do K-8 teachers.)
- Math educator: a person who might have a degree in math but whose advanced degrees are frequently in education or math education (both of which can be surprisingly light in actual math). Math educators usually are involved in teaching people how to teach math to others.

When you're presented with arguments or evidence, consider the person's background. Those who teach how to teach math tend to think about math differently from those who solve math problems for a living.

A local teacher is one of the pro-reformers who argue that engineers and mathematicians shouldn't comment on K-12 math curricula because they "don't know how to communicate" or they "don't know how to teach math to children." A local administrator said parents weren't invited into curriculum adoptions because "they don't have the necessary background." Another said parents have nothing to tell him about their children's math education. Reformers often make these comments in a matter-of-fact way, as if they were obvious truths.

This author has literally offered a suitcase of pertinent research from mathematicians, cognitive scientists, and other professionals—only to have administrators brush it off like a stray hair on their jacket. These tactics have worked for them. Instilling doubt about the credibility of people who know math or who know the students causes everyone to trust reformers. But if students aren't graduating with enough math skills, how does it help the students to argue that math professors don't know how to teach math to children? That's just shooting the messenger.

Lie 2: Reform math and constructivism are better than traditional math.

People who are pro-reform say that reform math programs and discovery learning styles get students to "think mathematically." With discovery, children supposedly explore, create, make connections, communicate, collaborate, build their own strategies for solving problems, and become "math literate," all while having fun. A traditional approach to teaching mathematics, they say, doesn't work, doesn't meet the students' needs, and isn't useful in the twenty-first century.

It's bizarre. Traditional math took us to the moon and constructed bridges, railroads, skyscrapers, computers, microscopes, and airplanes. What reformers have been doing has not worked well for the students. Yet, administrators keep pouring time and money into reform math, letting teachers and students swing as they run into the west looking for a sunrise that will never be there.

Despite these lovely claims of participation, collaboration, and communication, there are few statistically supportable claims about improvements in skill. That's because the amount of math being learned in reform classrooms is typically miniscule, shoved aside by group work, art projects, and overuse of calculators. So little fact-based knowledge is accumulated in these classrooms, students can do little else but guess and check as a problem-solving strategy.

Opponents of reform math often cite R. Hill and T. Parker's 2006 study of college students who had taken *Core-Plus Mathematics Project* in high school. The study found that the *Core-Plus* students tended to place into increasingly lower-level college courses, and the grades they earned tended to also be below average.

Aspects of reform can be beneficial in small doses. Students should learn to apply mathematics. Occasional math projects can help cement understanding. But constant discovery and group work take up too much time and don't allow for enough time on skills. Skills must come first. Students can't apply something they don't know how to do. The most efficient methods must be taught first as the primary skill.

Lie 3: Reform math is not the problem.

Reformers blame America's math problem on students, parents, social issues, and—illogically—"traditional" math, yet obstinately refuse to question how American schools have taught math for the last few decades. What good is their noisy, busy methodology if it doesn't get students where they need to go? People who love reform can't seem to look beyond themselves to see that it isn't working for the students.

The problem is bigger than the curricula, however. Various administrators have said 64 percent pass rates on math tests might be good; it's okay to set math "proficiency" at 53 percent achievement or less; it's okay to set a D as a passing grade. Some districts have policies of not giving grades below 50 percent. Others offset achievement grades with grades for "effort" or "work habits." Standards-based grading can allow nearly everyone to pass. Some districts don't give grades. Reform math is a problem, but it's perpetuated by people whose philosophy also is a problem.

Lie 4: It's good for students to struggle.

This lie might be the most pernicious and damaging of all. This broad generalization carries a grain of truth, so it's used to justify a terrible process. It's rarely good for young students to learn academics by struggling. It can be okay for older students to struggle with a few challenging problems, but not all day and not every day. It's easy for reformers to stand aside, watching students struggle, pretending that something good is happening. They should walk a mile in the students' shoes, spending years struggling to understand the process, day after day, after day, after day. The Geneva Conventions should outlaw this kind of "struggling."

Lie 5: Students love discovery classrooms.

Actually, students give clear indications of being supremely frustrated with reform and discovery. Student feedback to Spokane's 2009–2010 curriculum adoption committee was crystal clear that most wanted a math program with examples, explanations, clarity, rigor, and structure. But even those students who love discovery still aren't getting enough math. At the end of the day, that's what matters. To reject that is to obstinately reject the truth.

In 2010, a middle school student discussed the ubiquitous group project:

> When it comes to group projects, children must regulate and manage each other. The teacher chooses a leader for each group, who then becomes a leader, enforcer, manager, editor, rewriter, presenter, and communicator within and without the group. Not only is this a great stress on the child, it also sets the child apart from other students, as: More intelligent, teacher's pet, unfair, tattletale, bossy, and many other negative adjectives, all because of a lazy teacher. One teacher said of a group of students wanting to do individual projects, "Great. Now I have more crap to grade."

Lie 6: Reform math works if teachers get enough training.

No, it doesn't. Teachers are shuffled through endless, expensive "professional development" (PD)—typically courses in constructivism and specific reform curricula. But all of the PD in the world won't create missing content or turn bad curricula into good.

Volunteers without education degrees or PD in reform approaches capably teach chess, reading, arithmetic, algebra, and geometry. How unintelligible must a program be if reasonably intelligent adults—who have college degrees and teaching experience—can't teach it to children? Teachers should be trained in subject content, but the PD they get postcertification is often just indoctrination in reform. It's a cash cow for state and district budgets, curriculum coordinators, and PD providers, however. Guess who pays for it.

Lie 7: Students learn math better when they write paragraphs about it.

In reform, students discuss and write about math. It's known as "communicating (or thinking) mathematically." But without useful symbols and equations, it's like talking about Morse code versus actually using Morse code. In a 2008 e-mail to this author, mathematics professor Dr. Lawrence Gray discussed the term "mathematical thinking": The term can be "used in a way that is almost divorced from mathematical content, and hence it covers up the fact that the content is missing. 'Mathematical thinking' is very important to me, but only if it is connected to actual content. In particular, the phrase 'mathematical thinking' is properly connected to mathematical content only if it means that students need to know why particular math methods work, and when to use them."

Lie 8: Students learn better when they discover for themselves.

This fiendish lie built the theory of constructivism, and a grain of truth keeps it going despite all contrary data, research, and public opposition. A 2000 *New York Times* article said students in reform classes were to "count a million grains of birdseed" to appreciate size, use straws (not protractors) to measure angles, and add fractions by folding paper (Hartocollis 2000). How much time was spent, and how much real math was learned, with these activities?

Parents and teachers tell astonishing tales of students being chastised for using a formula or standard algorithm. For example, a class might be asked to determine the length of the "long side" of a ninety-degree angle. The terms "hypotenuse" and "Pythagorean theorem" wouldn't be presented; nor would the standard algorithm ($a^2 + b^2 = c^2$) be offered. Students would be asked to form groups and discuss possible ways in which they could answer the question.

Students who knew the Pythagorean theorem, however, and who provided it to their group would be met with disapproval from the teacher for not allowing group members to spend the period trying to figure out a method. Students would be expected to apply skills they didn't have, supposedly as a way to gain "deeper understanding" and "relevance."

Try arguing against this. Say to reformers, "Students need to learn how to do something before they can apply it." Hear them say, "You don't understand." Try saying, "Some discovery is good—a little, perhaps, at the end of a lesson." Watch their eyes change, assessing you now as an outsider, as someone who doesn't believe. The students' constant stumbling around isn't a big deal for reformers because it's expected. Efficiency and accuracy are not the goals.

Proficiency isn't a goal either. A local reform teacher gives grades of 100 percent when students get a 94 percent or higher and has said that earning forty-eight out of sixty on a test shows mastery of the subject. (Do you suppose that teacher would mind having surgery done by doctors whose operations were successful forty-eight out of every sixty times?)

A sixth grader said her math teacher accepts hand-drawn angles as long as they're within five degrees of the actual angle. But in math, five degrees is huge. Contrast this with a more traditional process, where students gain computational fluency and where accuracy and efficiency are emphasized. This fluency later leads to confidence in trying challenging word problems, activities, and applications.

Lie 9: Students are helped by using calculators.

Some people think calculators should be on every K–12 desk. Anti-reform group Mathematically Correct (which is opposed to this philosophy) explains the thinking: "The idea is that students shouldn't have to be bogged down with mundane things like addition and subtraction, since calculators can do these things for them." The group warns that students become reliant on calculators and are unable to do simple arithmetic.

In 2002, Wilfried Schmid, professor of mathematics at Harvard University, wrote a letter to legislators telling them that the *Investigations in Number, Data, and Space* curriculum was "extreme" and "unbalanced": "In this brief message I cannot describe all the defects of 'Investigations.' Let me mention only that the authors strictly oppose the teaching of all standard algorithms . . . and discourage memorization of basic number facts, e.g., memorization of the multiplication table. Instead, students are made dependent on calculators and mental crutches, including . . . counting on fingers."

Bob Dean, math department chairman at Evergreen High School, Vancouver, Washington, has noted that the state math test would require work without calculators, even though math classes weren't teaching to proficiency without calculators. He said, "That sounds like the foundation of a successful lawsuit to me."

Lie 10: Students learn better when they learn from each other.

Reform math leans hard on the "cooperative effort." Children are supposed to work together to develop answers, processes, or proofs. Some teachers have a mantra of "ask three before you ask me," as in ask three of your classmates before you come up here and bother me.

It's unreasonable to expect students to teach math to each other (except occasionally). Students should not learn math from their peers. This is for several reasons.

First, the peers generally don't know the math either.

Second, collaboration can be a slow, frustrating process that teaches ineffective and incorrect ways first. Even if better ways are learned later, the law of primacy says the new information will always be secondary to whatever was learned first.

Third, as children "reinvent" thousands of years of math, they often "discover" (or are given) multiple inefficient methods. Those methods might work for them at that point in time, so students become comfortable with them and prefer them. But later, the methods will be a hindrance. Besides being inefficient, those methods generally are not applicable to all problems. It's criminal that teachers can't provide students with the most efficient methods from the beginning. It's astounding that so many administrators adamantly refuse to acknowledge the benefits or the efficiency of traditional algorithms.

Fourth, in today's classrooms of wildly different levels of ability and skill, it would be a miracle to have equal effort and achievement. What's more likely to happen is that the more advanced students will tend to do most of the work, and less advanced students will lean on their peers. This is okay with reformers, who expect students to teach their peers (and to help manage classes, students, and material).

Last, the approach is illogical and ironic.

If teachers need constant professional development in order to teach math, how is it that children can teach math? The kids should get a salary.

The administrators disallow direct instruction of children, yet their professional development is directive. Teachers are not allowed to discover their own methods for teaching, and direct instruction is not considered to be equal to discovery. Students are to discover their own methodologies, and all methodologies are equal . . . except traditional algorithms. For some reason, those are not considered to be equal.

(One is inspired by George Orwell, author of *Animal Farm*: All approaches to mathematics are equal, but some approaches are more equal than others.)

According to Missouri's *Columbia Daily Tribune*, a district math coordinator said that if a student already knows a traditional algorithm (having picked it up at home, apparently), "the way 'Investigations' works is that we're going to highlight that child and ask him to show other children what he's doing and how he's doing it" (Heavin 2007).

Uh huh. Because the teacher is doing . . . what? Sitting on the couch eating Twinkies and watching daytime television? While the children try to teach the rest of the class something the teacher hasn't been allowed to teach, they are not being taught. This is a heavy burden to place on the students. They worry about it. A sixth grader wondered if she was passing on correct answers to her classmates. "I think I am," she said, "but I'm not sure. I'm not their teacher."

This student was asked whether she preferred the *Connected Mathematics* she got in school or the more traditional *Singapore Math* she got at home. She said, "In a way, *Connected Mathematics* is easier because you don't have to know as much math, but in a way, it's harder because you have to know more. You have to know exactly what they want."

She explained it this way: Students gather to discuss a problem. They don't agree on what's required. Many don't have the necessary skills. Some become frustrated or bored. Trying to help each other, some confuse the others. Without practicing the new concept, the class moves on. *Singapore Math*, on the other hand, "might be harder as far as the math goes," she said, "but at least you know what they want." Told that her explanation was articulate and enlightening, she said, "That's because they teach it, but I'm the one who has to learn it."

There are other, subtler consequences to discovery and group learning that are just beginning to be felt. More and more teachers, tutors, and advocates are saying that students no longer know how to take notes from a lecture, can't sift out pertinent information from extraneous information, have a difficult time sitting quietly and thinking or doing quality individual work, and are not skilled at memorizing things. Additionally, when teachers say, "Let's think about this," the students instantly start talking. They do it because group discussion–not quiet thinking–is the typical routine in discovery classrooms. Students cannot concentrate.

Students also have developed a disturbing tendency to see adults as equals. And why wouldn't they? They're in control of the learning, and teachers have been shunted aside–told to be "guides on the side." But students still need direction and discipline. Thus, behavior also is becoming a problem in many classrooms. This is not the students' fault, but they (and their parents) will be blamed for it. Laura Brandt, parent and cofounder of Where's the Math? said, "It's ironic that pro-reformers advocate for 'real world' problems while not preparing students for the real world. When expectations are set at a low level to ensure everyone succeeds, students are learning in a safety bubble. How does a reform classroom prepare students to compete in the 'real world' where the cream is allowed to rise to the top, hard work and competence are rewarded, and apathy usually results in a demotion or job loss?"

Lie 11: Long division is too hard and isn't even necessary. Students don't need to practice basic arithmetic skills (such as long division).

Long division typically gets short shrift in reform curricula. The elementary math coordinator for Columbia Public Schools, Missouri, said in 2007, according to the *Columbia Daily Tribune*, that, with *Investigations in Number, Data, and Space*, "division can become a pattern of subtraction and multiplication" (Heavin 2007). But this is true only in a sense. Division is the process of breaking a whole into equal parts. To do that, one must subtract and multiply.

Long division has been called the "nemesis" of schools because, supposedly, it's difficult to learn. This is patronizing to children and teachers. When an effective teacher directly teaches a math concept, gives students a chance to practice it, answers questions, and ensures students really have it before going to the next topic, the children get it—if not all of them, then most of them. Long division isn't a nemesis; it's a skill. It takes practice, but it isn't hard. Students' lack of skill in long division isn't a failure in learning. It's the failure of schools to teach an important mathematical concept that's a building block of so many others.

A sixth-grade student said her teacher told the class she didn't like long division, so she wasn't going to teach it. The homework disallowed calculators, so the student was asked, "How are you supposed to do these problems?" The student shook her head. "I don't know. My teacher has her own method, but I don't understand it." The student later learned long division from a tutor.

Dr. Shannon Overbay wrote in 2007,

Many [reform] programs, such as Investigations (TERC) do not even cover topics such as long division and routine computations with fractions. By the time these students come to college, they are unable to go into technical majors and have to struggle to pass even elementary math classes designed for nontechnical majors. . . . There are often gaps and holes in their mathematics background that would require years of remediation to fix. For most students, that is not a reasonable option. . . . We are faced with a 20 percent decline nationally in the number of engineering majors in recent years. It is devastating.

You can't blame teachers. For decades, they've been taught that practicing of skills, accuracy, efficiency, and speed aren't important—and could even be counterproductive. But in math, accuracy is everything. Math concepts can't be meaningfully developed without it. Efficiency and speed are helpful, especially in advanced math. Muddled process produces muddled understanding. Additionally, knowledge isn't static; it requires constant refreshment or it turns into "Gee, I used to know how to do that." The brain needs work to stay strong.

Ongoing practice and drill are necessary. They're critical to the learning of any skill, including mathematics. Dr. David Klein notes that no one questions the amount of practice that goes into being an athlete or a musician. "Arguably the most hierarchical of human endeavors, mathematics also depends on sequential mastery of basic skills" (McKeown, Klein, and Patterson 2000).

Lie 12: Research supports reform math. Traditional approaches don't work.

Important questions to ask when reviewing research are, Who did it? and Who paid for it? When research is done or funded by those with financial or personal interests in the matter, it can create a conflict of interest. Results can become skewed. Research should therefore be objective and disinterested. You'd think objective and disinterested studies would have been done before taxpayer dollars were spent buying reform curricula. But in 1996, advocacy group Mathematically Correct said there was little persuasive supporting documentation: "One might reasonably expect that such radical departures from traditional methods would be based on clear, well-documented, overwhelmingly compelling, quantitative evidence of their superiority. Sadly, this is not the case at all. In fact, the lack of research support is striking. Perhaps the most unifying feature of these new programs is that they are all experimental."

So, okay, maybe public education jumped the gun on reform, but supporting research should be available now. Because reform replaced traditional math—not just supplemented it—it's important to find scientifically conducted, replicable, peer-reviewed research that supports conceptual, discovery-based approaches as being effective replacements for traditional approaches. A dedicated search found materials such as the following:

1. Opinion pieces, written on behalf of reform or on behalf of the NCTM Standards.
2. Articles published in the *Journal for Research in Mathematics Education*, an official publication of the National Council of Teachers of Mathematics. The NCTM published the standards on which reform curricula claim to be based. Nonmembers can't see those studies unless they pay for them. (This is common practice for journals, but it is difficult for parents and nonmember teachers to determine what the studies say.)
3. Articles written by people associated with the NCTM, with specific reform curricula, or with the National Science Foundation (NSF) (which helped fund the reform movement).

In 2004, the National Academies Press report "On Evaluating Curricular Effectiveness: Judging the Quality of K–12 Mathematics Evaluations" was released (Confrey and Stohl 2004). This analysis of 698 studies of the thirteen NSF-funded curricula and six other commercial curricula found that no determination could be made about "the effectiveness of individual programs with a high degree of certainty, due to the restricted number of studies for any particular curriculum, limitations in the array of methods used, and the uneven quality of the studies."

In February 2009, the What Works Clearinghouse (WWC) was unable to establish the effectiveness of *Investigations in Number, Data, and Space* (WWC 2009). Forty studies of *Investigations* were assessed; none met the WWC "evidence standards."

In January 2010, just one of seventy-nine studies of *Connected Mathematics Project* met the WWC evidence standards "with reservations" and could therefore be assessed. The other seventy-eight studies failed to meet the WWC evidence standards. The WWC found that CMP had "no discernible effects on math achievement" (WWC 2010a).

Support for reform math, therefore, tends to come via materials that are opinion pieces or that are procedurally questionable. Their sum total isn't convincing, and yet, somehow, they still manage to convince. This is a conundrum that perplexes anti-reform advocates. When everything about reform math points to failure, why do administrators keep seeing success? The answer is, They see it because they want to see it. The motto at a neighborhood school is "Believe it, and you'll see it." This motto provides wry amusement for several advocates.

On the other hand, the research that contradicts pure reform and discovery is crystal clear. K. H. Mayfield and P. N. Chase's 2002 study found that incorporating cumulative practice into mathematics instruction on basic algebra skills improved students' scores on application and problem-solving tests. R. E. Mayer's 2004 analysis of research on discovery learning found that a guided environment is more effective than one using absolute discovery.

In April 2008, J. A. Kaminski, V. M. Sloutsky, and A. F. Heckler of Ohio State University found that students are better able to transfer their mathematical understanding to new situations when they learn those skills with abstract symbols. (Traditional approaches to learning mathematics tend to favor the use of abstract symbols, whereas reform approaches tend to favor learning through supposedly "relevant, real-world" application.)

In his 2009 book *Visible Learning*, Dr. John Hattie, professor of education at the University of Auckland, New Zealand, provides a compilation of more than eight hundred meta-analyses on student learning and achievement. The critical goal, he said, should not be to simply determine which strategies have an effect. When the bar for a useful effect is set at zero (that is, if it has any effect at all), then everything appears to work. Instead, he said, the bar should be set high enough so that strategies that have an effect greater than this bar are the ones to warrant implementation.

Dr. Hattie's findings illustrate the apparent lower effects of most of today's reform and discovery-based strategies. These lower recorded effects don't necessarily confirm the strategies' lack of value, only that their usefulness should be carefully reevaluated, given their generally weak effects on student achievement, particularly as compared to many others with much greater effects. One of Dr. Hattie's conclusions—based on the data—is that active and guided instruction is superior to discovery.

In April 2010, the WWC assessed nineteen studies of the more traditional curriculum *Saxon Math*. One study met the WWC evidence standards; four met them "with reservations." The "extent of evidence for *Saxon Math*" was found to be "medium to large for math achievement." (WWC 2010b). All five studies found positive effects of *Saxon Math*; two found the effects to be "substantively important."

In September 2010, the WWC assessed three more studies of *Saxon Math* (WWC 2010d). The study meeting WWC evidence standards found "significantly greater" impacts for *Saxon* than for three comparison curricula. The other two studies met evidence standards "with reservations." In one, comparison teachers implemented a "variety" of curricula, including skills found in *Saxon Math*. In the other, a lack of student-level data prevented the WWC from making a clear determination.

In 2008, the National Mathematics Advisory Panel said that students need more emphasis on fractions, algebra, and math facts. "Difficulty with fractions (including decimals and percents) is pervasive and is a major obstacle to further progress in mathematics, including algebra," the report said. The panel added that teachers are best suited to determine which teaching method is appropriate for their class and that practice of math skills is necessary.

On the NMAP report's release, Dr. Tom Loveless, panel member and director of the Brown Center on Education Policy at the Brookings Institution, said in a *Washington Post* article, "I think the main message of this report is simple—content is king" (Glod 2008). Secretary of Education Margaret Spellings said, "This report represents the first comprehensive analysis of math education to be based on sound science" (U.S. Department of Education 2008a).

On May 27, 2009, Spokane's school board directors were given the NMAP report. The board president waved it away to a side table. A few hours later, on the advice of administrators, the board voted unanimously for an additional $90,000 of reform supplements.

Why would administrators and school boards persist in spending your tax dollars on curricula that have been heavily criticized for decades? Why would they reject the conclusions of sound research, pay no attention to parent complaints, ignore the implications of weak student test scores, and discipline brave teachers for speaking out? The next section offers possibilities.

THE NCTM, THE NSF, AND THE DEPARTMENT OF EDUCATION

Math professionals and advocates have criticized reform math for decades, yet math curricula based on reform and constructivism are embedded in school districts all over the country. Administrators and board members choose and maintain these curricula despite all learned opposition.

In this section, you will see how the work of the National Council of Teachers of Mathematics (NCTM), the National Science Foundation (NSF), and the U.S. Department of Education (ED) has virtually ensured that American K–12 classrooms are using reform math curricula.

National Council of Teachers of Mathematics

The NCTM offers conferences, professional development, materials, research, and publications regarding K–12 math education.

In 1980, the NCTM published "An Agenda for Action: Recommendations for School Mathematics for the 1980s." According to the Center for the Study of Mathematics Curriculum (CSMC), this twenty-nine-page document advocated, among other things, the use of computers and calculators in every grade (CSMC 2004a).

The CSMC said the 1980 NCTM document was "widely circulated among teachers, supervisors, parents, schools, school boards, and politicians. The document was a public relation(s) bonanza for NCTM as its release stimulated many editorials, much positive reaction across the United States, and a dramatic increase in the membership of NCTM."

In 1989, the NCTM published "Curriculum and Evaluation Standards for School Mathematics." This document, according to the CSMC, continues the themes from the 1980 publication, advocating for problem solving over computational skills, increased use of technology, use of manipulatives, conceptual learning, constructivist teaching, and "cooperative work" (CSMC 2004b). It also advocates for *decreased* attention on "rote use of symbols and operations," the CSMC said, "rote practice and memorization of rules, problems with one answer and one method, written practice" or "teaching by telling."

It's interesting to read the names of the people who, according to the CSMC, were involved in writing the NCTM documents—and then to read the names of those listed as being developers, board advisors, authors, and project directors of various reform ("inquiry," "standards-based," "student-centered") curricula. Many of the same names show up.

For example, according to the CSMC, members of the commission and working groups for the 1989 document included Drs. Thomas A. Romberg (chair), Christian R. Hirsch, Harold L. Schoen, Glenda Lappan, Shirley A. Hill, Daniel T. Dolan, Diane Briars, and Norman Webb.

- Thomas Romberg is listed as a developer of *Mathematics in Context* ("*Mathematics in Context*" 2001). Thomas Romberg and Daniel Dolan are listed as being on the advisory council for the *MATH Connections* curriculum ("It's about Time" n.d.).
- Christian Hirsch and Harold Schoen are listed as project directors for *Core-Plus Mathematics Project* ("*Core-Plus Mathematics*" n.d.a).
- Glenda Lappan is listed as a coauthor of *Connected Mathematics Project* ("*Connected Mathematics*" n.d.).

- Shirley Hill is listed as being on the advisory board for *Interactive Mathematics Program* ("Inside IMP" n.d.).
- Diane Briars was codirector of the Pittsburgh organization Prime Plus (which worked to implement NSF-funded materials in classrooms). She's listed as being on the advisory board for both editions of *Core-Plus*. ("Local Systemic Change Projects" n.d.; "*Core-Plus Mathematics*" n.d.a, n.d.b).
- Norman Webb was listed on the advisory board of the second edition of *Core-Plus*.

In 2000, the NCTM published *Principles and Standards for School Mathematics*, also known as the "Standards 2000 Project." Members of the writing team included Drs. Susan Jo Russell, Douglas H. Clements, Philip Wagreich, Joan Ferrini-Mundy, and Edward A. Silver (Ferrini-Mundy 2001).

- Susan Jo Russell and Douglas Clements are listed as coauthors of *Investigations in Number, Data, and Space*. Susan Jo Russell is noted as having directed its revision (TERC n.d.a, n.d.b).
- Philip Wagreich is listed as a developer of *Math Trailblazers* ("*Math Trailblazers*" 2001).
- Joan Ferrini-Mundy and Edward Silver are listed as being on the advisory board for *Connected Mathematics*. Edward Silver is listed as being a curriculum development consultant for *Core-Plus*.

Then there are the NCTM presidents.

- Dr. Gail Burrill, president from 1996 to 1998, is listed as coordinator, field materials, for *Mathematics in Context* and as senior curriculum developer of *Core-Plus Mathematics Project*.
- Dr. Glenda Lappan, president from 1998 to 2000, served on the NCTM commission that produced the 1989 standards document and also directed the grades five to eight working group. She is listed as a coauthor of *Connected Mathematics Project*.
- Dr. Lee V. Stiff, president from 2000 to 2002, is listed as a curriculum development consultant for *Core-Plus*.

- Dr. Johnny Lott, president from 2002 to 2004 (according to a University of Mississippi Web page), was codirector of *SIMMS Integrated Mathematics* ("Director" n.d.).

Despite indications that NCTM documents did advocate for procedural fluency, there also appear to be clear ties and connections between the authors of the NCTM Standards and the principles of reform math and constructivism as articulated in various reform curricula.

School districts say they're following the NCTM Standards as they adopt reform curricula that claim to be based on (or associated with) the NCTM Standards. Proponents of reform consistently cite the NCTM Standards as a motivation for the choice of program. Various people on the writing teams for the NCTM documents also have written papers, books, and other publications making clear connections between the words "reform," "NSF-funded curricula," and the "NCTM Standards."

As it endorsed several reform curricula in 1999, the ED said that "43 states have adopted or substantially incorporated recommendations from the national standards documents into their own standards and curriculum frameworks" ("Expert Panel Selects" 1999).

This author was not granted permission to quote from it, but everyone should read the 2004 comments (published on the NCTM website) from Dr. Cathy Seeley, titled "Hard Arithmetic Is Not Deep Mathematics." Dr. Seeley is a former NCTM president and a senior fellow at the Charles A. Dana Center at the University of Texas, Austin, and she was a member of the writing team for the 1989 NCTM Standards. More recently, she was a "facilitator" for the 2007–2008 rewrite of Washington State's mathematics standards.

From her 2004 comments alone, you can glean a sense of the problem we face.

National Science Foundation

The NSF is an "independent" government agency tasked with supporting research and education in science, mathematics, engineering, and other fields. It has a big wallet. In 1998, the NSF appropriation was $3.429 billion. Ten years later, it was more than $6 billion. In 2009, the NSF received an extra $3 billion from the American Reinvestment and Recovery Act, bringing its 2009 appropriation to $9.49 billion ("FY 2010 Budget Request" n.d.).

In 1991, the NSF launched several "systemic initiatives" in order to "kick-start" education reform. "Through these programs," the agency said, "NSF grants funds to local school systems with well-thought-out plans for how to reform K–12 science and mathematics education at the state, city, or regional level" ("Education: Lessons about Learning" n.d.).

The NSF also funded reform math curricula. A search of its awards pages shows billions of dollars spent over the last few decades on various projects that include reference to the National Council of Teachers of Mathematics or the NCTM Standards. In an undated article from Borasi and Fonzi (that had to have been written in 1999 or later), the NSF listed the curricula it had funded and considered to be "exemplary":

High school (grades nine to twelve):

- *Contemporary Mathematics in Context (Core-Plus)*
- *Interactive Mathematics Program* (IMP)
- *MATH Connections*
- *Mathematics: Modeling our World* (ARISE)
- *SIMMS Integrated Mathematics*

Middle school (grades five to eight):

- *Connected Mathematics Project* (CMP)
- *Mathematics in Context* (MiC)
- *MathScape*
- *Middle Grades Math Thematics*
- *Middle School Mathematics through Applications Project* (MMAP)

Elementary school (grades K to five):

- *Everyday Mathematics*
- *Investigations in Number, Data, and Space*
- *Math Trailblazers*

In case this list doesn't give away the NSF's philosophy, the paragraph directly below the list articulates it exactly:

> In order to be considered "exemplary," a unit or comprehensive curriculum must be consistent with the NCTM Standards, designed by groups of specialists in mathematical content and pedagogy, and revised based on field tests in various instructional settings.

In their 2006 study of *Core-Plus*, Hill and Parker said there was concern that "the NSF-sponsored curricula moved from pilot testing to large-scale implementation without sufficient independent evaluations of their efficacy in preparing students for college mathematics and science courses." While studies of the curricula had appeared to yield "promising results," Hill and Parker said, there were concerns over methodology. They noted that most of the studies were done "by persons associated with" writing the curricula or with implementing them.

You'd think that, as an independent government agency, the NSF would take care to remain objective in its approach to funding research. You'd think the agency would do all it could to avoid looking like it actively pushed particular programs, philosophies, or organizations. You'd think so, but the NSF also has funded several large, ongoing initiatives that encourage school districts to adopt reform math programs and curricula.

In an undated publication, the NSF extolled the supposed virtues of discovery: People are "moving beyond the kind of learning-by-doing that asks students to conduct experiments or manipulate mathematical equations with the simple goal of getting an already-determined result—doing things the 'right' way to get the 'right' answer. In the new 'inquiry-based, problem-oriented' curricula, students become participants in discovery by using fact-based knowledge to think through open-ended problems in a variety of ways" ("Education: Lessons about Learning" n.d.).

Criticism of reform and constructivism in the years following the development of reform curricula didn't slow down their nationwide implementation, and here's why.

Department of Education

Before the NSF listed its thirteen exemplary curricula, a U.S. Department of Education expert panel endorsed ten math programs as being "promising" or "exemplary." This event was worth a great deal to groups whose curricula made the list. According to the expert panel's undated "Guidelines and Materials for Submitting Mathematics Programs for Review,"

> Programs designated as promising or exemplary by the Expert Panel will be fed into a larger system . . . established by law to "create, validate and disseminate to educators, parents, and policy makers those education programs that have potential or have been shown to improve educational opportunities for students." . . . Programs can benefit . . . through publicity and professional networking opportunities, including commendation by the Secretary of Education, potential invitations to present at professional conferences and in front of other educational audiences, and recognition in professional journals. Various funding opportunities may also arise from a program's designation as exemplary or promising.

A Department of Education press release said the final panel members included "15 mathematicians, scientists, educators, and policymakers from around the country" ("Expert Panel Selects" 1999). An archived list from the ED said one of the panel's members was Janice Earle from the NSF ("Mathematics & Science Education Expert Panels" 2001). The panel's "guidelines" were clear about the basis for submissions: "Submitters are encouraged to refer to state and national standards documents (such as the NCTM Curriculum and Evaluation Standards for School Mathematics and Project 2061 Benchmarks for Science Literacy) for guidance in identifying their learning goals. Examples of learning goals that are appropriate for this submission include . . . any actual NCTM standard, actual NSES standard, or Project 2061 benchmark."

When all was said and done, the expert panel settled on ten math curricula that supposedly "met the highest standards set by our nation's leading mathematics experts and educators." The "exemplary" programs were these:

- *Cognitive Tutor Algebra*
- *College Preparatory Mathematics* (CPM)
- *Connected Mathematics Project* (CMP)
- *Core-Plus Mathematics Project* (CPMP)
- *Interactive Mathematics Program* (IMP)

The "promising" programs were these:

- *Everyday Mathematics*
- *MathLand*
- *Middle School Mathematics through Applications Project* (MMAP)
- *Number Power*
- *University of Chicago School Mathematics Project* (UCSMP)

Do you recognize any of these curricula? You probably do. The expert panel, the ED, and the NSF all appeared to connect reform math to the NCTM Standards. It also appears that the NSF had a seat on the panel that would determine which of the programs it had funded would be called "exemplary" and financially and practically supported by the U.S. government.

The ED assured America that it would be happy with the choices: "These programs work, and we encourage teachers, administrators, and policymakers to learn more about them as potential additions to their curriculum. The promising programs have great potential and strong but preliminary evidence that they too can serve our students well" ("Expert Panel Selects" 1999).

The next month, Drs. David Klein, Richard Askey, R. James Milgram, and Hung-Hsi Wu publicly addressed a letter to then secretary of education Richard Riley, asking him to withdraw federal endorsement. The letter was endorsed by more than two hundred other professors and professionals, "including seven Nobel laureates and winners of the Fields Medal, the highest international award in mathematics, as well as math department chairs of many of the top universities in the country, and several state and national education leaders." They had concerns with the programs, the letter said, and they felt more research was necessary (Klein et al. 1999).

But the reform gravy train steamed ahead. Already, *Connected Mathematics Project* was "being used in more than 2,200 school districts across the country" ("Education: Lessons about Learning" n.d.). After the endorsement, the U.S. government helped promote these curricula to districts everywhere.

Nowadays, the ED's Doing What Works website hosts a disclaimer, saying that posting examples of education products "should not be construed as an endorsement by the Department of any particular teaching tools—including any products named in materials from schools or found on websites referenced on Doing What Works. The Department cannot endorse specific activities, products, programs, or curricula" ("Welcome to the Doing What Works Website" n.d.).

Yeah. That cash cow already left the barn.

On April 5, 2008, the NCTM president was asked where the NCTM stands on reform, how the NCTM is funded, and how it would advise school districts now. An NCTM employee responded, but a 2010 request to quote that response was politely refused. No worries. You can figure out these things for yourself.

About the word "reform": The word "reform" is all over the NCTM website, embedded in documents and practically carrying a banner and noisemakers. Plug "reform" into the NCTM's search engine, and dozens of pages come back, some from past NCTM presidents.

About funding: Do searches on the Internet and on the NCTM website, using certain terms together ("NCTM" and "Texas Instruments" for example). Several large corporations have given practical and financial support to the NCTM. Additionally, an NSF spokesperson said the NSF has supported NCTM activities to the tune of several millions of dollars for conferences, research, travel grants, teaching materials, and projects.

The NCTM website also has products for sale, including the 2007 NCTM book *Perspectives on Design and Development of School Mathematics Curricula* (Hirsch et al. 2007). The fifteen curricula discussed in this book include *Everyday Mathematics*; *Investigations in Number, Data, and Space*; *Connected Mathematics Project*; *Mathematics in Context*; and *Core-Plus Mathematics Project*. The book was funded in part by the NSF and written in large part by people associated with developing the curricula (including NCTM past presidents).

About guiding districts now: As the Common Core Standards initiative gathered steam in 2009–2010, the NCTM released commentaries on that initiative, including

- "Guiding Principles for Mathematics Curriculum and Assessment" (June 2009)
- "NCTM Public Comments on the Common Core Standards for Mathematics" (n.d.)
- "NCTM Supports Teachers and Administrators to Implement Common Core Standards" (June 2010)

Read through these and other NCTM articles, particularly the June 2, 2010, "Common Core State Standards Joint Statement: Mathematics Education Organizations Unite to Support Implementation of Common Core State Standards."

The NCTM's goals, underlying philosophy, and long-term strategy are all there—in black and white and made abundantly clear.

LEARNING STANDARDS

"Those who torment us for our own good, will torment us without end for they do so with the approval of their own conscience."

—C. S. Lewis

It's important to understand the connections between learning standards, learning materials, and standardized tests. The standards (or learning expectations) are key to how tests and materials are built and adopted. If the standards don't make sense or aren't effective, then nothing else is likely to make sense or be effective. Therefore, the standards must be clear, concrete, achievable, measurable, and rigorous. They should be structured so that college or trade school is a conceivable option for all capable students, without the need for remediation.

This section offers one example of how reform standards and curricula retain their grip on classrooms, despite all contrary research and data.

When parents talk about college readiness, many educators interrupt with, "Not all students will go to college." That's true. There is a great deal of opportunity in nondegree fields. But some critical careers require college degrees. College degrees can make tens of thousands of dollars of difference in annual income. Additionally, the skills necessary for college frequently are necessary, or at least useful, in nondegree fields. Students should be prepared for college or a trade, whether or not we (or they) think that's where they'll go.

Learning standards provide accountability. They tell us what the children are supposed to learn. Standards also are important to curriculum, which is a corner of the Square of Effective Learning. Unfortunately, they're now also political tools, huge moneymakers, shell games, and handy vehicles for education ideology. It's dangerous for parents and teachers to blindly trust that learning standards are sufficient. Be sure. Know whether they're enough.

In Washington State, learning standards have changed multiple times, resulting in administrator complaints. A draft of a 2006 Office of Superintendent of Public Instruction (OSPI) publication says Washington's math standards (at the time) were guided by several publications, including one from reform advocate Dr. John A. Van de Walle, and these three from the NCTM: the 1989 *Standards*, the 2000 *Standards*, and the 2003 *A Research Companion to Principles and Standards for School Mathematics* ("Mathematics [Edition 2]" 2006).

Another document used was OSPI's 2000 publication "Teaching and Learning Mathematics," which summarizes studies on the teaching of K–12 mathematics. On page 66, author Jerry Johnson of the University of Washington cites a study listing six "observations" of how elementary math and science were taught, including these three:

- "Teachers believe that elementary school mathematics is traditional arithmetic, which is comprised of basic skills and computational algorithms."
- "Teachers depend on textbooks as their curriculum guide."

- "Teachers tend to use direct instruction or demonstration, followed by paper-and-pencil exercises to be done individually."

All of that sounds reasonable and helpful, but Dr. Johnson wrote, "We can only hope that these results are dated and no longer valid!"

In some of the research cited for that OSPI publication, we see the beliefs that children should invent their own methods and that standard algorithms can be harmful. It's astonishing, but there it is. Many administrators continue to believe these things, rejecting the algorithms that the rest of the world knows, along with direct instruction and procedural fluency. They continue to sway learning standards and curriculum adoptions toward reform math and constructivism.

By 2007, a consistent 40 to 60 percent of Washington students weren't passing state math tests. State legislators voted against math being a graduation requirement and ordered the State Board of Education to have the math standards reviewed by an "expert national consultant" and advisory panel ("Certification of Enrollment" 2007). The national consultant—Linda Plattner of Strategic Teaching—compared Washington's standards against those in California, Indiana, Massachusetts, Finland, and Singapore. After praising aspects of Washington's (then reform-based) standards, Plattner was frank about their shortcomings:

> There is insufficient emphasis on core mathematical content. Some math should be taught earlier in a student's schooling, and some crucial math is missing completely. Simply put, Washington is not focused enough on the important fundamental content topics in mathematics. This is shown in the early grades in which Washington standards do not ensure that students learn the critical algorithms of arithmetic and continues throughout the standards until it ends in secondary school with minimal expectations that are missing most of the algebra, geometry, and trigonometry found in other places.

According to Plattner, Washington's students were seeing 68 percent of the content found in other standards documents. By grade twelve, it dropped to 40 percent. Recommendations included fortifying the content, increasing rigor, clarifying the importance of standard algorithms, and increasing the "clarity, specificity, and measurability" of learning expectations.

Clearly, more content was required.

The next step was to rewrite the standards. OSPI contracted with the Charles A. Dana Center to oversee the process. In March 2008, this author began querying Uri Treisman, Dana Center executive director, about the contract. The answers did not come that way, but they did eventually come from OSPI (after a formal request and seven weeks). The value of the Dana Center contract was $769,943, plus another $110,000 to extend the contract. Education Service District (ESD) 113 also was hired to handle logistics.

Contrast the Dana Center payment—$879,943—with the unsuccessful bid from StandardsWork (just $129,403, plus expenses related to assembling a team). StandardsWork had already assisted Indiana and California with aspects of their standards. Why then was the Dana Center chosen at a substantially greater cost to taxpayers?

It's worth noting that Dr. Treisman is listed as an advisor to *Connected Mathematics*. Dana Center employee Susan Hudson Hull is listed as a member of the advisory board for *Connected Mathematics 2*. The Dana Center has hosted professional development in *Connected Mathematics 2* ("Charles A. Dana Center Professional Development for Teachers" 2010). Senior fellow Cathy Seeley is an NCTM past president. She was a member of the grades nine to twelve working group for the 1989 NCTM *Standards* (CSMC 2004b).

Drs. Treisman, Seeley, and Hull were "facilitators" of Washington's Standards Revision Team. Of the sixteen other "national" members of the team, five had ties or former ties to the Dana Center and ten to the NCTM ("Standards Revision Team Biographies: National Consultants" n.d.). These included Diane J. Briars (who was on the 1989 NCTM *Standards* writing team and also on the advisory board for *Core-Plus*) and Angela Andrews and Susan Eddins (who were on the writing team for the 2000 NCTM *Standards*).

The Dana Center team's first draft came under heavy attack from math advocates, who said it was unclear and lacking in core content. After subsequent rejected drafts, the SBE rehired Strategic Teaching to oversee completion of the work. Strategic Teaching's original contract was for $194,400, plus an additional $180,600 to monitor the rewrite. Add those amounts to the contracts for the Dana Center and ESD 113, and the costs to assess and rewrite the K–12 math standards came to at least $1,654,943.

The next step was to conduct a review of K–12 math curricula. You would think after all of this, reform math would be a dead issue, but OSPI placed *Core-Plus* third on a list of curricula meeting the newly revised standards—even though it had placed sixth overall in the preliminary review. Ranked second was the inquiry-based *Discovering* series, which had ranked poorly in the preliminary review for its geometry section.

In 2009, as math advocates continued to push, OSPI recommended just one curriculum, *Holt Mathematics,* because it had been chosen in all reviews. But, OSPI assured districts, success in math could come from several different avenues, and districts were under no obligation to adopt *Holt*. Freed from the obligation to change what they were doing, many districts didn't.

Soon, these conversations about state learning standards and curricula will be moot. In 2009, the Department of Education began pressuring states to sign on to Race to the Top, a competitive grant program. As they compete for these "grants," states benefit from adopting a federal vision for public education, including adopting "common core standards."

In July 2010, despite the $1.6 million spent developing rigorous math standards, OSPI "provisionally" adopted the national standards. The math portion is weaker in many respects than Washington's standards. (See "Divert Our Attention to National Standards, Tests, and Curricula" in chapter 9.) With the advent of national standards, anything we want to say about what the children are learning will have to be said to strangers in Washington, D.C.

HOW REFORM CURRICULA ARE ADOPTED

Before its website was changed in 2009, Spokane Public Schools explained the process by which *Contemporary Mathematics in Context*

(*Core-Plus*) was chosen in 2006 as the district's new high school math curriculum. The adoption committee's goals were "deep alignment" with the state's learning standards and College Readiness Standards, as well as "promotion of hands-on, applied (constructivist) learning strategies" ("Parent's Brochures" n.d.).

You can see by the goals that a traditional, direct-teaching approach was never on the table. Parents, teachers, and advocates could have argued for it all day long—it was not going to happen. But parents and advocates weren't included. When school districts eliminate dissenting voices, and their rules eliminate traditional approaches, we're going to get a reform curriculum.

As part of their support for choosing *Core-Plus*, Spokane administrators claimed it had helped students in other districts, including neighboring district Central Valley (CV), be "more successful." But in 2005, CV's pass rate on the tenth-grade state math test was 65.1 percent. A year later, it dropped to 56.7 percent. In 2009, it was 50.8 percent. By 2010, CV had scrapped its main reform math curricula, including *Core-Plus*.

Choosing a curriculum because another district chose it is analogous to choosing a medication because neighbor Bob uses it. You don't know Bob's medical history, so you wouldn't choose his medication because he can now run six miles in thirty minutes, and you wouldn't avoid his medication because his hair suddenly turned green. You might listen to Bob's story (especially if you want your lawn mower back), but what you want is properly conducted research on that medication and a professional medical opinion on whether it's right for you.

Testimonials aren't research. Students in other districts might be smarter, or they might be in tenth grade for the seventh time. Perhaps some had tutoring or all of the answers taped to an eraser. A few probably had brave teachers who closed the door every day and taught what they felt best. Proper research would account for these and other variables. But what if administrators don't know what good research is, or don't care to know?

Kristine Lindeblad, former secondary curriculum coordinator in Spokane, said in an e-mail that when Spokane chose *Core-Plus* in

2006, it "considered about 20–25 textbooks" (the website said it was twelve), narrowing them to four finalists. (Three of these finalists were on the ED's 1999 list of "exemplary" or "promising" programs. All claim to be based on, or informed by, the NCTM Standards.) Lindeblad listed materials that had supposedly helped with decision making, including—naturally—the NCTM Standards.

And yet, while this adoption process was going on, studies and commentaries were available suggesting that *Core-Plus* was flawed. Anyone who did even a surface assessment of the program couldn't help but fall over them. In fact, parents and math professors who spoke to Spokane's school board in February 2006 brought some of the research with them ("Minutes" 2006). The board thanked the parents and professors for speaking and then, based on advice from administrators, voted unanimously for *Core-Plus*.

According to board minutes, the superintendent said opportunities would be provided for "dialogue" regarding the adoption of *Core-Plus*, but no one can say when that happened.

Advocates hear that a lot: "Don't worry. We'll keep the lines of communication open. We're doing it provisionally. We can always say no later." When you hear that, keep an eye on the process and your wallet. Even if these things are said with the best intentions, the process is moving forward as they say it, and it's rarely, if ever, revisited.

Despite the abject failure of reform and constructivism, administrators still trumpet constructivism and reform math as "best practices." In May 2009, this author gave the Spokane school board research and reports supporting the adoption of more traditional curricula. Without examining the material or asking a single question about it, the board voted—on advice from administrators—for more reform materials.

On May 31, 2009, Spokane Public Schools responded to a formal request for public information that asked for the research and data supporting the reform math curricula being used. Karin Short, associate superintendent of teaching and learning, said the district hadn't kept it. Spokane's curricula align well to the new standards, she said, offering the names of a few tests and organizations—including the NCTM—that "influenced" the adoptions.

It's astonishing that Short would say Spokane's reform curricula align "well" to Washington's new standards and performance expectations. In 2009, when the state released its final list of curricula that align well to the revised math standards, Spokane's math curricula weren't on it. Two weren't even on the preliminary list. Despite several requests, she offered no data, research, or specifics. Pressed, she issued an invitation to look at some of their materials on "how to teach mathematics." Copies could be taken, she said, at fifteen cents per page.

In October 2009, facing weak on-time graduation rates and high dropout rates, Spokane formed another adoption committee—just three years after *Core-Plus* cost taxpayers at least a half million dollars. This author was chosen as a parent representative on the committee. In the first meeting, administrators gave each member the book *How the Brain Learns Mathematics,* by David Sousa. The committee was to use it as a resource for decision making.

Dr. Sousa has a bachelor's degree in science and advanced degrees in education. His book discusses how cognitive science supposedly supports reform math philosophy. The book is dismissive of traditional approaches and flawed in its logic. Cognitive scientists who were asked about some of the views in Dr. Sousa's book did not support them.

Listening to administrators talk, and looking at Dr. Sousa's book, it appeared that the best possible outcome might be to resign from the committee, publicly complaining all the way out the door. But one can be pessimistic yet still throw one's heart and soul into the process. In the end, the committee chose one of the better available math curricula, and the next March, the school board adopted it.

This happened not by luck but by fighting the Delphi Technique at every turn.

BEWARE OF THE DELPHI TECHNIQUE

"To me consensus seems to be the process of abandoning all beliefs, principles, values and policies in search of something in which no one believes, but to which no one objects—the process of avoiding the very issues that have to be solved, merely because you cannot get agreement on the way ahead. What great

cause would have been fought and won under the banner 'I stand for consensus'?"

—British prime minister Margaret Thatcher,
in a 1981 speech

In its 2004 annual report "Building on a Legacy," the RAND Corporation said the company designed the Delphi Technique in the 1950s as "a methodology for eliciting the intuitive judgments of experts and for building a group consensus."

Unfortunately, the technique is now often used to subtly force a diverse group to come to consensus on a predetermined conclusion. In 2009, some version of it was used on a curriculum adoption committee in Spokane. When a description was posted on the Betrayed blog, teachers and parents responded, "I've seen that!" An elementary school teacher said the district uses the technique "to get everyone 'signed on' to things they don't really want." It keeps people off-balance, she said. They're too confused and busy to engage in thoughtful dissent.

Here's how any committee can achieve "consensus" without actually achieving it.

The committee is split into small groups. Each group contains different "types" of committee members. Thus, like-minded individuals are separated from each other and spread around the room. Their influence is lessened and more easily "managed."

Rules for behavior ("norms") are set up so that real debate is disallowed.

Each group contains people loyal to the institution's agenda. One grabs for the pen to be the official recorder; another monitors behavior for adherence to the "norms."

Oppositional or problematic comments are eliminated. Recorders politely but persistently "interpret," reject, ignore, rewrite, or "reframe" unwanted comments.

Requests for debate or discussion are ignored or rejected. Monitors politely but persistently delay debate and redirect conversations. There's a lot of writing and talking in groups. Many tiny pieces of papers are filled out, discussed, ordered, and tacked onto other sheets of paper. The constant activity gives the appearance of productivity and debate, but it serves to fill time, prevent real dialogue, and produce desired cue words.

Each recorder produces a "summary" or "synopsis" of comments. The summaries virtually eliminate problematic comments. Remaining challenges are dismissed as being the minority view. Even clear oppositional statements can be questioned—"What does that mean, anyway?"—thus casting doubt upon them and lessening their influence.

From these summaries or synopses, the institution creates a "perception" or a "perspective," supposedly drawn directly from what committee members said, yet rephrased or "clarified" to shade comments to the preferred view.

Persistent questioners are ignored or admonished for operating outside of the "rules," refusing to accept the "consensus," or being unreasonable pains in the neck.

Most people find it difficult to combat all of this. It's uncomfortable being the odd one out. It's exhausting to fight for every inch of ground, every word, every phrase, every idea . . . and then look up to find that what was said isn't there. It's hard to go back and do it again the next day. And if one's job as a teacher or principal depends on getting along with those who run the committee, it can be a devastating choice one makes to try to get a solid word in edgewise. Most employees won't dare fight that battle and risk their jobs.

And so, some people get quiet or suddenly find they have time conflicts and must drop out. Those who remain tend to be supporters of the institutional agenda, they're willing to go along to get along, or they become convinced they're being heard. Dissent evaporates, and things quiet down. The few who continue to present an opposing view are easily managed and dismissed. Voila! Consensus.

The first time the members of Spokane's 2009 high school math curriculum adoption committee met was September 29, but it wasn't until December 9—more than ten weeks later—that committee members (including this author) finally were allowed to examine the curricula. What was the agenda on the other days? It could have included discussions of the new state standards, the various curricula assessments that had been done, the National Mathematics Advisory Panel report, any curricula that had arrived at the district, the suitcase of data and research this author brought for the committee, or various perspectives on how K–12 mathematics should be taught.

But the standards, curricula assessments, and NMAP report weren't discussed in depth, the suitcase of research wasn't discussed at all, and debates over teaching methodology were actively discouraged. Instead, the committee was forced to endure twenty-three hours on the following:

- How to speak with each other nicely. Committee leaders even "redirected" discussions as if committee members were six-year-olds. One expected them to say, "Now use your words."
- "Consensus"—what it means, that it was the goal of the committee, and how committee members were to go about achieving it. But views were diverse, and debate of critical issues was disallowed. True consensus, therefore, was usually not reached. Dissenting comments were often ignored, rewritten, or removed altogether.
- A new definition of "dialogue." Concerned about the lack of debate, this author asked that "dialogue" be added to the "norms" (rules for behavior). The word was added, but at the next meeting, the secondary math coordinator explained at length how "dialogue" means to *not* discuss the issues. In each group, he said, a person was to say something, and tablemates were to respond, one by one, each with a thought that was brief, not an opinion, and not a challenge. Everyone was to then move on.
- Discussions of the district's education "research." The district consistently handed out research that was poorly written, illogical, adamantly opposed to anything traditional, or uncritically supportive of reform math or extreme constructivism.

Although administrators kept saying that cognitive science supports current education theory, they offered nothing written by actual cognitive scientists. (This is probably because actual cognitive scientists say it's premature to base curriculum decisions on cognitive science.) A few committee members objected to some or all of this education research, but those objections were generally ignored, rewritten, or reframed as questions.

Committee members were to discuss perceptions of Spokane K–12 math and to state a preferred vision. That feedback was rewritten (committee members were told this), and original notes were tossed out (committee members weren't told that). Most comments that were supportive of a "traditional" approach were minimized or eliminated.

Despite having to suffer with this dodgy process, the committee chose two of the stronger curricula as finalists, and ultimately the district adopted one of these. It happened that way because several committee members understood what the students needed and resisted the manipulative use of the Delphi Technique.

HOW TO INFLUENCE A CURRICULUM ADOPTION COMMITTEE

In 2009, perhaps for the first time, Spokane Public Schools invited parents to be members of its high school mathematics curriculum adoption committee. For this author, after two and a half years of unsuccessful advocacy, it was a welcome opportunity. Trying to influence math instruction via the school board can be a bit like trying to move the back end of a donkey. (Once it plants its feet, nobody moves.) The front end of the donkey is the curriculum adoption process. Influence that, and you can influence generations.

Many districts discourage or prevent community participation. They say it's because parents don't know anything, but it's more likely that they worry about what we know. Unless we're on the payroll, we aren't under their thumb.

Influencing an adoption committee doesn't mean that one must influence administrators. (That's the back end of the donkey again.) The people to influence are other committee members, and that's doable. Some of them are already on our side.

Reformers don't have statistical support for their argument; even so, they continue to influence decision making. They know the players, and their arguments are comforting and familiar, with a common language and shared experiences. It's important, therefore, to be at every meeting. Things happen quickly, and once they're done, they're done for good.

The first time members of the Spokane committee were allowed to openly argue an unscripted slate of issues was in the last few hours of the last meeting. This author has always advocated on behalf of all of the students, but on that last day—in those final hours—the battle was for one child. Probably many tactical errors were made on that committee, but the last few hours of that last meeting proved to be a persuasive best.

Following is a list of suggestions for how you can influence a curriculum adoption:

Be there.

Community advocates write eloquent, informed letters, make phone calls, bring research, and speak to school boards. These are good things to do, but that information is easily dismissed, ignored, filed, and forgotten. Being on an adoption committee, however, and being knowledgeable, willing, and able to argue point by point with them is some of the most effective advocacy you can do. Teachers and staff members must be careful with vocal dissent, of course, but your presence and your vote allow you to have input.

Being on the Spokane committee meant being able to give the committee real data and statistics about student achievement, as well as information about the national standards. It meant knowing that a vote for one of the curricula was more of a fallback position. (They wanted a reform curriculum. If they couldn't have that, then they wanted to wait. If they couldn't have that, then they wanted the publisher to build a special book just for Spokane.)

It's important to be on time, to not leave early, and to not miss meetings. Being thirty minutes late one morning in Spokane meant missing the entire discussion about changing the weighting for textbook requirements. No notice was given that this would be discussed, and after just thirty minutes, it was done. Instead of "content" representing 40 percent of a textbook's total score, it was knocked down to 25 percent, tied with "what teachers do." That brought the two finalists closer together in scoring, encouraging the committee to consider adopting neither. Efforts to revisit the change in weighting failed.

Attend every school board meeting in which the academic subject or the adoption is being discussed. This shows that you're committed, and it allows you to develop relationships, determine leanings, and keep up with new developments. Be there when the board votes. Bring information and arguments, just in case. Once that board vote takes place, the deal is done.

Be informed.

Passion and personal anecdotes are great, but take care to establish yourself as knowledgeable. Learn educator jargon and preferred terminology. Use or reference pertinent reports and statistics, and feel free to ask for help from the (typically generous) academic, business, and advocacy communities. Use provable numbers and real reports. Bring in reports if you can, and hand them out on paper or on discs with embedded links for easy reference.

Keep up on developments at local, state, and federal levels, particularly with respect to curriculum assessments, adoptions in other districts, and national initiatives. You don't need to know everything in order to advocate. Parents know their children; teachers know their classrooms. You can talk about what you know. But the more you know, the more easily you can deflect incorrect information, unhelpful suggestions, and the big, fat lies.

Be polite and respectful, but don't allow bad ideas to take root.

Some people will deliberately try to rattle you to damage your credibility. Keep your eyes on the prize and swallow your anger. If someone says things that cause you to look like you're chewing on a lemon, hide your expression or go for a walk.

Focus on critical points, and don't become distracted with extraneous issues. It's hard to catch it all. You might miss things and make tactical errors, but go to meetings with a plan and ideas, and think about each point as it's raised, asking yourself, Do I need to address this? Will I get a chance later? Is it a deal breaker, or is it just annoying? Will someone else address this? If they do, will it be enough?

Mass telling (telling the whole room at once) and one-on-one discussion are useful for different things. Mass telling gives witnesses and encourages administrators to be polite. One-on-one is better for persuasion. You hear the objections, and you can deal with them right away.

When you're tired or cranky, be careful. For example, if someone wonders out loud what should happen with the old reform books, don't mutter that you have a match. (This was an impulsive response in a moment of weakness and is not recommended.)

Beware of the Delphi Technique.

Administrators often use the Delphi Technique to control meetings and people (see the previous section). Remember that you're an adult with autonomy. You don't have to sit down when they tell you to. You don't have to follow rules that prevent discussion. When they say, "We want only positive comments today," you can choose instead to work through the issues. When your words are rephrased, politely ask that they be written as stated. When they still don't go down properly, stand up during a break and write them down.

If the committee's "research" is all reform, bring in citations on math and direct teaching and give everyone a copy. Put the list and research on discs for each committee member. Even if the discs are never referred to again, everyone will have one.

Feel sympathy for committee members who are kept in the dark about how things are in math, in research, and in their district. In Spokane, this author told committee members that cognitive researchers say "cognitive research" isn't at a point where it can be used for curriculum adoptions. When the district's "summaries" of teacher, student, and parent feedback were inadequate, committee members received compilations of original comments. When administrative types said the math situation in Spokane wasn't too bad, the group received unflinching and unparsed statistics that reflected the students' reality.

On decision day, committee members received a list of two years' worth of various curriculum assessments, including the results of the district's curriculum pilot. As the committee prepared its scoring criteria, a few members fought for language that better represented the student, parent, and teacher feedback.

At every moment, you can examine the arguments and provide information and clarity. The clearer the picture, the less reasonable reform curricula will appear. Even if your arguments ultimately fail, you'll know you did all you could to provide the committee with the information it needed to make a decision that really is best for students.

Find allies and cultivate them. If you can, have allies on the school board. It's even better to have a school board filled with allies.

Being an advocate is difficult. At the end of the day, you won't be everyone's favorite person. Still, you can keep it from getting personal. Stay focused on the needs of teachers, students, and parents. One day in Spokane, a teacher confided to this author that the adoption committee contained several allies. It was good to hear. Up until then, everyone had been quiet, and it wasn't apparent there were any. Don't blame teachers and staff if they're quiet; it's risky to be vocal in front of entrenched administrators who can affect their job or paycheck.

A hallmark of the Delphi Technique is to spread out dissenters so they can't build momentum. Anti-reform advocates usually are surrounded by administrative types. Identify your allies but avoid calling them out or talking with them in front of administrators. Just because you can't see or hear them, it doesn't mean they aren't there.

Let go of minds that will never be won. Engage only when those minds argue for something that will take the committee in a wrong direction. If reformers continue to agitate, don't become angry or talk about them personally. Focus on what needs to happen.

See if you can enlist the help of a friendly board member who can attend the meetings. If a board member is there, you can reference board meetings, you'll have a witness to adoption committee meetings, and administrators are more likely to treat you politely, even if through gritted teeth. That politeness can help you get necessary information in committee members' hands. And if you have a school board with a quorum of allies, you are truly blessed.

Call on math advocates. The people with Where's the Math? (a Washington State math advocacy group) were a constant source of information and inspiration. Other math and science professionals across the country and from as far away as the Netherlands and New Zealand generally responded promptly to calls for help.

Support the teachers.

Teachers are told what, how, and when to do everything—and then they're blamed for the weak results. They're disrespected in myriad ways. This is an unfortunate administrative tendency that will not abate with the federal push to tie teacher pay to test scores. Teachers can be more receptive to your message than administrators who don't work in the classroom and who are paid and assessed differently.

Many teachers aren't aware, however, of how subjects are taught in other grades or of how hamstrung the parents are. They therefore have an incomplete picture of why the students have a hard time. Clearly state your support for them throughout the process.

On the last day, the Spokane committee heard that a vote for *Holt* represented support for piloting teachers (who had almost unanimously chosen *Holt*) and for all teachers who were desperate for a book. At some point, the voices on the other side of the argument began to look unreasonable, dogmatic, and worse—unsupportive of the teachers.

Give them information to take home.

Committee members are busy, and spoken arguments are easily forgotten. Give them citations and research on paper, as easy to read as you can make it, or better yet, on a disc with embedded hyperlinks. They can then think about it, take it home, and show it to others. Give them no rants, personal attacks, or cluttered layouts.

Spokane committee members also received feedback from students and teachers, unparsed statistics on student achievement and enrollment, and results from various recent curricula assessments (including the curriculum pilot).

Watch out for unhelpful ideas.

Adoption committees can go in unplanned directions. Unhelpful rubrics can be built, weightings can be modified, and committees can ultimately vote to change nothing.

When the committee voted on a recommendation, the first vote was slightly in favor of the other textbook—the one whose publisher offered the option to build a book. (The committee could essentially have voted for a book it hadn't seen or assessed.) Then there were tie votes, and some people argued for waiting. Effective arguments against that included these: The board expected a recommendation, teachers desperately needed a book, and weak student achievement and dropping enrollments necessitated a change. A teacher wondered how it would look to the staff and community if the committee did nothing. Would people continue to support the levy?

Pick your battles. Don't be distracted by extraneous arguments.

It's tempting to worry about everything and to try to deal with all of it. Don't do it, and don't allow anyone else to do it. Keep the committee away from issues of cost, implementation, supplementation, textbook publishers, jobs, tutoring, and dissent. Avoid muddying the waters. Leave these issues for another day. The more complicated it gets, the more attractive it becomes to "wait." Deal with the one curriculum adoption and nothing else.

Don't think that when the board votes, it's over. Watch your back.

Two months after Spokane's board adopted *Holt Mathematics*, administrators were telling teachers that *Holt* was just a "resource." The district would "supplement" this resource with its own materials, they said, pulling everything together with its own "program guide." People who had opposed the adoption of *Holt* were building these district materials, and early drafts published on a high school website revealed heavy elements of discovery.

Asked about this, Superintendent Nancy Stowell confirmed that *Holt* was just one "support" for the curriculum and that the curriculum was actually the state learning standards.

This author wrote about it on the Betrayed blog and mentioned it to the school board. Shortly thereafter, information about the new program disappeared from the school website.

From May 2010 to September 2010, this author tried several times to obtain information about the school district's plans for high school math in the fall, finally filing a formal request for public information. Despite *Holt Mathematics* being vetted by the adoption committee, preferred by piloting teachers, and adopted by the school board, a reform math program still was being built. The administrators persisting with this reform program were not fired for flouting the intent of the committee and the school board.

Reform is like black mold; it always comes back. Insubordinate reformers are rarely fired, and they can always get a toe back in. Advocates must remain vigilant.

6

CORNER 3:
THE LEARNING
ENVIRONMENT

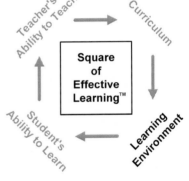

As of September 2010, several motivational posters are affixed to the wall of the women's bathroom at a neighborhood elementary school in Spokane, Washington. One says, "The aim of education is the knowledge not of facts but of values."

That's an idiotic statement. One would hope no teacher actually believes it. It's particularly galling to see a poster like that when one is a volunteer, running the school's chess club, reading with first graders, grading math homework, and volunteering to tutor young students in math—in math facts.

Schools that teach values in addition to facts suffer from "mission creep." But schools that teach values instead of facts have truly perverted their mission. Parents teach the values. Schools are supposed to be about academics. What schools can legitimately do relative to values is enforce societal norms and expectations, such as don't cheat, do your best work every day, treat your classmates and teacher with respect, and don't talk back. Schools can enforce these societal norms while teaching academics.

In 2007, staff members were asked to remove the poster, but as of fall 2010, it was still there, bleating its wrongheaded philosophy in its happy, colorful way. The poster is small, yet significant. The concept behind it is endemic to the nation's approach to education. Rather than turning out competitors, administrators intend to turn out their vision of nice people—People 2.0. This goal is unethical, and it helped create schools in which the focus is not on academics.

Public schools are filled with capable students who can't reliably do arithmetic or work with fractions. Many can't read at grade level, write a coherent sentence, or pass state tests. Their homework is a series of small, silent tragedies. Every day (except for late starts, holidays, long weekends, and teacher-training days), they spend about six hours a day at school. What are they doing? In 2006–2007, at a neighborhood school, they did the following:

- Students cheered on a local basketball team during a special assembly. At the end of the season, they watched college games on television during class time.
- At an assembly, a tape of *American Idol* contestants exhorted students to sell a product to raise money for the school.
- Students celebrated Dr. Seuss's birthday by spending the morning in their pajamas, reading, and listening to a local author talk about his new book.
- One week, there were two large assemblies, and there was no time for math tutoring. Then the class had a party for the student teacher. No time for tutoring. Then it had a party for the partner teacher. No tutoring. Then it had a party for the main teacher. No tutoring.
- A parent's request for a spelling bee was rejected, supposedly because teachers had time for just fifteen minutes of spelling per day. Meanwhile, there were computer classes, parties, character classes, assemblies, computer games, field trips, days off, and late starts.
- In April 2008, Washington legislators decided students should be talking about people with disabilities. Legislators passed a bill that requires schools to spend October recognizing the disabled ("Certification of Enrollment" 2008). Robert Crabb, a public school administrator with Riverside School District, wrote in a 2008 *Spokesman-Review* column: "It's very simple math. Start

with six hours of instruction. Subtract however much time you want schools to spend on Disability History. Subtract the time you want them to spend indoctrinating students on moral issues or values. Take away the time needed for any other special agenda that sounds good. What's left over is the time the school has to teach reading, writing, mathematics, social studies, health and all the rest. It's a finite number of minutes."

As state and federal legislators force schools to take time away from academics in order to specially acknowledge various groups, they're interfering with the process that would help the people in those groups succeed in life. Instead of being taught to fish so they can eat for a lifetime, these kids are being groomed to accept a fish a day for the rest of their lives.

In 2010, with Senate Bill 6696, Washington State joined other states in pushing schools to make room for dental care, food banks, and clothing banks. And thus, the mission creep continues. How does one say no to dental care for children from low-income families? One doesn't, but people who care about the effectiveness of the classroom can push for it to be done in its rightful place—social services.

These aren't the only activities interfering with the learning process, however. They might not even be the most disruptive things. That dubious honor might be given to standardized testing—not to the fact of it but to the way it's being managed.

HOW STANDARDIZED TESTING AFFECTS LEARNING

"We have technology now, we have brighter lights, it's warm all the time, we have a better environment to work in, but we still have kids that come to us yearning for knowledge, yearning to be able to read, to be successful, to see success in themselves. . . . If we continually tell them, 'You didn't pass the WASL. You got an F. You didn't pass the WASL. You got another F.' How long are we going to kick the dog before the dog bites us back?"

—Elementary school math teacher, Spokane

In some of America's more affluent school districts, high schools lure students to their programs with cool electives. In other districts, students stare bleakly at a narrow range of classes that focus almost entirely on "written, taught, and tested" subject matter. Even within those classes, the material is hammered down to whatever is likely to be on the tests.

Teachers have said if something isn't on the standardized tests, it doesn't show up in the curriculum—or if it does, not much time is spent on it. No civics, geography, grammar, or trigonometry on the tests means little to none in the classroom. If math tests call for paragraphs of writing, there are lots of paragraphs in the math classroom. Meanwhile, lunch breaks are wasting away, music and art programs are shrinking, and social studies struggles at the fringes. After years of dismal test scores, K–12 curricula have largely become Petri dishes for the tests.

In 2000, researchers from RAND and the University of Colorado reported on the effects of standardized testing in Kentucky and Washington State (Stecher et al. 2000). Their survey of teachers suggested that, following the implementation of standardized testing, the classroom focus changed to concentrate more on tested subjects, more on tests than on the standards, and more on the types of writing and problem solving that were found on the tests.

Instruction began to reflect "open-response questions with many right answers—just like on the standardized tests," the researchers said. "Students were asked more frequently to write *about* mathematics, to explain their thinking to other students, and to represent things in graphs."

As schools focus on "written, taught, and tested" subjects, other subjects (civics, communication, geography, economics, and languages) have largely disappeared. Additionally, students have neither the skills nor the time to experience the joy of learning or the satisfaction of accomplishment. It's ironic, considering the messianic zeal of today's hordes of math reformers and social experimenters to engage in what they like to call "deeper thinking" and "conceptual understanding." Every day, students waste hours reinventing the wheel in math and playing games designed to foster their self-esteem and deliver someone else's values.

George Nethercutt, former congressional representative and author of *In Tune with America: Our History in Song*, advocates for civics literacy. In 2007, after the Nation's Report Card gave low marks in civics to students in grades four, eight, and twelve, he said, "The civics report card showed that American schools—especially American students—are failing in the area of civics education, and young people are not becoming informed, engaged citizens of our country."

Other reports bear that out. We hear that many students can't name the vice president, don't know when the Constitution was signed, or don't know when the Civil War took place. A local teacher confirmed that her sixth-grade students aren't required to know the names of the states, much less the state capitals.

In each of two consecutive years, the Intercollegiate Studies Institute (ISI) surveyed fourteen thousand college students to determine their civics literacy:

- In 2006, freshmen scored an average of 51.7 percent, and seniors scored 53.2 percent.
- In 2007, freshmen scored an average of 51.4 percent, and seniors scored 54.2 percent ("Our Fading Heritage" 2008).

In 2008, ISI surveyed adults. The average score was 49 percent. Fewer than half of the adults could name all three branches of government. Elected officials scored worse than other adults: Their average score was 44 percent, and 30 percent didn't know that "life, liberty, and the pursuit of happiness" are the inalienable rights referred to in the Declaration of Independence.

Read the ISI report, titled "Our Fading Heritage: Americans Fail a Basic Test on Their History and Institutions," and see how little your leaders knew (Cribb and Bunting 2008).

Supreme Court Justice Sandra Day O'Connor said in a 2008 *New York Times* article: "Knowledge about our government is not handed down through the gene pool. Every generation has to learn it, and we have some work to do. . . . Two-thirds of Americans know at least one of the judges on the Fox TV show 'American Idol,' but less than 1 in

10 can name the chief justice of the United States Supreme Court" (Schiesel 2008).

The lack of civics instruction in the schools has long been an issue, but those who grew up in the 1940s, 1950s, and 1960s will remember greater expectations with respect to other subjects. Many of us took math, grammar, science, social studies, a foreign language, health and fitness, history, and music—and still had time to walk home and get a hot lunch. We didn't have "character" classes, calculators, or parties. Students who misbehaved were suspended. Those who failed were retained. We didn't get "character" awards—character was expected. Academic awards were rare and valued. There was no test "prep." The material was taught, and we were tested. Period.

Robert Archer, a Spokane teacher, commented in a 2007 *Spokesman-Review* column that students come to his ninth-grade class unprepared to work. He wants students to learn a work ethic—timeliness, preparedness, organizational skills, responsibility, socially acceptable behavior, integrity, respect, honor, and diligence. These concepts are discussed in elementary school "Character Counts" classes, but talking about them isn't the same as expecting them.

Every generation looks at the generation that follows and says, "That never happened when I was a kid." But today's students have been raised to play games, grab for technological toys, defer to classmates, and talk instead of think. With fewer math and science skills, fewer prospects, more foreign competition than any generation before it, and an education bureaucracy that refuses to tell it the truth, it's definitely an at-risk population.

Fred Strine, a now retired teacher who taught in North Bend, Washington, wrote in a 2007 *Spokesman-Review* column that language arts, Shakespeare, and other classics were taking "a back seat" to test prep. He offered a chilling view of how Washington's test, the Washington Assessment of Student Learning (WASL), affected his classroom: "Teachers drill, drill, drill until students follow the exact format of proven WASL responses. Practice forms duplicate WASL templates. Past WASL questions become new writing prompts. Precise WASL vocabulary is practiced weekly. Two weeks before each year's real WASL, school-wide cramming begins in all disciplines covered by that test. . . . Regular learning in real classrooms screeches to a halt."

Strine described eight annual "WASLettes," which also had students "practicing" for the state tests. All told, he said, two full months were displaced due to test prep.

In an announcement for Washington State's 2007 "Schools of Distinction" award, principals explained how their schools achieved success on the state tests ("Stories from 2007 Schools of Distinction" 2007).

A principal said, "The most important thing we do is make the WASL a regular part of our day. . . . Since we use the testing formats and the processes every day in our classes, the test is not intimidating or different for our students." Another said, We have "WASL Thursdays in grades 3–6 to give students practice with test format and build confidence." Another said, "Working from their fourth-grade scores, we work with students to develop skills and activities that require results in the WASL. Therefore, assignments are scored much like the WASL."

It's ironic. Amid their vociferous opposition to "rote" learning and "drill and kill," administrators support excessive test preparation using rote drill. A parent said this prep began for her child in first grade. But test prep detracts from the Square of Effective Learning. What it aims to add should already be there, developed through instruction and practice.

A poster at a local school purports to quote Mark Twain: "Knowledge without experience is just information." Here is a corollary: Experience without sufficient content knowledge leads to students not having the skills they need to go to the next grade level, to go to college or begin a career, to be good citizens, or to run their lives properly.

This situation used to call for remedial help, tutoring, or retention. Not today. In today's kinder, gentler education system, students are hounded to pass meaningless tests, then passed through to the next grade, regardless of their skill level—ostensibly as a way to help them, but really as a way to hide the reality of their poor education.

SOCIAL PROMOTION

"The safest road to Hell is the gradual one—the gentle slope, soft underfoot, without sudden turnings, without milestones, without signposts."

—C. S. Lewis

With confusing curricula, inefficient approaches, and insufficient focus on academics, many children won't be ready for the next grade. They're probably going there anyway.

Many districts have policies that students can't be held back. In Spokane Public Schools, Procedure 4425 says, "No student shall be retained more than once during K–8 grades except in special cases." According to this procedure, "Research demonstrates that retention does not help students who do not succeed because they have low potential; have social, emotional, or behavioral problems; or lack motivation" ("Policies and Procedures" 1988). Actual research is not cited.

This procedure sounds reasonable, but the reality in Spokane, as in many other public school districts, is that retention is as rare as a comet. Parents and students know that all K–8 students will almost certainly be promoted to the next grade, regardless of how well prepared they are to be there. A 2006 study by J. P. Greene and M. A. Winters assessed the effects of a "test-based promotion policy." The study found that two years after Florida students had been retained, they had "made significant reading gains relative to the control group of socially promoted students." The socially promoted students continued to fall farther behind.

In his 2009 book *Visible Learning*, however, Dr. John Hattie said he found an extremely negative influence of retention policies on student learning and also on the likelihood that students will drop out. One factor in poor outcomes for retention, he said, could be a failure to modify the program. (In other words, if a program isn't helpful the first time, it's unlikely to be helpful the second time. A local elementary school teacher said about this, "If you continue to do what you've always done, you will continue to get what you've always gotten.")

For administrators, the argument often ends there, but something has to happen for these students—something different from what happened before. It doesn't help them to ignore the fact that they didn't learn what they needed to know. Policies against retention can work if students have opportunities to get caught up, but for many, there is no targeted, structured remediation. Unless parents or teachers make special effort on their own, students are passed to the next grade without the skills needed to be successful there.

Eventually, students are passed through to twelfth grade, at which point everyone can bemoan the fact that "students are graduating from high school not knowing how to read and write or do basic math." But many won't make it through twelfth grade. In 2009, Dr. Robert Balfanz of Johns Hopkins University conducted a study of grades five through eight to determine the role that the "middle grades" had on graduation and achievement gaps. Certain notable factors had a dramatic impact on the likelihood that a student would graduate on time: "We found that sixth graders who failed math or English/reading, or attended school less than 80 percent of the time, or received an unsatisfactory behavior grade in a core course had only a 10% to 20% chance of graduating on time. Less than 1 of every 4 students with at least one off-track indicator graduated within one extra year of on-time graduation."

Being held back probably doesn't feel good at the time, but that doesn't mean the better thing to do is socially promote the child. Falling short in something is a normal, natural part of life. It can be instructive—to the student, the family, and the school. If students don't have the skills for the next grade, then something must change—with the student, teacher, curriculum, or general learning environment.

Spokane teacher Robert Archer wrote in a 2008 *Spokesman-Review* commentary that students come to his class "below grade level" in reading comprehension and vocabulary. "What exactly is going on in grades 1–8 in Spokane Public Schools?" he wondered. "If the students are so lacking in basic academic and work skills, how are they even making it to ninth grade?" They're making it there because they were neither retained nor helped.

How good can it be for students' self-esteem to be promoted when they aren't ready? Do you suppose they'll eventually get the idea that no one's ever going to fail them, that maybe they don't ever have to learn, that maybe there aren't any real consequences for not trying?

"What are they going to do about it? Fail me? They can't fail me," one fourth grader said. What he didn't realize is that the district is failing him—not in the legitimate, honest way he's imagining but in a dishonest, illegitimate way, by passing him through and then blaming him for failing to learn, which it will continue to do until he either graduates or drops out, in either case totally unprepared for college or the workforce.

Meanwhile, long-suffering teachers wind up with evermore challenging classrooms, stuffed with twenty-eight to thirty students of widely varying degrees of ability. As everyone laments the situation, many of the students sadly (and falsely) come to believe they're incapable of learning. The policy against retaining children and the failure to provide them with sufficient remediation are both destined to fail them. How can this possibly be about self-esteem?

Remember the classic episode of *I Love Lucy* in which Lucy and Ethel worked in a chocolate factory? Their job was to wrap chocolates and put them back on the conveyor belt. They were warned that if even one chocolate went by unwrapped, they would be fired. Initially, everything went well, but before long, the belt was moving too fast, the chocolates came by too quickly, and they couldn't keep up. In a panic, they began stuffing chocolates in their mouth. When they heard the supervisor coming, they got rid of the chocolates in whatever way they could—down their shirts and even in their hats.

When she came in, the supervisor could see there weren't any chocolates on the belt. She praised Lucy and Ethel for their work and called out for the conveyor belt to go faster.

Children in American public schools are like the chocolates. They're sent down the conveyor belt before they've been properly wrapped. But rather than slow down the belt or figure out a better system, workers are hiding the unwrapped chocolates. Doesn't it bother you to think about students being passed through, not ready, while plant managers stand around, nodding their heads, saying how wonderful the production lines are, passing out plaques, winning awards, and congratulating each other? Doesn't it make you angry?

Teachers must be angry as they survey their students, knowing that 40 to 60 percent don't have the skills to do the work they're about to assign. They must be angry knowing they could get into trouble for telling parents how it is, knowing that administrators refuse to accept responsibility or blame. A high school math teacher said he's angry: "I don't want my picture in the paper. I don't want awards. I don't want all that stuff. I want kids to say, 'You know what? I took a math class from [him]. I learned a lot.' That's all I want, but now that's not to be, and I'm angered by that because the philosophy has changed. All of a sudden I'm not such a good math teacher anymore. Well, I don't like that. It makes me mad, and after I get over my initial anger and I start looking around, my poor kids are getting shafted."

EQUITY VERSUS EXCELLENCE

"Sad, isn't it? We are definitely the world's first industrialized third-world country."

—Burma Williams, math tutor and retired math teacher

America's education establishment has tunnel vision, focusing on its vision of "equity," almost to the exclusion of all else. Equity means to give all children the same education opportunities, provide extra assistance to the disadvantaged, and close achievement gaps between the more and less fortunate. Unfortunately, equity has come to mean equity of results, rather than what it should be—equity of opportunity. Equity of results is where the research, time, and taxpayer money are going.

(Equity of opportunity actually was an original thought, but others used the term before this, such as Alfinio Flores in a 2007 paper "Examining Disparities in Mathematics Education: Achievement Gap or Opportunity Gap?")

Equity of results as a goal denies the reality of the human condition. Some students can excel academically, a majority can achieve sufficiently, and others will perennially lag behind. It's impossible for students to achieve more than they're capable of achieving. Therefore, if all students are to do as much as they can do, there must be achievement gaps. Yet, the entire education establishment has repeatedly stated its intention to "close" achievement gaps. How are they to force this utopian desire on the children?

The only way to close gaps associated with ability is to inhibit academic achievement. If capable learners would just tone it down a bit, the gaps would be closed, all students would meet a minimal standard, schools would meet government requirements, and everybody (in administration) would be happy. You wouldn't think educators would deliberately impede students in this way, but just look around you, at the dumbing down of the standards, the easier tests, the lowering of passing scores, and the redefinition of "honors" classes.

The amount of taxpayer money spent on special education programs in this country is a biblical flood compared to the pitiful drops going to gifted programs. Decision makers have said that it doesn't matter about highly capable students ("they'll learn anyway") and that "even if a program doesn't help the students, it won't hurt them either." Except that not helping the students *is* hurting them.

Not all students are capable of academic excellence. If all are to be challenged to their best potential, the "achievement gaps" can never be legitimately closed. So let's stop pretending. It will be such a relief, like ceasing to pound ourselves on the head. This isn't elitist or giving up; it's simply a truth that many are loath to say. If we acknowledge this truth, then we can move forward, toward the different types of excellence that are possible. Academic excellence isn't the only kind of excellence out there.

If we actually offered students equity of opportunity, most would find their own ways to excel. As administrators and legislators persist in forcing "equity of results" on the children, few students have the chance to excel in any of the ways they might.

One day, a young boy at a local school didn't want to do math; he wanted to play. So his tutor found some manipulatives, and the boy used them to build forts, shoot cowboys, and blow up buildings. He built up the fort (adding and multiplying), and he tore down the fort (subtracting and dividing). The process worked well for him, but it would have been excruciating for other students. Why should they have to do it just because he needs to? The philosophy in many districts is that, because he needs to, they all have to.

We can't always have what we want, but we can appreciate the children for who they are. Children will be gifted musically, visually, mechanically, or athletically—or in astonishing ways that haven't occurred to us. We must stop trying to stuff eight- and ten-year-old square pegs into round holes developed by PhDs. We have the ability to nourish the children's talents, whatever they are. Academics might say, "Well, duh. That's what we're going for." If that's so, then they've failed.

Some kids are talented in math but not in writing long paragraphs about their "mathematical thinking." Shy children can feel tormented by endless group projects. Deep thinkers can be frustrated by the lack of focus or practice. Is it fair to say that because these students can't articulate their thoughts on cue, they must not have any? Who will know what they could achieve if they weren't stuck in noisy, lockstep classrooms, where if it's Thursday, they're all doing *this*? It's ironic that administrators are so critical of "lockstep environments." They have produced a worse version of that which they criticize.

What about the small faces at the heart of the matter? Many administrators are so busy chasing preferred ideology, pretend percentages, and graphical illusions of minute improvement, they have ceased to really see the children. Meanwhile, students who rebel are quickly labeled as "at-risk," "behavioral," "struggling," "special education," "bad apple," or "dropout." How many just have academic needs that aren't met?

Gifted and Talented Students Are Neglected

Whatever its flaws, Spokane Public Schools has accommodated different needs—through gifted programs, honors classes, Advanced Placement, Running Start, cooperative programs, and others. The effort is laudable. The district states its philosophy toward gifted education in a brochure titled "Gifted Education Programs for Highly Capable Students." "We believe that gifted students need a qualitatively differentiated program that takes into consideration individual learning styles, special abilities, and their need to interact with one another. Providing programs and materials for students gifted in intellectual, academic, creative, artistic, kinesthetic, or leadership areas is an integral part of this commitment."

The National Mathematics Advisory Panel agrees, at least with respect to math. In March 2008, the panel said it supports "acceleration" for the mathematically gifted and that students should be allowed to learn at their own pace. On a national scale, however, this is a pipe dream, at least for now. Gifted and talented (GAT) programs generally have waiting lists, and their future is always at risk. The federal government typically leaves GAT funding to the states, and not all states provide it. Some provide a pittance, just a few hundred dollars per student per year.

Gifted programs, therefore, tend to depend heavily on levies, private donations, fund-raising, and grants. Every year, the question weighs heavily on educator minds, Will gifted programs be around next year? In 2009, Washington legislators made gifted education part of the definition of basic education . . . but didn't provide sufficient funding. In the governor's 2010 proposed state budget, funding for gifted education was suspended ("2010 Budget Highlights" n.d.).

In a 2008 report from the Thomas B. Fordham Institute called "High-Achieving Students in the Era of NCLB," Dr. Tom Loveless indicated that from 2000 to 2007, America saw much larger academic gains for its less capable learners than for top students. For the same report, S. Farkas and A. Duffett conducted a survey of nine hundred teachers, plus qualitative surveys from five focus groups. Most teachers said they don't believe advanced students are "a high priority" at their schools. Meanwhile, 73 percent said, "Too often, the brightest students are bored and under-challenged in school—we're not giving them a sufficient chance to thrive" (Loveless, Farkas, and Duffett 2008).

Bored and underchallenged for long enough, students begin to misbehave.

Equity of results won't help the country produce high numbers of internationally competitive graduates. It's important to acknowledge the cost of current education policy to the country's overall intellectual capability. Highly capable students score significantly lower than similar students in other countries, including Singapore, Finland, and Japan. People fret about our competitiveness in the world markets, yet

America generally neglects its students' individual needs and talents. As a result, an increasing number of parents seek out academic excellence for their children through private or charter schools, alternative programs, or homeschooling.

In 2005, according to former *Orlando Sentinel* columnist Peter A. Brown, Harvard president Larry Summers was worried that public educators were dumbing down curricula for higher-level courses in order to help lower-achieving students. Summers reportedly said that few of former president Bill Clinton's aides sent their children to public schools. President Clinton's own daughter attended Sidwell Friends School—a private school in Washington, D.C., that has taught children of other presidents, plus granddaughters of Vice President Joe Biden.

Brown said his own children weren't in public school, adding that "top students attend academically rigorous private schools out of parental concerns that the public schools do not sufficiently challenge them, because of the attention rightly focused on poor learners."

Before Senator Barack Obama won the presidency in 2008, his two daughters attended the University of Chicago Laboratory Schools (UCLS). In 2010, tuition at the UCLS ranged from $14,142 to $23,928, plus additional fees ("Tuition" n.d.).

After he won the presidency, President Obama's daughters enrolled at Sidwell Friends. In 2009–2010, tuition for Sidwell ranged from $29,842 to $30,842 per student per year, plus additional fees for dues, textbooks, labs, and equipment ("Tuition and Fees" 2010).

All parents—including elected officials—have the right to choose what they think is a better education environment for their children. This author's family has done it, by homeschooling in math and by choosing a nonregular program within the public school district. A choice for private schools, homeschooling, or alternative programs typically is a rejection of the current process, structure, philosophy, or policy of regular public programs.

At the same time, the long-term effect these decisions will have on public schools and on the children who go there is worrisome. If decision makers choose private schools for their own children, how well will they truly understand how to solve the problems that afflict the public schools?

INCLUSION VERSUS DIFFERENTIATED INSTRUCTION

Because of their single-minded focus on "equity of results"—and also because of lawsuits—governments and administrators have implemented a policy in many of our public schools called "inclusion." It requires all types of learners to be taught together, regardless of what they're capable of learning and regardless of what they've learned to date.

Additionally, as noted, social-promotion policies (where students are advanced to the next grade or class regardless of what they've learned) also lead to complicated classes. And current teaching philosophy leans heavily on "cooperative" work, where students work in groups to teach and guide each other.

It's a pleasant delusion that all of this togetherness helps everyone excel. What often happens is that the more-advanced students do more of the work, and the less-advanced students do less. Students know their abilities are on display every day at nearly every moment for all of their friends and classmates to see, discuss, and "peer-review."

It should be okay in this world to be an average kid—with gifts in some things and average abilities in others—but in today's classrooms, there is no place to hide. It can be a heavy burden for the students. Embarrassment can stunt any child's desire to keep trying. Additionally, if inclusion is allowed to take precedence over learning, it will impede the schools' primary mission of academics. All of the good intentions in the world won't change that bare truth.

Some inclusion is necessary. After all, classrooms hold twenty-five to thirty individuals, all with different talents and needs. However, with an "inclusive" classroom, teachers must simultaneously teach all levels of learners, as well as students who have physical, emotional, behavioral, or learning disabilities. It's a lot to manage. We can tip our hat to teachers' extraordinary efforts, while asking how many students are actually able to achieve their personal level of excellence.

Some parents support inclusion because they believe it's best for their children. Depending on how it's done, placing more-capable learners in classrooms with less-capable learners can be good for both groups. More-capable learners can gain by helping, being patient, learning self-restraint, and hearing different ideas. Less-capable learners can gain by being with all of their peers, having more help, and having more rigorous material.

With only one or two adults to a class of twenty-five to thirty diverse learners, however, the more-capable students often must wait. And wait. And wait. They can read or do extra work while they wait, but that isn't the same as being actively challenged. It's easy for adults—who aren't the ones waiting—to say, "Well, it's good for them to learn to wait." But while students are waiting, their brain—active and eager for new information— is forced to slow down. They become bored and frustrated. Some will step back so they don't stand out. Others will misbehave.

Some teachers try to challenge their more-capable students by having them help teach, but children have neither the skills nor the rhetorical sensitivity to manage and teach other children—especially those with learning or behavioral challenges. Additionally, while they're "teaching," they aren't being challenged as children. Eventually, they can become weary and resentful of this teaching role. While bored, they pick up bad habits.

It isn't any better for the less-capable learners, who are confronted daily with the gap between what they can do and what others can do. As the class moves forward, less-capable learners might be given different tasks to do, told to wait, sent into the hall, or sent out to different classes where they learn different things. Many don't appreciate being pulled out of class in front of everyone to attend special instruction; nor do they enjoy waiting while classmates engage in activities they don't understand.

Cheney Middle School in eastern Washington made a decision to teach special education students in a separate class—not as a way to stigmatize them but as a way to offer respite, according to a 2009 *Spokesman-Review* article (Leinberger 2009). Students were finding that leaving regular classes for special education made them feel different and "kind of stupid." But, housed in a class of all special education students, they felt more comfortable.

"I like to brag about this model," the coprincipal said.

Separating groups of learners is a "new way" to teach special education, the reporter said, supposedly the "brainchild" of a district committee. But it's really an old way that was tossed out on its ear.

It can be most difficult of all, however, for students in the middle of the learning spectrum. Their needs can be neglected entirely as teachers battle to manage the extremes.

Students in any class should begin at about the same place. It's why the military has boot camp and colleges have entrance exams. It's why we separate students by age, why we have classes for English and for art. It makes no sense to put students into advanced calculus when they've tested into remedial math, but K–12 administrators continually plunk children into classes for which they aren't ready. Concerns are dismissed with "They'll learn just by being there." Ill-prepared students do learn—to be frustrated and embarrassed. They often learn to give up and drop out.

Those who have outside help can persevere. A few will muddle through on their own, causing administrators to say, "See? It works!" Meanwhile, the quality of the classes can be negatively affected for everyone else. But for the administrators, this appears to be immaterial. Inclusion takes precedence over academics.

Internationally, the practice of placing together those with similar needs or abilities—otherwise known as tracking—is commonplace, but in America, relatively few K–12 students are taught full-time in classes that are built for them—in "gifted," "behavioral," career-related, or other special classes. When these classes are available, sometimes they're available just for an hour at a time or for one day a week. But children are the way they are all of the time—not just for an hour, not just on our schedule, not just when we approve of it, and not just when the budget provides for it.

Adults who wax poetic about inclusiveness should remember three things:

1. School is about what's best for the students. It isn't about us.
2. School is about academics. The primary mission is to teach information that prepares students for life and helps them assume responsibility for the country's future. Student learning is the point. It doesn't serve the students to pretend that things are going well academically if they aren't.
3. Children need to feel accepted and to feel they fit in. For the children, this is more important than academics. Educators and

parents ignore this need at their peril. It doesn't stop being a need just because adults want something different to happen. Behavioral classes, detention centers, and jails are full of people who never felt they fit in.

It's taboo to discuss doing away with inclusion, however. It's taboo because of the federal laws governing inclusion, because questioning inclusion gets one called "elitist" or "prejudiced," because parents have sued to have their children included in regular classes, because no one wants to admit failure, and because if we debate this properly, administrators might have to do something about it.

In March 2008, a parent wrote to Spokane Public School's online "Chat with the Superintendent" to ask about middle school honors classes ("Chat with the Superintendent: Curriculum" 2008). The parent said that the honors classes contained students who weren't ready for that material, that there were many discipline issues, and that academic learning for the other students was suffering.

The superintendent's response was to explain the concept of the honors class (as if the parent had asked, "Why do we have honors classes?"). The superintendent didn't address the parent's concern, which was that the honors classes weren't working the way they should.

In 2007, Spokane superintendent Brian Benzel and administrator Karin Short were given the scenario of a classroom of twenty-eight students in which six could consistently do the work, six were considered challenged, and the remaining sixteen need academic help to greater or lesser degrees. How does one teacher teach all of the children what they need to know so they can meet the standards and pass the tests?

The administrators said teachers just need to do differentiated instruction.

Differentiated Instruction

"Differentiated instruction" is when children in the same class are taught according to what each can do. Obviously, every teacher in every classroom engages in this to some degree every single day. However, the term can be used as a way to blithely dismiss impossible scenarios: "Just do differentiated instruction, and everything will turn out." It sounds great on paper, capturing the rose-colored imagination of everyone who sits comfortably in an office.

Somehow, different instruction is supposed to get all students to the same place at the same time so they can pass the same tests on the same day.

Consider the requirements of the 2001 No Child Left Behind Act (NCLB). By 2014, 100 percent of public-education students were to be "proficient" on state standardized tests (or some acceptable alternative). Although 100 percent proficiency is impossible due to the diverse nature of the human condition, everyone must pretend it's possible. The only way to handle inclusion and NCLB is to downgrade expectations.

Teachers have said that—because of the curriculum, teacher scripts, standardized tests, and administrators hovering over them—they can't stop the presses to help children who haven't gotten the concept. Sure, they try. Teachers do their best to accommodate all of the learners. But when a child doesn't "get it" in the time frame allotted, teachers must eventually push on and leave that child behind. It isn't their choice; it's district policy. And when some children have gotten it already and want to move on, teachers are often unable to accommodate them with anything more than busywork.

Differentiated instruction can be a wonderful, helpful choice that teachers make, but it's a choice they make over meeting other requirements set for them by district, state, and federal governments. Even as the Spokane administrators recommended it, they must have known that differentiated instruction is a devil's choice. Why would they say teachers should do something that conflicts with everything else they're mandated to do? Probably because Policy 4426 said it: "Differentiated instructional practices will address the individual learning needs of students. All programs, including those of special needs students, will be aligned with the district curriculum and designed to meet the specific learning needs of the students. When assessments and classroom performance indicate that progress is not sufficient, a student learning plan will be developed to address areas of needed improvement" ("Policies and Procedures" 2005).

So, all students will be taught together, through differentiated instruction, but everyone will still pass the same test on the same day. A teacher laughed when asked about differentiated instruction. He said the phrase is meaningless, just a "buzz phrase." Administrators can keep the phrase handy, however, for whenever they want to make the entire thing the teachers' fault.

Those who like and respect the students want them to feel okay as the people they are. Some will go faster academically, which is something they already know, even if administrators refuse to say it. Hiding the truth doesn't remove it. What many students don't know is that it's okay for them to be who they are. They're all gifted and challenged in their own ways. They'll learn what they can. They'll go where they can go. We can help them to the best of our ability, but we mustn't lie to them.

This brings us back to these large, complicated classes. If differentiated instruction is a devil's choice, then what is the best solution? Some say the obvious solution is all-day grouping: tracking. Put like learners together, and teach them the same things. Spokane Public Schools seems to agree. Policy 4423 says,

> It shall be the policy . . . to encourage flexible grouping patterns to better meet student needs. Creation of groups should be based upon, but not limited to, the following: age, grade level, achievement in the basic skills and/or student learning objectives (SLOs), grades, teacher recommendation, academic potential, ability to cooperate with the group, physical development, similarity of interests, current academic grouping, behavior, leadership qualities, and personal and emotional maturity. ("Policies and Procedures" 1982)

Yet, in the very next breath, the policy says something different:

> Special education students shall be grouped for instruction with regular students to the greatest [extent] possible. . . . Special education students shall not be grouped together for self-contained instruction solely on the basis of a common handicapping condition (label) except (1) in case of rare and/or severe handicaps; and (2) with the prior permission of the

superintendent or designee. Special education students may be grouped together for instruction during portions of the school day, based upon the criteria adopted for the grouping of regular students.

So, grouping is okay, even on the basis of academic skill, except that special education students can only be grouped for part of the day so as to avoid labeling them. Of course, some labeling must be done, otherwise how do we know which students qualify? It's that conundrum of labeling people that always bites well-meaning folks in the rear. You have to identify groups of students so you can address their particular needs, but you can't address their particular needs in such as way as to accidentally label them. You can label them, but you can't label them. You can group them, but you can't group them.

Policy 4423 is reminiscent of the pushmi-pullyu—pronounced "push me pull you"—from the classic Dr. Doolittle stories. The animal has a head at both ends and tries to go in both directions at once—thus being unable to go anywhere. A general policy of inclusion results in classrooms that try to go in several directions at once.

Let's set aside the pretend reason of building "self-esteem" and look at pragmatic reasons for favoring inclusiveness.

1. Decreased costs. As a math advocate noted, "Placing previously segregated children into regular classrooms results in larger, but fewer, classes." The district gains by having fewer specialized teachers.
2. Decreased liability. Some families have sued for inclusion.
3. Focus on closing achievement gaps. Stated goals at all levels of government are to close achievement gaps and bring all children to a minimal standard. This has become more important than meeting the academic needs of the majority. Everybody gets a little, even if no one gets enough.
4. An anti-intellectual bias. Americans are better at cheering athletes and musicians than they are at cheering the academically capable. In movies, academically capable students are often derisively portrayed as nerdy and socially inadequate. When it comes time to support them financially, enthusiasm is lacking.

5. Section 612(a)(5) of the Individuals with Disabilities Education Act requires "to the maximum extent appropriate, children with disabilities . . . be educated with children who are not disabled." Additionally, "public agencies are strongly encouraged to place a child with a disability in the school and classroom the child would attend if the child did not have a disability."

6. Fear and punishments. Educators fear students will be labeled or get stuck in these groups. The way to avoid that, of course, is for schools to be responsive to the children's needs. Some teachers will resist grouping, not wanting an entire class of less-capable learners. Additionally, the federal push to tie teacher pay to student test scores could be a financial nightmare for teachers of the less capable.

7. A misunderstanding of the children's needs. Administrators claim without proof that children appreciate being in classes with students who learn more quickly, and also that nobody needs to worry about highly capable students because they'll learn no matter what. Neither of these statements fits with personal experience.

Public education is a grand notion. It helps students learn to see the world as it is so they don't suffocate in a false world someone created for them. However, things are what they are. If public education isn't working well academically, then something must change. Academics are the primary mission of schools and must be the priority.

How have these classroom challenges skewed our perception of what it means to be "gifted" or "special education"? How many children might be gifted if they weren't so frustrated and bored? How many children might not be "special education" if they had the learning environment they needed? What would happen if all children had the opportunity to be all they could be—if public schools stopped trying to force them into the same little classroom box?

Ironically, Dr. Benzel and Karin Short are probably right about some benefits of differentiated instruction. Homeschooling is, after all, the ultimate differentiated instruction.

7

CORNER 4:
THE STUDENT'S ABILITY
TO LEARN

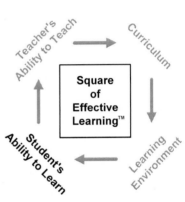

Corner 4 of the Square of Effective Learning is the student's ability to learn. It has to do with students being at school on time and ready to begin absorbing information. It's the responsibility of parents or guardians to make it happen.

Did students get enough sleep? Did they eat breakfast? Do they have lunch, or money for lunch, and something hydrating to drink? Do they have warm and clean clothes? Do they have school supplies? Did they get their homework done, and do they understand it? Have they received health care (vision, hearing, and dental)? Do they have a stable home where they're loved? Are they learning a work ethic and helpful attitudes?

In February 2010, at a legislator's town hall meeting in Spokane, Washington, several education professionals blamed parents for problems in education, complaining that we aren't involved enough. The comments were made in front of several very involved parents.

The same month, this author was invited to participate in a thoughtful BAM! Radio Network talk show. The topic was "How Involved in Your Child's Education Is Too Involved?" At issue was the "helicopter parent," an ill-defined term used to describe hovering parents who can't let go. Some parents fit this mold, although (1) the term is often used to scare off parents, and (2) parents need to be involved enough to ensure that classrooms work well for their children.

Administrators tend to plead for parent involvement, then contradict their pleas by pushing parents away. The messages to parents are paradoxical. Be involved. Don't be irritating. Help out. Don't hover. Communicate with us. You have nothing to say. We need parent involvement. It's your fault, not ours.

A 2004 Johns Hopkins University report from R. Balfanz and N. Legters said 12 percent of high schools nationally were "dropout factories," meaning that 40 percent of the students enrolled as freshmen didn't make it through their senior year. In response to the report's release, some administrators blamed parents for not being involved enough.

For many parents, it's annoying to hear that. We volunteer in the classrooms, drive the carpools, help with extracurricular activities, monitor the homework, and raise our children properly. When we can't make it to parent-teacher conferences, sometimes it's because we're single parents, working, taking care of the baby or grandma, driving the teen to soccer, or getting a root canal. Most parents are doing their absolute best to support their student's ability to learn.

On the other hand, some parents are really great, they love their children truly, but they say goodbye to them in the morning, feed them dinner at night, and put them to bed—and never once look at their schoolwork or make a move to help them figure it out. "That's what school is for," they say. "That's the teacher's job. I parent; they teach. I can't do it all."

And then there are other parents who—for whatever reason—are not very good parents. It's true that a great deal in education (although not everything) would improve if all parents worked with their children on academics—teaching, guiding, and supporting them as they develop their own sense of responsibility over learning.

Education Secretary Margaret Spellings said in March 2008 that she hoped parents would take to heart the findings of the National Mathematics Advisory Panel: "I hope parents will seize upon this finding," she said, "and, just as we encourage with reading, they also spend time with their children working on numbers and core mathematics concepts" (U.S. Department of Education 2008a).

In some families, it isn't going to happen. Parents aren't around, or they don't have time, they don't like math, or they would rather be doing something else. Some say their children are predestined not to be good in math because *they* aren't good in math. In other families, children are allowed to watch too much television, to play too many video games, and to favor extracurricular activities and sports over academics.

Helping children manage schoolwork isn't in the same league as feeding them, clothing them, and not allowing them to play in traffic, but children will learn better if parents help. That doesn't mean doing work for them. It means going over it with them and making sure they understand—or finding someone else who can help: a teacher, family member, friend, or paid tutor. What's the point of allowing children to sink or swim on their own? The goal of an education is that they learn, so by golly, let's teach them. It's just school, not some big secret. It doesn't have to be a constant trial or tortuous process.

With parent and teacher support of the learning process, children can do more. We want children to have every option available to them. They aren't born knowing what good work looks like, so we all have to teach them about their corner in the Square of Effective Learning. Every bit of reinforcement helps. School is important to their future, but they won't believe it if parents don't model that belief. It's easy for parents to accidentally close doors without realizing it.

Parents are an important aspect of the Square of Effective Learning—outside of the Square, yet dramatically affecting the students' development of responsibility over this corner. Ask any teacher what happens when parents

- help children to set goals, do research, have a schedule, and get homework done on time;
- explain what doesn't make sense, check to see if homework is done properly, make sure corrections are made, and encourage practice;
- help children learn to ask questions of the teacher;

- make sure children come to school having sufficient rest, food, medical care, school supplies, and appropriate clothing;
- model an attitude of caring about the children, about the learning process, about school, and about the schoolwork:
  - "It matters, so you must work harder and do it properly."
  - "It matters, so if you can't figure it out, I'll help you figure it out."
  - "It matters, so let's go back to school and get the textbook you forgot."
  - "It matters, so you won't play Nintendo until it's done."
  - "It matters, so don't cheat."
  - "It matters, so I'll take you to the library so you can do some research."
  - "It matters, so find the joy in doing the best work you can do."
  - "You matter, so show me what you learned and what you have to do next."

When parents do these things—and the thousand other things they do as loving and supportive parents—they teach their children to have a hand in their own education and to incrementally take responsibility for their learning. If you're a parent who is like this, then thank you. Teachers can always use more parents like you.

TURNABOUT IS FAIR PLAY

It's only fair, then, to talk about the barriers between the administration and the public. Some parents want to be more involved in the learning and administrative processes, precisely because they recognize their role in their student's education. But they're kept neat and quiet on the side. Administrators complain constantly about the lack of parent involvement, but what they want is happiness and stability. They don't want parents to be involved enough to rock the boat.

When parents intuitively recognize that a corner of the Square of Effective Learning is deficient and that their child's ability to learn is negatively affected, they have the right and responsibility to raise the matter with administrators. The education bureaucracy, however, tends to resist this kind of involvement and not to appreciate parent questioning of its collective wisdom. Administrators say it's unusual for parents to ask questions, yet they refuse to provide public settings in which parents can engage in dialogue. Pressed, administrators will agree to private meetings, yet they tend to dismiss parent concerns as being uninformed or isolated.

Another problem is that statistics from districts and states generally point to excellence, progress, and all-around administrator brilliance. It's hard to sort the wheat from the chaff. Everything is great, students are always promoted to the next grade, and everyone is in "honors" classes. Parents are kept in the dark about how things really are.

Parents who want honest and forthright discussions with administrators must overcome resistance and demand more. They must fight for it—when they don't have time, when they don't know everything they need to know, when they aren't sure of themselves, and when they keep hearing how wrong they are. It's a hard thing to do.

Open debate is healthy. It's constructive and reasonable. Administrators affect our children's lives through their impact on all four corners of the Square of Effective Learning. They use, and are paid with, public money. The public has a responsibility to expect and demand accountability, and administrators have a responsibility to explain themselves.

Be a squeaky wheel. Find out what's going on. The education bureaucracy will resist, but you can push past that. Be an advocate for your child. As you advocate for yours, you will be advocating for everyone else's. It's a pretty good thing to do for the world.

REMEDIATION AND TUTORING

"This problem can't be solved by doing a little extra tutoring or starting a student learning plan once a student enters high school. This problem needs to be solved back in the 3rd and 4th grades."

—Chair of the Evergreen High School
Math Department Bob Dean

Public education is broken. Administrators generally don't say that, but—looking at the constant changes in standards and curricula; low test scores; high tutoring and remediation rates; high dropout rates; dropping enrollment; truckloads of money spent on testing, teacher development, and coaching; and booming enrollment in private schools, alternative programs, and homeschooling—it's a reasonable conclusion.

Many students leave high school with serious gaps in knowledge that require extensive remedial work to repair. College credit isn't given for this work, and they can't begin college-level classes in a subject until the requisite classes are completed. This process is expensive, frustrating for students, and often unsuccessful. Many students never do learn the necessary material. The gap is too large, and they decide it is simply too late.

In February 2008, sixty University of Washington (UW) faculty members issued a statement expressing concern about the "declining level of math competency" of students entering UW: "Many students arrive with poor mastery of essential mathematical skills, such as algebra, manipulation of fractions, trigonometry, and basic mathematical operations" (Mass et al. 2008).

The professors said they believe they must lower the level of their courses in order to accommodate the poorer skills of incoming students. Cliff Mass, UW professor of atmospheric sciences, said shifts in K–12 education toward "inquiry-based" teaching methods have left an increasing number of incoming students in need of remedial math.

No UW department of education professor signed the statement.

Brian Jeffries, graduation policy director for the state education agency, the Office of Superintendent of Public Instruction (OSPI), was asked about his estimate that just 2 percent of Washington's graduates needed remedial work at UW. A few weeks later, he e-mailed to say, "Assembling the data files in a readable format has been a challenge for our data folks"—thereby blaming the data folks—"but they are working on it. Sorry for the delay." That was the last communication from him.

In reality, there is no one "correct" number. Remediation rates depend on which classes, colleges, students, and years are being counted. It's the sheer depth and breadth of the rates among recent high school graduates that point to a serious problem in K–12 education. Mass noted that the remediation rates at UW don't take into account "the fact that 1/3 of our students are transfers from [community colleges] where most had remediation."

Asked if they'd received a response from OSPI, Mass said there was nothing directly, but he believes the statement triggered media interest and influenced legislators. You'd think that when sixty university professors write a statement asking for something different in K–12 education, administrators would at least give them a call.

The professors' concerns are well supported by remediation rates in math at two Spokane community colleges: Spokane Falls Community College (SFCC) and Spokane Community College (SCC). For students who enrolled in 2008–2009, remediation rates were as follows:

- 90.5 percent: all recent high school graduates enrolling at either SFCC or SCC
- 96.3 percent: all recent high school graduates enrolling at SCC
- 87 percent: recent graduates from six Spokane high schools, enrolling at either SFCC or SCC
- 100 percent: recent graduates from four Spokane high schools, enrolling at SCC (CCS Institutional Research 2010a, 2010b)

Jeffries's 2 percent figure seems low. If the remediation rate in mathematics actually was 2 percent, it's doubtful anyone would complain. The question becomes, What to do about it?

Tutoring Industry Booming

You can trust in American businesses to sniff out the next opportunity. The tutoring business is a multi-billion-dollar industry and expanding.

Kumon Math and Reading Centers has benefited. In its fifteen hundred plus tutoring centers in North America, Kumon focuses on a process that looks distinctly more traditional in its approach to learning. The company is a big name in a growing pool of tutoring options for parents that include public and private tutors, nonprofit organizations, and online tutoring. The tutoring requirements of the No Child Left

Behind Act (NCLB) no doubt played a role in the development of these options, but many parents turned to them on their own, in desperation.

Tutoring can work because typically, it's done one-on-one or in a small-group setting. Students get immediate and personal feedback. It also works because private tutors tend to directly teach the material. They have a small window of time to clear away confusion, the meter is ticking, and everyone's in a hurry. They have to be accountable for results, and they tend to use the most efficient, effective approach. That's direct instruction.

Short-term tutoring isn't a replacement for a proper education, however. It also costs money. How much tutors charge depends on several factors, including where they live, what they teach, and whether they operate as individuals or within a center. Costs cover a broad range—anywhere from free to hundreds of dollars per hour. A January 2010 *New York Times* article reported that some tutoring companies in New York charge less than $100 per hour for one-on-one tutoring, while other tutors charge as much as $350 per hour (Gardella 2010).

If one of the goals of education is to close achievement gaps between higher- and lower-income families, a dependence on tutoring seems destined to fail. It turns out that the federal government thought of that—for Title I schools, anyway.

School Choice and Supplemental Education Services

Under the 2001 NCLB Act, if a Title I school fails for three consecutive years to meet targets for yearly progress, students become eligible for Supplemental Educational Services (SES). This can be tutoring or after-school services, and it's free to students and their families.

Initially, parents were restricted to tutors from outside the district, but because of the high numbers of families that qualify, the Department of Education began allowing districts to tutor from within. Spokane Public Schools was approved as an SES tutor and began offering the service in 2009. Essentially, taxpayers pay the district twice to teach the same material, and students are dragged through it twice. Is the second time the charm? Who knows?

In a December 2009 school board meeting, Spokane administrator Karin Short said she doesn't have enough staff to determine which of the district's intervention programs work. Earlier that year, administrators told the board they don't know how to fix the math problem ("Minutes" 2009). These moments of administrative honesty appeared to faze no one on the school board. Meanwhile, others do know how to fix the math problem. They're called parents, mathematicians, engineers, advocates and teachers, but who listens to them?

Where else but in public education does the consumer pay people for things they tell us they don't know how to give us? Where else do consumers fork over increasing amounts of money for things we don't want? And where else do consumers meekly accept all blame for everything that goes wrong?

Most students won't receive any tutoring until they officially become "at-risk." It would probably be cheaper in the long run to scrap public education and just tutor everyone. As it is now, private tutoring can mask the depth of the problem. Any improvements likely will be interpreted to reflect well on public schools. If tutored students were removed from certain sets of data, however, scores and pass rates would almost certainly drop even farther.

Help from the Community

With all of the need for tutoring and remediation, you'd think administrators would be delighted when people stepped in to offer help. In 2007, two men sought to hold their math tutoring programs at area schools. Both told this author they were refused. Jim Harrison, an elementary math teacher, wanted to tutor at a Spokane school outside of regular school hours using *Saxon Math*, a traditional curriculum. Local businessman Andrew Holguin tried to arrange for children to obtain free tutoring in math at a school in Central Valley School District.

In a November 2007 interview, Spokane's elementary curriculum coordinator said Jim Harrison was denied the use of school property because his plan was to "supplant" the district program, not to "supplement" it. This explanation is odd for several reasons.

It's okay to supplement. It's a subtle difference—supplanting versus supplementing. They both start with *s* and both end in *ing*. But one is okay with administration, and the other is a no-no. How do teachers know when they leave the happy Land of Supplementing and arrive in the dreaded Valley of Supplanting?

Several Spokane teachers have said they believe they are not allowed to deviate to any degree from the required curriculum—not supplanting, not supplementing. They believe they'll get into trouble for doing so, and if they choose to be a renegade and do it anyway, they must hide it from principals and supervisors.

The tutoring was to take place outside of regular school hours. If the district's concern really was supplanting versus supplementing, the fact that the tutoring took place outside of the regular school day should have assuaged it. The curriculum coordinator didn't mention any union or district prohibitions against teachers using other curricula.

It's just math. The tutoring wasn't in witchcraft, drug abuse, or pornography. It was in math—addition, subtraction, multiplication, division, fractions, ratios, geometry, and algebra. It involves skills people need when they balance checkbooks, make budgets, figure out mortgages, go to college, or begin a trade. We want students to learn these skills. Administrators have acknowledged that different methods work for different students, and yet they said no to supporting this tutoring because the plan was to use a different method. So, they didn't mean what they said? Or what, exactly?

Several requests from this author to borrow district facilities in Spokane for free math tutoring have met with resistance. If a tutoring program is supported in any way by the school, this author was told, the district's curriculum, approaches, and policy must be followed, and a paid certificated teacher or staff member must supervise.

You'd think administrators would be thrilled if parents, teachers, retirees, and university students organized free math tutoring—that they'd offer rooms and resources and say, "Wow! What a wonderful idea! How can we help? What do you need? Paper and pencils? Coffee and doughnuts? What can we do?" For heaven's sake, we aren't trying to subvert the children's minds; we want to teach arithmetic.

After the school district turned him down, Harrison took his program to a church. Holguin worked with Gonzaga University's John Dacquisto, associate professor of engineering, and Shannon Overbay, associate professor of mathematics, to arrange for college students to tutor the children directly at Gonzaga.

Meanwhile, advocates continue to try to hold administrators and school board members accountable for the results of their decisions. It's a tricky business.

8

ADMINISTRATIVE ACCOUNTABILITY

"We are not afraid to entrust the American people with unpleasant facts, foreign ideas, alien philosophies, and competitive values. For a nation that is afraid to let its people judge the truth and falsehood in an open market is a nation that is afraid of its people."

—President John F. Kennedy, twentieth anniversary
of the Voice of America, 1962

This author's philosophy toward authority generally centers around one word: accountability. There are two main kinds: small *a* accountability and capital *A* Accountability. In public education, there is a lot of one and almost none of the other.

Small *a* accountability is accountability to the system.

With this kind of accountability, there are statistics, reports, numbers, factoids, and figures. These numbers bounce around the organization, heading farther up the chain and occasionally shooting out to the public in the form of headlines. Change takes place because of these numbers, but the public typically isn't involved. Publicized numbers are usually supportive and positive about the overall effectiveness of the system.

In a seeming gesture of openness, administrators might gather to talk among themselves in public. They occasionally answer questions briefly and sociably. The public is allowed to attend their meetings and get copies of minutes, newsletters, and e-mails. We're invited in to listen and occasionally to talk but never to debate. We can call them on the phone or meet with them individually when they have time. They will smile and say, "How nice to meet you."

With this accountability, there are "challenges" to meet, but overall everything is "fine" and definitely on the "upswing." There are pats on the back, plaques, and photo ops. The public doesn't learn anything that is troublesome to hear.

Capital *A* Accountability is accountability to the public.

With this kind of Accountability, administrators speak the truth. They're held responsible for their actions and performance. If things aren't working, they say so. Employees are encouraged to speak freely and aren't forced into silence nor bullied into compliance. Nonperformers are released without undue wrangling or excessive cost. Records are made public—without the need for Freedom of Information Act requests. Pertinent input is welcomed, even if it's uncomfortable. Administrators acknowledge their mistakes and learn from others.

In order for capital *A* Accountability to thrive, the public must be engaged.

Public education is a bureaucracy, however, and it tends to be impermeable and self-serving. The public has been purposefully blocked from most of the process. The establishment spends billions of dollars each year studying students, teachers, schools, and families—dutifully reporting its picked-over version of reality and probably cutting down an entire rain forest of trees each year to publish the results. All the while, it fails to tell the public it's in a dark place where 30 percent of students drop out, and most of the rest require extensive remedial help before beginning college coursework.

Without capital *A* Accountability, administrators need not own up to their failures, parents remain uninformed, and problems—such as teachers' inability to speak freely with parents—can remain hidden behind an institutional smoke screen.

INSUBORDINATION VERSUS COERCION

The most obvious sources for information on public education are the teachers. They're on the front lines of education; who better to enlighten? But many teachers are afraid to speak frankly lest they be disciplined or fired.

Those who spoke with this author spoke carefully, as if the walls had ears. Some agreed to talk if they could meet outside of the school. Several said they'd been disciplined, with letters in their file, for talking with parents. One spoke with his lawyer before agreeing to meet. Almost all spoke on condition of anonymity. Three began to talk, then decided the risks were too great. A few gave the gist of their concerns but wouldn't allow note taking or taping. Several expressed sympathy yet refused to talk about their experiences.

A frequent explanation: "I just have a few more years to go to retirement. I can't afford to get into trouble."

Bob Dean, chair of the Evergreen High School Math Department in Vancouver, Washington, and a math advocate, said he's familiar with the fears. "I know that many teachers are afraid to speak out. . . . Some admire my outspokenness and others think I am crazy to 'rock the boat.' I have seen gag orders put on teachers and intimidation used to silence them. Anyone who dares to challenge the latest educational fad is labeled reluctant, out of touch, and a non-team player."

A high school math teacher in the Spokane area said he's been disciplined—including verbal reprimands and a letter in his file—for telling parents he thought they should petition the school board about an issue regarding college-preparatory classes: "I want to find a way to discuss the present situation with parents who can do something about it. I want to give them the information I have regarding the poor performance of students in college-level mathematics classes [who have] spent their high school days immersed in the curriculum we are using. While I don't mind making enemies, I don't want to lose my job."

Talking with parents about their child's academic situation is part of a teacher's job. When teachers aren't allowed to do it, children lose an important ally, and parents lose an essential element of Accountability. In February 2008, Spokane superintendent Nancy Stowell was told about these teacher comments, and she said it didn't surprise her.

"Certainly, you know, [there is] a wide variety of teachers out there," she said, "some of them very, very successful, and some less successful. And so, you know, people have issues along that continuum." If teachers have issues, she said, they should go to their principals. "It's the principal who really knows the teacher, and how good the teacher is, and we all want, you know, excellent teachers." She went on to say that "change is difficult." Some teachers will embrace new ideas while others will be "more resistant."

The high school teacher said administrators don't seem to want his ideas:

> There is no longer a professional discussion of these and other problems regarding high-stakes testing and related curriculum issues. Teachers of an "old-school" philosophy who are critical of the so-called "fuzzy math" and discovery-based learning . . . are vilified, ostracized, and sometimes subject to disciplinary action. Techniques that work, like direct instruction and drill and practice of basic skills, are ridiculed, and those that use them are seen as incompetent and ineffective teachers. . . . Collaboration has become coercion.

You'd think the union would stand up for teachers' right to express their views, and it probably does, but the language in the Spokane teachers' 2009–2012 collective bargaining agreement makes it sound as if teachers don't have any freedom the district doesn't want them to have (Spokane Education Association n.d.). Under the part titled "Academic Freedom," the agreement affirms "the principle of the employee's freedom to think and express ideas and concepts on issues, including controversial issues." But in the end, it says, the schools "are not the appropriate forum for personal causes or points of view held by an employee."

The prohibition against willfully complaining to students and parents is understandable. On the other hand, teachers should have avenues for questioning policy and curricula. They should not be disciplined for properly going up the chain of command or for giving parents their professional opinion on issues directly related to a child's academic learning.

SCHOOL BOARDS: CHECKS AND BALANCES

School boards are the "bosses" of the school districts. They approve the policy. It can help to liken district school boards to the Congress of the United States. It's an imperfect, yet useful analogy.

The Congress of the United States is analogous to the top "board" in the country. If legislators do their job properly, then Congress inherently checks excesses of the other two branches of government: the executive and the judiciary. The head of the executive branch is the president of the United States. The president and the administration propose such rules and legislation as befits their agenda. As the executive branch, they administer the execution of passed legislation. The president proposes budgets; Congress passes them (or not). The president proposes treaties; Congress ratifies them (or not).

The third branch of the government—the judiciary—sees evidence, hears arguments, and passes judgment on laws and rules made by legislators and the administration. Together, these three branches of government form a balance—a brilliant system of "checks and balances." The public ultimately functions as the judiciary of them all. It's our responsibility to examine the evidence, pass judgment, and make "rulings" through our involvement, our voice, and especially our vote. When all else fails, we can try to seek redress through a court of law.

Applying the analogy, we see that superintendents (or commissioners) are akin to the president. School boards are akin to the legislators. The federal government attempts to be an education judiciary through the No Child Left Behind Act (NCLB) and other measures of accountability, but teachers, parents, and community members are the better judiciary. Our best evidence returns home every afternoon with a backpack and hungry stomach. At some point, our evidence won't be able to get into college or begin a trade without substantial remediation.

We're supposed to gain other types of evidence via the testing process, at district meetings, and through the media, but we don't get to see all of the information. We don't get to hear all of the arguments. And most of us aren't involved in passing enough judgment.

The Administration

School boards generally have one employee: the superintendent. In Procedure 1000, Spokane's *Policies and Procedures Manual* says, while the school board is responsible for establishing policy, the responsibility to administer policy "is delegated to the superintendent of schools, who serves as the board's chief executive officer" ("Policies and Procedures," 2010). (Managing an entire school district by managing one person, however, is a bit like trying to manage an elephant by holding its tail.)

Superintendents and staff propose policy as it suits their agenda, school boards approve or disapprove, and staff members implement board decisions. In Spokane, that process is nearly airtight. It's difficult to ask questions in public of board directors, the superintendent, or her staff. Private meetings can be arranged, but there's a better way. All board members and top-level administrators should have regular forums that are open to the general public, where they listen to questions, answer the questions, listen to follow-up questions, and answer those. They should do it because it's respectful, and it's their role in providing capital *A* Accountability.

Most district administrators are hired, not elected. Other than going public with complaints or suing them, teachers and parents have no real "hammer" over them. We depend on the board to monitor the superintendent, and we depend on the superintendent to monitor everyone else. It's a real leap of faith. We hear about removing "ineffective teachers." When do we ever hear about removing ineffective administrators? It's as rare as a budget surplus.

The School Board

In January 2007, this author went to a board meeting to ask about test scores. The president said it was a business meeting, and they wouldn't answer questions. The district hadn't reached all of its goals, the superintendent said, but had made huge gains over ten years. He said someone would be in contact. They went back to their meeting. It should have been obvious this would be the process. This statement is included on meeting agendas: "The board's role will be to receive comments. No formal action will be taken on comments at this time."

(Right. Always read the directions.)

Several administrators have been asked if the public can ever have two-way conversations with the entire school board in a public setting, and the answer is, "No." But part of the school board's mission is community relations. If "community relations" doesn't mean relating with the community, what does it mean? District board directors spend money, set policy, hire superintendents, and make decisions about curricula and budgets—all with little public discussion with the people for whom it's being done.

Parents and teachers can get angry and frustrated all they want—the only hammers they have are to vote (but a lot of people must vote with you), go public with concerns (a cumbersome process—risky for some), or file a lawsuit (a very expensive, very risky process).

Do not depend on school board minutes to keep you informed. In 2008, this author went to a meeting to ask for five things—three regarding accountability and communication, two regarding math. When the minutes were posted on the school board website, the presentation was winnowed down to a few sentences noting the fact of the presentation ("Minutes" 2008c). There is nothing there to tell the public what was requested or why.

In February 2009, the Spokane board agreed to host a public meeting called a "Coffee and Conversation." The meeting was fairly well attended, considering the weak public notice. A quorum of the board was there, along with some media. Several people asked for better math instruction, and the superintendent took notes. The school board's website didn't offer minutes of this "conversation." Asked about it, the superintendent said it didn't have to.

Have you seen those strange, sad people who haunt public meetings to rant passionately about obscure things? Most education advocates aren't strange; we're persistent. We slog on, determined to find a way. Our reputation and credibility are always at risk, however.

If you advocate, take care to follow the rules, be respectful and polite, avoid ranting, keep it brief, stay focused, avoid personal attacks, don't swear, don't take it personally, and don't go to every meeting. With school boards, sometimes less is more.

School Board Voting Patterns

School boards have "personalities" that depend on the members, structure, issues, and available resources. Some boards are contentious;

arguments occur right up to board votes. Others aim for "consensus"; everyone underwrites the decision before the vote.

From June 8, 2005, to December 3, 2008, there were just a few lonely contrary votes from Spokane board directors on what should have been controversial issues (sinking enrollment; changes in curricula, superintendent, and staff; budget problems; cutbacks in programs and services; school renovations; bonds and levies; lawsuits; and a school closure). With new people on the board, the voting became less predictable but is still heavily influenced by administration.

Advocates must understand their school boards. Arguments must be presented early, particularly if the board's goal is to achieve consensus. Arguments made on the day of the vote often are made too late; the most eloquent arguments are unlikely to change decisions. You also can try to persuade individually outside of board meetings, and this can be more effective. It's less formal, and you can inform privately. (Board members know they can't be experts in everything, but many still don't appreciate being educated in public.)

Because they don't debate issues with the public, many board members fail to learn from their constituents. Despite the state's poor scores on math tests, high remediation rates in math, revisions in the math standards, and controversy over reform math, in February 2009, according to board minutes, a Spokane board director said the "frustration is that no one has figured out how to solve the [math] problem" ("Minutes" 2009). This comment was made in the face of the district's wilful refusal to replace its reform math curricula.

In March 2010, after Spokane's high school math adoption committee chose *Holt Mathematics*, the piloting teachers chose *Holt*, the students chose *Holt*, and the state had recommended *Holt*, the president of the school board voted "nay" to adopting *Holt*. She said "nay" to the one reasonably good thing to happen in this district mathematically in a decade. Why did she do it? No public Accountability was required for that vote ("Minutes" 2010).

When we can't get public Accountability from administrators or school board members, we might obtain it from standardized tests. Given a good curriculum, adequate teaching, parent support, and an effective learning environment, the students will learn. The first necessary bit of public Accountability is to get away from the convenience of "It's the students' fault."

Standardized tests are great for this. When you hear someone blame a district-wide 40 percent failure rate on the children or the teachers, you aren't hearing a reason. You're hearing a flimsy excuse. You're hearing someone cover a behind.

Standardized tests are all about capital A Accountability, whether or not anyone agrees with that and whether or not anyone uses them that way.

THE PROOF OF SUCCESS DEPENDS ON YOUR DEFINITION OF "SUCCESS"

> *"A lie told often enough becomes truth."*
>
> —Vladimir Lenin

These exasperating experiences in Spokane are echoed on advocacy websites and blogs across the country. For decades, mathematicians, professors, and math advocates have complained about "discovery" teaching styles, yet here we are, awash in discovery teaching styles. For decades, they've refuted the effectiveness of reform mathematics, yet here we are, awash in reform curricula. For decades, parents have tried to address their concerns with administrators and board members, only to be consistently rejected as uninformed, uneducated, unknowledgeable, and alone in their complaints.

Standardized testing is a good thing. Really. Done properly, testing tells us if students know what they need to know. Unfortunately, it isn't done properly. The public doesn't see the truth. Rather than being used to determine something, tests are being used to prove something.

Nowadays, a lot is riding on those scores (most of it money and control). A parent asked, "With so much at stake, what would administrators be willing to do to get the scores to 'go up'?"

- Prepping: In some classes, test prep takes place every week.
- Interfering: In 2009, a Spokane principal was accused of pressing students who had finished their tests to go back and answer

missed questions. The district acknowledged inappropriate behavior but did not remove the principal at that time.

- Dropping the cut scores (the passing scores): Dropping a cut score has the effect of allowing more students to pass, even though they have lower scores.
- Giving students multiple chances to pass the tests and also multiple ways to "meet the standard" without actually having to take or pass the tests.
- Pressuring parents to participate: Parents who take steps to opt out of testing might be warned that the school's overall test scores will include a "zero" for their child.

Other ways to get scores to go up (or at least stop going down) include

- not giving grades below 50 percent;
- offering just four grading levels so that nearly everyone gets a three or four;
- using new grading terminology (such as "achieving synthesis," or A, B, and "not yet");
- giving grades for effort or work habits;
- offering fun electives that allow GPAs to go up without too much effort.

In Washington State, student-achievement data has been plucked and parsed until it says something positive. Statistics have excluded students whose inclusion would have detracted from the numbers. When scores dropped, administrators focused on the few that went up or said the scores didn't go down as much as everyone else's. Students were flunking the math tests, but according to administrators, they were excelling at communicating mathematically.

Academic Achievement Awards

This section isn't a slam against teachers or students. They have challenges, and everyone tries hard. But some awards are given to schools for fine statistical distinctions that mean little in terms of actual school improvements or student learning. Compare achievement awards in your school district against actual achievement data, and see if the data merits an award.

In 2007, Shaw Middle School in Spokane was one of four schools to win a Title I Academic Achievement Award. (Just eight were given out in the state.) In November 2006, Shaw also was named a Title I Distinguished School for its reported success in closing the "achievement gap" ("Two Spokane Schools Earn" 2006; "Four SPS Schools Earn" 2007). Figure 8.1 shows Shaw's 2006 Washington Assessment of Student Learning (WASL) pass rates.

Grade	Reading	Math	Writing	Science
7th Grade	43.1%	41.1%	54.8%	——
8th Grade	54.2%	35.0%	——	33.6%

Figure 8.1. Shaw Middle School WASL Pass rates, 2006.
Source: Data extracted from Washington State Report Card, Office of Superintendent of Public Instruction

No disrespect to Shaw or to students who attend Shaw (this isn't their fault), but how badly did other schools have to do to not win an award ahead of Shaw?

At an October 2007 board meeting, two elementary schools won a 2007 Learning Improvement Award and the designation "School of Distinction" ("Stevens and Whitman Honored" 2007). The two schools were among eighty-six in the state to receive such status and the only two in Spokane County. Figure 8.2 shows Whitman's 2007 pass rates. Figure 8.3 shows Stevens's pass rates.

Grade	Reading	Math	Writing	Science
3rd Grade	54.5%	58.2%	——	——
4th Grade	77.8%	56.8%	38.3%	——
5th Grade	64.9%	56.8%	——	32.4%
6th Grade	67.2%	43.3%	——	——

Figure 8.2. Whitman Elementary School WASL Pass rates, 2007.
Source: Data extracted from Washington State Report Card, Office of Superintendent of Public Instruction

Grade	Reading	Math	Writing	Science
3rd Grade	64.2%	64.7%	——	——
4th Grade	80.0%	65.2%	46.2%	——
5th Grade	66.7%	47.4%	___	17.2%
6th Grade	66.7%	33.3%	___	——

Figure 8.3.   Stevens Elementary School WASL Pass rates, 2007.

Source: Data extracted from Washington State Report Card, Office of Superintendent of Public Instruction

How did these pass rates merit achievement awards? Were they looking at some trend, some infinitesimal appreciation in numbers, some tiny flicker of improvement? These scores are a "snapshot" in time, but things look no better if we follow students from one grade to the next or compare grades from year to year. Scores dropped in nearly every way and nearly every category. How does a school get an award for doing a worse job?

But awards make everyone happy, and that's what we want—for people to be happy (and not be running around rebelling and stuff). Awards were given out, pictures taken, compliments given. Watching the show, however, one wonders how the awards help the students. Many come from low-income families. Some have behavioral issues or parents with legal problems. Some live in shelters or barely speak English. They don't benefit from platitudes or false praise. They benefit from an education system that works for them. They in particular need a solid education if they're to escape the difficulties that dog their innocent lives.

Many of them get one shot at a good education. Pretense doesn't help them.

The "Next Step" and the "Next Level"

On August 26, 2008, the Washington State superintendent announced that the classes of 2009 and 2010 were "on track" with respect to graduation requirements ("Classes of 2009 and '10 on Track" 2008). But those requirements didn't include math or science, and the data didn't include certain students who were behind in credits.

In the press release, Superintendent Terry Bergeson didn't say, "OMG! We've been going in the wrong direction for an entire decade, wasting your money and putting your children's futures in jeopardy." Instead, she said a "major reinvestment" was required to take education in Washington State to "the next level."

Ah, the "next level"—a cousin of "the next step." It isn't that the level we're on is broken, in the wrong place, or imaginary. No, this is a logical, expected order of events. What we need to do is just go higher, if you can believe it, up to the "next level."

It's a perennially Pollyanna attitude that brushes all bad news off the table like so many leftover crumbs. It's like trying to talk to a friend about a car accident you've been in, and you say, "It was terrible! My brand new car was totaled, and every bone in my body was broken except one in my inner ear. The insurance company won't answer my calls, the other driver has psychotic tendencies, and the police told me not to leave town."

Whereupon your friend smiles and says, "But you saved your hat!"

The Learning Gaps Are Being Closed

Parents and teachers keep hearing that achievement gaps are narrowing, but in 2008, Dr. Donald Orlich, professor emeritus at the Science Mathematics Engineering Education Center at Washington State University, took issue with that. In a *Spokesman-Review* commentary, he separated into ethnicities the 2007 WASL pass rates for tenth graders (see figure 8.4).

Students	Reading	Math	Writing	Science
All students	80.8%	50.4%	83.9%	36.4%
Black	37.0%	14.2%	39.3%	9.2%
Limited English	38.3%	10.7%	37.7%	2.9%
Am. Indian	68.4%	31.3%	72.4%	19.3%
Hispanic	66.1%	25.6%	68.6%	15.5%
Low Income	68.2%	30.5%	72.3%	18.7%

Figure 8.4. Achievement Gaps & Ethnicity in Washington State.

Source: Data extracted from Don Orlich, "Eliminating WASL First Step to Equality," *Spokesman Review,* January 31, 2008, p. 7B

These numbers are for Washington State, but you can safely extrapolate similar numbers to practically any district, any state in this country. The National Assessment of Educational Progress (NAEP), the SAT, the

ACT, and various international assessments all consistently record huge achievement gaps, particularly in math and science. We can argue over why the gaps are there and how to remove them, but—clearly—decades of reform twaddle have not gotten these kids where they need to go.

NAEP Scores Prove That Students Are Doing Great

In a 2007 *Spokesman-Review* article, Washington State's superintendent said the state was fourth in the nation on the NAEP (Roesler 2007). Figure 8.5 shows actual data comparisons against other states from 2005 and 2007.

Grade and Subject	2005	2007
Grade 4 students in reading:	13th	19th
Grade 4 students in math:	12th	18th
Grade 8 students in reading:	23rd	22nd
Grade 8 students in math:	8th	21st

Figure 8.5. Washington State Student Ranking among 50 States by NAEP Scores, 2005 & 2007.

Source: Data extracted from National Center for Education Statistics, "NAEP State Comparisons," http://nces.ed.gov/nationsreportcard/state-comparisons/

But those numbers are relative and do not discuss proficiency. See figure 8.6 for how many Washington students tested at proficient or better in math and reading on the 2005, 2007, and 2009 NAEPs. It isn't pretty.

Grade and Subject	2005	2007	2009
Grade 4 students in reading:	35%	37%	33%
Grade 4 students in math:	42%	44%	43%
Grade 8 students in reading:	34%	34%	36%
Grade 8 students in math:	36%	36%	40%

Figure 8.6. Percent of Washington State Students Scoring at Proficient or Advanced Level on the NAEP, 2005, 2007, and 2009.

Source: Data extracted from National Center for Education Statistics, Nation's Report Cards 2005, 2007, 2009

One wonders why these pitiful numbers aren't blaring all over our local media. It's partly because state test results tend to offer a rosier view of student proficiency. More than once, the U.S. Department of Education has "mapped" state testing data against NAEP data. In 2007, Secretary of Education Margaret Spellings called the results of the most recent mapping "sobering" (2007b). She said, "Many states' assessment standards do not measure up to the rigorous standards of The Nation's Report Card."

When Washington's data said 36 percent of its black and Hispanic fourth graders were proficient in math, the 2007 NAEP said it was 16 percent for black and 13 percent for Hispanic. When Washington's data said 66 percent of its low-income fourth graders were proficient in reading, the 2007 NAEP said it was 21 percent. Similar disparities were found across the country.

Jack Jennings, president of the Center on Education Policy, testified in 2007 to a subcommittee of the U.S. House of Representatives that state data necessary for reaching "definitive" conclusions about achievement "were sometimes hard to find or unavailable, or had holes or discrepancies," that "states show more positive results on their own tests than on NAEP," and that states showing the "greatest gains on their own tests" tended not to be the states that "had the greatest gains on NAEP" ("Testimony of Jack Jennings" 2007).

But even the NAEP gives pause. In 2009, fourth-grade students needed to reach just 249 on a scale of 0 to 500 in order to test as "proficient" in mathematics, and eighth-grade students needed to reach just 299 on a scale of 0 to 500.

In a 2010 book review published in *Education Horizons*, Dr. David Klein of California State University, Northridge, was critical of NAEP content:

> The prerequisites of the NAEP math questions for fourth and eighth grade are minimal. They allow the use of calculators on a substantial portion of the exams. Some questions, which closely resemble IQ test items, do not measure math achievement, especially the questions that ask students to complete a pattern or to fill in geometric shapes with other geometric shapes, like puzzles. Some test insignificant vocabulary only; some are so vague they require guessing the intent of the questions. The NAEP exams favor students who have used constructivist math programs with little substance but a greater emphasis on patterns, pictures, and other low-level content.

The students scored poorly on scales that didn't appear to ask for much. All of these tests indicate serious gaps in knowledge.

In April 2008, Superintendent Bergeson was "excited" about scores on the 2007 NAEP in writing. "Washington's young writers are outpacing the nation," she said. "These students are not only prepared to meet the rigor of a high school curriculum, they are prepared to communicate well no matter what career they pursue" ("Washington 8th Graders Show" 2008).

Here's the reality. On the 2007 NAEP in writing, eighth graders posted an average score of 158—in the middle of the NAEP scale of 0 to 300. As a group, they scored at a "basic" level of ability (considered to be a "partial mastery of the skills needed for proficient work").

Let's see how it sounds now: I'm very excited that Washington students have gained a partial mastery of the writing skills they'll need for proficient work.

(Yeah. Not as good.)

The SAT and ACT Prove That Students Are Doing Great

The SAT

In August 2007, the Office of Superintendent of Public Instruction (OSPI), Washington's state education agency, issued a press release saying that, for five years running, Washington's average SAT scores were "among" the highest in the nation ("State SAT Scores" 2007). You have to read the press release carefully. This is not a straight comparison of fifty states.

In 2006, about 55 percent of Washington students took the SAT. In other states, it was as few as 3 percent or as many as 100 percent. For its press release, OSPI had compared Washington State against states with similar participation rates (thus excluding twenty-nine states). Among the twenty-one states with more than 50 percent participation, Washington State students scored better than everyone else. But of all of the states, twenty-four actually scored better than Washington ("Table 3" 2007).

The ACT

In August 2008, Washington students supposedly scored "far above" the national average on the ACT ("State ACT Scores" 2008). Massachusetts' high score was 23.6. The national composite was 21.1. Washington's composite score was 23.1. The superintendent called it "wonderful" news: "It shows our top students are more college ready than their peers around the nation."

Except that just 17 percent of Washington students took the ACT in 2008. Also, Washington's composite score is 64 percent of the total possible score of thirty-six. Washington students did better on the ACT than students in most other states, but collectively they achieved an overall D in terms of academic achievement. Additionally, achievement gaps between white or Asian students and black, Hispanic, or American Indian students ranged from around thirty to forty points ("ACT High School Profile Report" 2008).

Also, the SAT and ACT are taken by students from other districts, other schools, and other countries and also by those educated through remediation, tutoring, homeschooling, supplementing, private schools, and alternative programs.

What do these tests say about any state's public-education system? It's hard to know.

Advanced Placement Scores Prove That Students Are Doing Great

In December 2008, Richard Pan reported on a disturbing trend with respect to the Advanced Placement (AP) Program, noting a dramatic increase in the number of students taking AP exams from 1997 to 2007—and particularly from 2004 to 2007. It appeared to be a national tendency to boost AP participation even though more students were failing AP tests and even though overall grades were weakening.

In February 2007, an OSPI press release said Washington State was among the top four states for how many in the Class of 2006 scored a three or higher on AP tests ("Advanced Placement Report: Washington

State" 2007). The state superintendent said, "This report offers more evidence that we're among the national leaders in creating a public education system that strives for excellence and equity."

Again, read the press release carefully. What put Washington State in "the top four" was its increase from 2000 to 2006 in the percentage of all students in the entire class of 2006 who took an AP test and who scored three or higher. (The entire class includes the students who took AP classes and those who didn't. So, if the entire population decreased in size, then the percent taking AP classes would increase.) Looking at just the population of students who took AP classes, however, the percent who scored three or higher on the AP tests actually dropped.

"The quality of performance on the AP work is climbing, even as the program expands to more kids," said OSPI's Advanced Placement program supervisor. "Many more students are taking the tests and doing well on them." But it all depends on how one works those statistics.

Spokane mirrors Washington State. In Spokane, AP enrollment and exam taking increased from 2000 to 2008 despite a drop of about two thousand in full-time enrollment (see figure 8.7).

Technically, Spokane administrators can say that the number of students passing AP exams has increased (and they do tend to say this). In 2000, 81.3 percent of

	2000	2008
Number of students	368	1093
Number of exams	636	2028
Number of course areas	15	27
Number of exams passed	517	1099
Percent Passing	81%	54%
Percent Failing:	19%	46%
Average Grade	3.45	2.72

Figure 8.7. Spokane Public Schools AP Class Data, 2000 and 2008.

Source: Data extracted from Spokane Public Schools Advanced Placement Exam Results, 1992–2008

636 student exams were passed, for a total of 517 exams passed. In 2008, 54.2 percent of 2,028 student exams were passed, for a total of 1,099 exams passed. In effect, 582 more exams were passed in 2008 than in 2000.

Technically, however, it also can be said that the number of students failing AP exams has increased (they don't tend to say this). In 2000, 18.7 percent of student exams (119 total) were not passed, while in 2008, 45.8 percent of student exams (929 total) were not passed.

In effect, 810 more exams were failed in 2008 than in 2000.

According to school board minutes ("Minutes" 2008b), when presented with evidence that AP pass rates in Spokane had dropped, board director Rocco Trippiedi "recalled past discussions about the value of encouraging students to take the more challenging AP classes, regardless of the grade the student received or whether he or she even took the test."

Folks, if we aren't concerned with pass rates or AP tests, how do students know when they've achieved what they want to achieve? How does the district know when it's failed to do its job? The universities know. Whitworth University, Gonzaga University, Eastern Washington University, Washington State University, the University of Washington, and Spokane Community College all have indicated that—depending on the subject—they give credit for passing scores on the actual AP test of three or greater (or sometimes four or greater).

State administrators know too. Students had to obtain at least a three on an AP math exam in order to use the class as an alternative to the tenth-grade state math test (the WASL).

Passing State Tests Means Students Learned What They Need to Know

Parents have complained that their child passed standardized tests, got As in honors math, passed calculus in high school, and then tested into remedial math in college.

Dr. Tom McKenzie, chair of the Department of Mathematics at Gonzaga University, said he doesn't care about scores from Washington's standardized math test. What he cares about are math skills, and in his experience, the math skills of local high school graduates have been weak.

Teachers and parents continually hear how the scores are going up, 90 percent passed this, and 80 percent passed that. "We're on track," we hear. "Everyone's looking to us."

In Washington State, an OSPI publication called "2007 Report to Families" touted these kinds of figures. The data from that publication—which focused on students who were scheduled to receive a diploma in

2008—is cumulative, gathering pass rates from three testing sessions. Also, the figures don't include students who dropped out, who didn't take the test, or who—after three years of high school—didn't qualify as juniors.

If you take out everybody who didn't take or pass the test, you can say, "Wow! 100 percent of the students who passed the test have passed the test."

When information on the Class of 2008 was released, the state superintendent was pleased that 91.4 percent of twelfth graders had achieved the new graduation requirement, and that 85.5 percent of juniors in the Class of 2009 had as well ("Classes of 2009 and 2010 on Track" 2008; "More Than 90 Percent" 2008). But the graduation requirement was in reading and writing, not in math or science. Cited figures were again cumulative, gathering data over several attempts and several test alternatives. They didn't include students who dropped out or who fell behind on credits.

A few months later, the superintendent said she was pleased that students were "continuing the momentum" set by the Class of 2008. "We know there's still plenty of hard work ahead, but these results are very encouraging to me" ("Classes of 2009 and '10 on Track" 2008).

It's perplexing how she could be encouraged by results that show students continuing to have difficulty. Why would she have been pleased in the face of continuing achievement gaps, high dropout rates, and high remediation rates?

The Curricula Are Not the Problem

In a November 2007 interview, Spokane's elementary curriculum coordinator was asked if she thought the district's K–6 reform math curricula were good. She said, "I don't think we'd have the curriculum in place if we felt it wasn't appropriate." Logically, then, administrators must believe the programs are appropriate—since they're still here. But that's weird, inundated as they are with a wealth of empirical and anecdotal evidence that says otherwise.

If someone says the grass is green, and all evidence indicates that it's brown and dead looking, then we have to think that

- the person doesn't understand what we're asking;
- the person has a different definition of "green";
- the person doesn't want to know what color the grass is;
- the person is being deliberately deceitful;
- the person is foolish, unknowledgeable, or stupid;
- the person has a self-interested reason for insisting that brown grass is green.

A 60 Percent Pass Rate Is Good

In January 2007, then Spokane superintendent Brian Benzel was offered a statistic:

"Forty percent of the students didn't pass the math requirement."

"But sixty percent did," he said encouragingly.

"I know, but if you're a parent of one of the sixty percent, then woo-hoo for you, but if you're a parent of the one of the forty percent . . ."

Dr. Benzel proceeded to blame the students: "If there's a problem after fourth grade, this thing called 'free will' comes into play," he said. "The choices that students make take on grave power in a person's willingness to learn. Up through fourth grade and ten years old, kids tend to do pretty much what we tell them to do."

Are you shocked? Other administrators—and some teachers—have blamed culture, a sense of entitlement, hormones, bad attitudes, a lack of foresight, video games, and parents. Students just don't want to learn, we're told. They don't think school is worth their time.

Perhaps students don't think school is worth their time. Those who tutor all grades of students will notice an unmistakable drop-off in interest around fourth and fifth grade. It never seems to occur to administrators that the reason might have to do with district policies on curricula, grading, remediation, retention, inclusion, or teaching methodology.

Instead of whining about social issues over which they have no control, administrators should focus on their mission. Install rigorous curricula, allow the teachers to teach, and remove distractions (including themselves) from the learning environment. If they did just those three things, all at once, from K–12 (and not piecemeal, with disconnected programs here and there), things would begin to make sense, and student engagement would improve.

Spokane administrators have been shown district pass rates in math and how they dropped grade after grade until grade ten, where fewer than half the students passed. Some said those pass rates might be good, depending on where the groups began. If the situation weren't affecting children, the statements might be funny. It isn't all that often that 60 percent is "good." If you expect a score to be zero, and instead it's 60 percent, perhaps 60 percent is a huge relief. But it isn't good.

- It isn't good on a battlefield. ("Sir, 60 percent of the men have guns and ammunition.")
- It isn't good in a hospital. ("Ma'am, 60 percent of our patients lived through the night.")
- It isn't good at the dinner table. ("You get to eat 60 percent of your meals.")
- It isn't good in college. ("Sixty percent of you will get textbooks this year.")

It isn't good as a score on a math test or as a pass rate on a standardized test—especially considering how little those tests demand. What about the children who didn't pass? It isn't cause for celebration when 61.8 percent of students made it as opposed to only 59.3 percent last year. Both figures are pitiful. Why must we slowly eke our way up over three decades of struggle? There's no good reason why it shouldn't happen now, this year, on their watch. We've been teaching math and science in this country for hundreds of years. How did it suddenly get to be so hard?

It's a travesty when just 60 percent pass the math portion and even fewer pass the science portion. It's a complete district failure. Imagine how the students see themselves. It's shameful when, with a more effective curriculum and learning environment, most could have learned what they needed to know. How can we even communicate when we see a 60 percent pass rate as a district failure, and they see it as potentially good? It might be an improvement. It might be the best you can do. It's certainly better than zero. But it isn't good.

Try to tell administrators that. Watch them turn around and incorporate their shameful thinking into their "standards-based" grading policies. In Spokane, there are now four achievement levels in the standards-based grading. Each in-class assessment—and there are many—is graded one, two, three, or four.

- A top grade of four isn't available on assessments with fewer than three points.
- On assessments with three to seven points, students must get all points to earn a top grade of four.
- From eight to nineteen points, students who want a top grade of four can miss just one point.
- Depending on the number of points available on the assessment, grades of three or four can cover a span of 51.6 percent achievement all the way to doctoral thesis.

Many of the classes lean heavily on group projects. "Peer reviews" are often part of the grading process. Students can be graded on "rubrics" that entail long lists of required and suggested items. Students have fretted and cried over this grading system. One capable seventh grader said that—despite "working my tail off"—her grades were slipping to threes.

What's a caring parent to do? Say, "Don't worry about the grades"? It isn't the message we want to be sending, but what are the alternatives? Stand by and watch our children be demoralized? Leave the district? Can't you just feel that achievement gap "closing"?

We're All About Excellence; We're Raising the Bar

Administrators have an aggravating habit of telling us how well we're doing: We're raising the bar, we're getting better—we're all about excellence for everybody. In her 2007 address, Washington State superintendent Terry Bergeson said, "Our math and science standards and our curriculum and teaching approaches have brought us to new levels of excellence." She said, "When we set out nearly 15 years ago to revolutionize the way we help kids learn, if we had dared to claim that students would be achieving the kind of success they are today, people would have called us crazy."

Hmm, yes. What can be said to that? When students couldn't meet the standard, OSPI lowered the passing scores. How does lowering the bar mean "new levels of excellence"? (Unless by "new levels," she meant new, lower levels.) It's a yawning maw between where advocates stand and where these administrators stand. Can a gap like that be bridged? It's as if advocates see a chair while administrators see a table, and we can sit and argue all day about it, but in the end, advocates will see a chair and administrators will see a table.

It's the Children's Fault; It's the Parents' Fault; It's Society's Fault

Administrators have a hard time publicly acknowledging the role of curricula, learning environments, or administration in the problems. It's difficult to get them to say anything's wrong. On the rare occasion they do, it's always someone else's fault. Superintendent Bergeson has blamed poor results on math teachers, teacher preparation, failure to align curricula with standards, remedial math courses, and funding.

In a 2007 column in the *Seattle Post-Intelligencer*, Dr. Bergeson said we have to "share accountability rather than leaving it solely on the shoulders of students." Dr. Bergeson went on to say, "We've already made significant progress toward solving what is truly a national problem in math education—a problem rooted in some 20th century math myths, including some outrageous ethnic and gender generalizations about which children have 'math minds.'"

Today's math problems are not rooted in "outrageous ethnic and gender generalizations." They're rooted in an outrageous failure to teach the children math.

After the tough spring and summer of 2007, which saw low scores on the tests, dropping SAT scores, dropping enrollments, increased pressure from math advocates, and legislative action on the learning standards, Dr. Bergeson said she was pleased with the state's progress.

"We've made incredible academic progress since 1993 and people all around the country are turning to us in Washington for answers," she said in her 2007 State of Education address. The 2008 graduates "will be the best prepared group of students in our state's history."

Those who resist her approach were called critics and naysayers. "The critics are getting louder," she said in her address. "Their negative messages are confusing people about that progress and weakening the consensus that has fired our success."

Due in no small part to efforts from advocacy group Where's the Math? the woman was voted out in 2008, and it would be nice to think the problems went with her. But in a June 2010 press release, under Superintendent Randy Dorn, OSPI said, "For the third straight year, more than 90 percent of Washington 12th grade public school students passed the state reading and writing exams prior to reaching their respective graduation ceremonies" ("Class of 2010 Maintains" 2010).

- The data to the side of the release touted reading and writing scores for the classes of 2010 and 2009 (those twelfth graders who should have graduated the year before).
- A full nineteen paragraphs down in the release was the fact that "just 43 percent of 10th graders passed the math exam."
- Don't be too excited about the twelfth graders' 69.2 percent pass rate in math. The release said, "A little more than 20 percent of 12th graders in the class of 2010 met the graduation requirement by earning two math credits after 10th grade" (not by passing the test).

Math "continues to be a challenge," Superintendent Dorn said, "especially at a time when education funding is being cut, crucial afterschool programs are being eliminated and class sizes are increasing. We will expect more than 90 percent of the class of 2013 to be proficient in math by the time they reach graduation. I'm not confident that will happen."

How can it happen if his concerns are money, after-school programs, and class sizes? None of these things has a direct and dramatic impact on the Square of Effective Learning.

The same message is delivered at local and national levels. People across the country built (and praise) this failing system. They watch as children fail tests; parents complain; teachers fret; science, technology, engineering, and mathematics professionals beg for something different; and families give up and leave. Even when legislators acknowledge obvious systemic problems, administrators support the status quo and blame things on children and their families. From 2007 to 2010, would central-office administrators in Spokane Public Schools acknowledge on the record that some of the fault might rest with the district? Not to this author, they didn't, and they had plenty of opportunities.

Here's a sneaky way to blame the students: Pay them for good grades. A 2008 *New York Times* article reported that students at thirty-one New York City high schools were offered $1,000 for doing well on Advanced Placement tests (Gootman 2008). The program was supported by private donations and was one of a number in the nation designed to boost attendance and achievement through financial incentives. After all, adults are motivated by money—why not children? Pay the children for doing better, and they'll be more motivated. Right?

Those who develop such programs operate with what they think are good intentions but that are actually cynical and wrongheaded. The message being sent is that

- children aren't achieving because they aren't trying hard enough;
- money will motivate them;
- no other motivation is more effective;
- properly motivated with money, the children will achieve.

But children aren't motivated by money the way adults are, and we don't want them to be. We want them to be personally invested in learning because it's honorable and in their best interests. Additionally, any lack of motivation in the children is generally a symptom of the problem, not the problem itself. Because the underlying issues have to do with things beyond the students' control, bribery won't fix them. You can give a child $1 million, and it won't matter. It's like trying to bribe someone with a car when all they know how to do is ride a tricycle. The children don't have the skills, the freedom, or the support to do what the bribery intends them to do.

Not surprisingly, the $1,000 incentive didn't work as intended. An additional 345 New York City students took the AP tests, and more students scored the highest possible score, but the number of students who actually passed the test dropped slightly. Similar money programs continue elsewhere. Some attempt to modify behavior; others just hand out the money.

Frequently, concerns about the wisdom or ethics of this strategy are just brushed off the table in the hope that the money will do the trick.

Jobs and Housing Are the Main Reasons Families Leave

In October 2007, Spokane administrators said the drops in student enrollment were bewildering. The district had lost more than two thousand students since 2001. In a *Spokesman-Review* article, officials speculated about factors such as jobs, demographics, new construction north of the city, and lower-cost housing (Leaming 2007). They did not publicly speculate about parent dissatisfaction. The 2006 loss of 350 students cost the district $1.6 million in revenue.

In a belated effort to find out why enrollment was dropping like a rock in a bathtub, district officials hired a demographer to conduct a study. In a May 2008 online "chat," Superintendent Nancy Stowell said the demographer projected another drop of 375 students, "mostly at the secondary level," for the following school year. Enrollment was projected to turn around in 2013, she said, "depending on economic and housing trends." In a board meeting, she also mentioned the demographer's recommendation that the district do a survey of families to determine "perceptions of local schools" ("Minutes" 2008a).

Strategic Research Associates conducted a survey in fall 2008. Drawing from 1,368 student transfers between February 2006 and August 2008, interviewers conducted 294 interviews. According to the report, five of the top six schools having out-of-district transfers were high schools (Strategic Research Associates 2008). Five of seven middle schools also were listed in the top fourteen.

Top destination choices were to online or homeschooling options or to districts less than ten miles away. (Private schools were not included in the survey.) Most families didn't appear to leave the Spokane area. Top reasons given for leaving were these:

- 33 percent: Quality of curriculum does not match your expectations.
- 26 percent: District class sizes too large.
- 22 percent: A transfer will make student more accessible to parent's work.
- 21 percent: Desired coursework is not offered in the district.
- 21 percent: Student doesn't feel connected to his or her current school.

Parents were asked to name ("unaided") the most important reason for the transfer. Three "dominant" reponses were summarized in the report's notes: "a preference for homeschooling, a desire to have the child closer to work (or daycare or their residence), and a seeming lack of quality or availability of curriculum (or academics) in Spokane." The notes continue, "Those with elementary or middle school students were more likely to want to homeschool; complaints about curriculum were most likely to originate from those with students attending middle school."

Just 13 percent said they left because they were moving to another district.

You would think these results would reverberate throughout the central-office building, but in January 2009, asked about the survey results, Dr. Stowell said better questions would need to be asked "if the information is to be valuable and actually inform our decision making." She said her priorities at that time were the bond and levy renewals on an upcoming election ballot.

Early in 2008, told that there seems to be no connection between parents' frustration and the district's perception of the situation, Dr. Stowell said she knew families would like more opportunities to be heard. She mused, "Sometimes I think people don't want to know [why families are leaving] because . . . when you know . . . you have to do something about it."

She's probably right about that.

The People Think We're Spending Their Money Wisely

Administrators like to say how carefully they spend taxpayer money. They seem to think the public agrees. Washington's former superintendent pointed in her 2007 address to a U.S. Chamber of Commerce report that gave Washington an A for its return on investment. She said the A was because of "the gains we've made with only minimal new buying power in the last 10 years." She added, "Ironically, one of the barriers to convincing people of our need for more resources is that we continue to achieve so much success with the money we do have."

Dr. Bergeson didn't mention the Cs given to Washington for "truth in advertising about student proficiency," for "rigor of standards," and for "postsecondary and workforce readiness."

Americans know education money hasn't produced well-educated students. They know that public education is a bottomless purse, a veritable black hole that sucks in all available money and produces just 40 to 60 percent of the possible light.

Washington's standardized tests, for example, have been a money hog. Dr. Bergeson's 2007 address (in which she patted herself on the back for frugality) came just months before she asked the state legislature for $15 to $25 million more dollars—on top of the $22 million already budgeted—to administer just one year of the WASL ("In Brief" 2008). The state planned to get rid of the tenth-grade math portion in 2014, but until then students had to keep taking it, even though they didn't have to pass it, and taxpayers had to keep paying for it while they also paid for the end-of-course tests that would replace it.

Does that sound like good stewardship to you? It boggles the mind to contemplate the $658 billion spent across the nation (from all sources) to enable a largely failing K–12 education bureaucracy. Taxpayer money isn't being spent wisely. The only people who think it is are the ones who are spending it.

Money Will Fix the Dropout Problem

In 2010, a *Spokesman-Review* report said Spokane Public Schools had a 60 percent graduation rate (Lawrence-Turner 2010b). If true, that made the district a "dropout factory"—a term coined in 2004 when Johns Hopkins University researchers R. Balfanz and N. Legters called schools "dropout factories" if the number of seniors in a graduating class was at least 40 percent less than when those students were freshmen. For the Class of 2009, however, Spokane's cohort dropout rate was actually 28.7 percent, and the newspaper later clarified that. Part of the confusion lies in definitions. Who is a "dropout?"

- Students who formally file papers saying they've chosen to drop out.
- Students who haven't been seen for a few months, so it's assumed they've dropped out, but no one knows for certain. Maybe they're foster kids, they've been in jail, they're living in abusive homes, or their parents are homeless, transient, or migrant. They do what they can. They don't know when or where they'll be going next.
- Students who graduate with a credential other than a high school diploma.
- Students who need more than four years of schooling to complete graduation requirements.

It's important to properly report dropout and graduation rates. Students who don't graduate are at high risk of having limited futures.

Speaking at a May 2007 summit called "America's Silent Epidemic," Secretary of Education Margaret Spellings said, "The United States has the most severe income gap between high school graduates and dropouts in the world" (Spellings 2007a). She criticized states' methods for reporting dropouts, saying they tended to inflate on-time graduation rates, reported only those students who said officially they were dropping out, or marked as "graduated" the students who left the school but promised to get a GED in the future.

The next year, Secretary Spellings took steps to "ensure that all states use the same formula" to calculate graduation and dropout rates, make the rates public, and tie graduation rates to annual NCLB targets (U.S. Department of Education 2008c, 2008d). She reiterated the message: "Over their lifetimes, dropouts from the class of 2007 alone will cost our nation more than 300 billion dollars in lost wages, lost taxes and lost productivity. Increasing graduation rates by just five percent, for male students alone, would save us nearly eight billion dollars each year in crime-related costs."

And so, administrators and journalists struggle to put together relevant and consistent data based on fine statistical distinctions and the vagaries of human beings. Besides the issue of how to define a dropout, there is the need to assign static numbers to mobile human beings. The desire for clarity requires multiple representations of the data. It's easy to misunderstand.

For the Class of 2008–2009, Spokane's on-time graduation rate was 62.1 percent. It had an estimated cohort dropout rate of 28.7 percent and an extended graduation rate of 65 percent, indicating that once students fell behind, they tended to be there for good. The remaining students in that "cohort" were "continuing," as in continuing to work on their diplomas.

Is Spokane a "dropout factory"? It depends on your definition. Even with a 28.7 percent cohort dropout rate, the district has a problem, and it isn't confined to high school. Spokane also has a dropout problem in middle school. Asked about the dropout rate at a February 2010 town hall meeting, the superintendent inexplicably pointed to the state's more rigorous learning standards.

In June 2010, a *Spokesman-Review* report discussed the myriad "disconnected" efforts to evaluate and/or lower the dropout rate. Working on this problem, the newspaper said, are Gonzaga University, the Children's Investment Fund (CIF) (which pushed a tax initiative), the school board, the district's "Graduation Task Force," and various local clubs. Supporters of the CIF tax initiative claimed without proof that it could improve the dropout rate by "up to 20 percentage points" through early-learning, mentoring, abuse prevention, and after-school programs (Lawrence-Turner 2010c, 2010d).

It's irritating and counterproductive. Three ideas the school district could easily implement right now that would help the students academically are these:

- Give the teachers and students better curricula that contain sufficient content.
- Allow teachers to actually teach the students, instead of forcing teachers to force students to teach themselves and each other.
- Remove from the school day 90 percent of activities that detract from academic learning.

These ideas—all of which have a direct impact on the Square of Effective Learning—would improve so much yet cost so little. But pushing for these things is like talking to the wind.

Everybody's on board. We're pulling together, working on a fix.

Despite what you might have heard, math advocates are not "yammering" malcontents stuck in an old way of thinking. Across the country, from New York to California, from the forty-ninth parallel to the Rio Grande, parents and teachers are fighting for a better public school system or choosing to leave the system altogether. Yet, their criticism often is neatly deflected.

In 2008, Terry Bergeson, Washington state superintendent, was up for reelection. In May of that year, the teachers union took the unusual step of voting no confidence in her (Cuniff 2008). It hardly made a dent in her attitude. In August 2008, Dr. Bergeson said that Washington had seen "tremendous achievement results over the past decade," that college graduates were "among the best prepared in the country," and that more money was needed for all students to reach their full potential ("Classes of 2009 and '10 on Track" 2008). Take a lesson, folks. That's some accomplished spin.

Meanwhile, administrators, researchers, politicians, and various education-related people rush around doing sundry disconnected things to "fix" the problems—basically experimenting on the students.

With each experiment, the public is supposed to applaud on cue. A few years later, parents can see it didn't work, but administrators have already moved on to something new. And what happens to the students in the failed system? They're blamed.

Over the course of a few years, administrators and legislators have, among other things, changed curricula, delayed graduation requirements, revised math and science standards and tests, revised grading systems, mandated more math in high school, implemented new data systems, revised employee evaluations, adopted national standards, and mandated Algebra II. Lord love a duck.

Adding advanced math is good as long as students who take it are prepared for it (which they aren't if they've had only reform math). Implementing new data, grading and evaluation systems does nothing to address the Square of Effective Learning. But public education is a bureaucracy, and this is how bureaucratic change takes place. Bad change happens speedily and completely, and when it doesn't work, bureaucrats push harder with more of it and at great expense. Good change happens glacially, in infinitesimal amounts (too little to make the needed difference), whereupon everyone says it doesn't work and scraps the whole thing.

There was nothing "glacial" about Chancellor Michelle Rhee. In just one year of running the District of Columbia Public Schools, Chancellor Rhee closed twenty-three schools and fired hundreds of administrators, teachers, and principals. She said, "We've come under fire for a lot of things over the past three years, from incorporating performance in a lay-off, to 'moving too fast' on all kinds of reform. Many people have said we should focus more on consensus and collaboration to reform the school system more gradually. But show me the parent who wants his or her child to wait in a sub-par school while we work slowly and collaboratively to fix it."

When one sits in an office, juggles financial interests, compiles data, and pushes paper, it takes determination and discipline to avoid becoming aligned with administrator colleagues at the expense of teachers and students, to spend taxpayer money wisely, to resist grabbing every new idea like it's a shiny toy, to ask tough questions, to speak frankly, and to not be afraid to say, "We goofed up." Love her approach or not, Dr. Rhee appeared to have the children firmly in mind. She also did something that rarely happens in public education. She fired administrators.

In Spokane, various top-level administrators have told board directors that no one knows how to solve the math problem ("Minutes" 2009), that there isn't a magic bullet, and that they don't know which of their intervention programs are even working. Yet, some still work there. In 2010, they received a raise.

One sits in awe of the perpetual motion and limitless expense, knowing that what administrators and board members need to do is let good teachers teach sufficient material in a distraction-free classroom. One can't help thinking, They truly haven't got a clue.

9

DEALING WITH DIVERSIONARY ISSUES

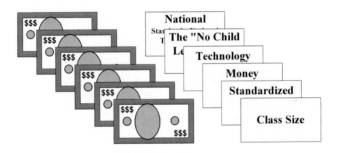

Generally, education administrators are good at keeping the public's focus on diversionary issues—things that they say have a negative effect on academics but which serve to divert attention from real problems. Their almost complete focus on these issues delays or prevents the implementation of real solutions, and it always seems to require billions more taxpayer dollars. If there is any sizable effect on the Square of Effective Learning, it's usually negative. Let's take a look at six of these diversionary issues:

1. Class size
2. Standardized testing
3. Money
4. Technology
5. The No Child Left Behind Act (NCLB)
6. National standards, tests, and curricula

DIVERT OUR ATTENTION TO CLASS SIZE

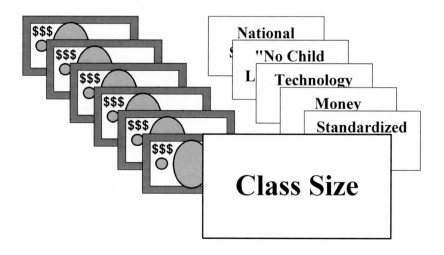

The idea behind differentiated instruction is to separate a class into smaller groups of children who need similar kinds of attention. That discussion naturally leads to one on class size. It seems like an intuitive thing—the smaller the classes, the more attention can be paid to each student and, therefore, the more each student can learn. Class size seems to be part of the Square of Effective Learning, affecting the learning environment.

Here's a different way to look at it. Class size is mostly a diversionary issue. Part of the reason is because taxpayers keep forking over money for smaller classes, but that money continually gets diverted to pay for other things. It should be illegal, this constant diversion of taxpayer money. Taxpayers trust administrators when they say, "We need that money for smaller classes." Then our money goes elsewhere, and classes are as big as ever.

Washington taxpayers have been hearing about smaller classes for years. At a May 2010 work session for the Spokane school board, the district superintendent mentioned maximizing class sizes as a cost-cutting measure. Board directors didn't argue.

Another reason class size is a diversion is because—although it matters—it isn't the thing that will fix the public school classroom. The benefits of small classes seem axiomatic. One hundred students per teacher clearly isn't a helpful ratio. Therefore, smaller must be better. It makes sense. Teachers definitely prefer smaller classes (one teacher said she preferred a maximum ratio of 25:1). Private schools tout their small classes. Legislators and administrators talk about reducing class size. But the research is contradictory. Other variables come into play.

The 1990 Tennessee Student/Teacher Achievement Ratio (STAR) study suggests that students achieve more in classes with teacher-to-student ratios below 18:1. Conclusions were that students in kindergarten and first grade did particularly well in reading and math if they were taught in smaller classes. Although small-class effects were less dramatic after the first grade, positive effects were still strong in second and third grade (Word et al. 1990).

Follow-up studies indicated that STAR students continued to impress. They were less likely to be retained and more likely to finish high school, graduate on time, and finish advanced courses. The National Education Association cited the Project STAR study in pressing for classes of about fifteen students per class. Yet, the STAR study, while influential, isn't the final word on class size. Its conclusions have been challenged.

In 2002, L. Wößmann and M. R. West reported on the math and science performance of eighteen countries as reflected in the Third International Mathematics and Science Study (TIMSS). Singapore, with an average class size of 33.2 students, scored the best of all in both math and science. Japan also didn't reflect noteworthy class-size effects in either math or science, and four other countries didn't show class-size effects in one subject or the other.

In fact, in just four of thirty-six total cases were there "statistically significant beneficial effect(s)" of smaller classes in either math or science.

The authors note that in Greece and Iceland, where smaller class sizes did appear to have "nontrivial" effects on performance, the students still performed "below average" on the TIMSS tests. Conversely, both Singapore and Japan (where class-size effects were completely ruled out) performed above average. It's not what you'd expect, but there it is. The question of the day is, Why? The authors were blunt: "The significant class-size effects in Greece and Iceland simply imply that class-size reductions would work to raise student performance within their current institutional environments, which as a whole are rather ineffective." In other words, smaller classes might assist a poorly performing system, but they won't save it. If the system is flawed to begin with, smaller classes won't fix it.

Another analysis suggests that Project STAR's positive effects hadn't assisted the students who need the most help. In 2008, Dr. Spyros Konstantopoulos said that "higher-achieving students" seemed to gain the most from being placed in smaller classes in the earlier grades. Although all types of learners did gain from the smaller classes, he said, the achievement gap was not reduced between the low and high achievers.

(For more on the achievement gap, see "Equity versus Excellence" in chapter 6.)

In his 2009 book *Visible Learning*, Dr. John Hattie found just modest support for reducing class size—not worth the billions of dollars it would take. He did note, however, that increasing class size probably isn't a good idea.

Other studies indicate positive and long-term benefits from smaller class sizes, especially in the early grades. And having smaller classes for kindergartners and first graders seems like a no-brainer. The little ones have a lot to learn, and they need a lot of hands-on help. However, as we've seen, efficient, effective learning can be done with much larger classes. It happens every day in countries around the world. What's the difference? Why can't Americans do that?

We can. We just have to do more than lower class size.

- Students need mastery of sufficient core skills. This will entail having better curricula, practicing of skills, and direct instruction.

  In 2005, an American Institutes of Research study conducted for the U.S. Department of Education (ED) examined the differences between how Americans typically taught math and how Singaporeans typically taught it. A. Ginsburg and colleagues found that Singapore's national program was "highly logical" and that its textbooks were "mathematically rich" and "problem-based."

Additionally, tests were "challenging," teachers were "highly qualified," and the goal was to teach "to mastery." Struggling students were provided with an "alternative" program and "special assistance from an expert teacher." Calculators were not embedded throughout the curriculum. America, meanwhile, was praised for its interest in reasoning, communication, applied mathematics, probability, data analysis, and statistics.

However, the study said, "If U.S. students are to become successful in these areas, they must begin with a strong foundation in core mathematics concepts and skills, which, by international standards, they presently lack."

- Teachers need to be in charge. Students must be better disciplined.

Not to stifle anyone's creativity or self-esteem, but the students must be more disciplined. They aren't to blame for misbehavior, poor manners, disrespect, unwillingness to persevere, or short attention spans. These are great kids, all of them. They get away with things because they can. School policy is often weak on discipline.

Therefore, schools must implement policies that support the teachers in better managing the children. All of the adults have a role to play—the parents who raise the children, the administrators who set and enforce the discipline policy, the elementary school teachers who set the tone for everything that comes after, and all of the other teachers, aides, and staff who must reinforce high expectations and consistent discipline. With better discipline, respect, and self-restraint, more can be done.

- Teachers need to be prepared and willing.

In 2006, Barry Garelick, a parent with deep concerns over the poor quality of math education, examined a pilot of the traditional program *Singapore Math* in four Maryland schools. Three of the four schools dropped out of the pilot a few years later, which Garelick blamed on a lack of preparation, planning, patience, and money. Philosophy also was a problem, he said:

> Taking on a program like *Singapore Math* meant going against what many teachers believed math education to be about; surely, it was not what they were trained for. Since the success of Singapore's programs relies in many ways on more traditional approaches to math education, such as explicit instruction and giving students many problems to solve, in some ways its very success represented a slap in the face to American math reformers, many of whom have worked hard to eliminate such techniques from the teaching canon.

Garelick quoted Dr. David Klein, a mathematician at California State University, Northridge, who had criticized claims that cultural differences prevent *Singapore Math* from being successful in America. Dr. Klein called those claims a rationalization: "Math reformers assume that math education is bad in the United States because the NCTM reforms were not properly implemented nor understood by teachers. They never consider the possibility that the NCTM standards themselves and the textbooks written for those standards are one of the causes of poor math education in this country."

In June 2007, W. Hook, W. Bishop, and J. Hook said a quality Asian/European elementary math curriculum was "successfully transplanted" to America. It provided "immediate and stunning performance improvements," even in at-risk populations, they said, and "virtually no special teacher training was required to achieve these results."

American students can have the same successes in math and science as students in Singapore and Japan, but changes must be made. Fiercely held notions of the benefits of reform and constructivism must be abandoned, and that's where the problem lies. Families are willing, but the education establishment is weak.

The optimal size of a class depends on many variables. Are students prepared for the material? Is the curriculum logical, efficient, and clear? Is the teacher allowed to teach the material—or do the students have to discover everything for themselves? Is the classroom environment friendly yet focused—or are there constant distractions to the learning process?

Are students allowed to practice to mastery? Are teachers and students in the classroom most of the time—or are there too many district-initiated absences? Each of these issues has an impact on the Square of Effective Learning.

Teachers can have a class size of one, but if the student isn't prepared, if the curriculum isn't logical, if the teacher refuses to teach, if the environment is distracting, if the student can't practice the material to mastery, if the teacher keeps getting up to make coffee or take phone calls, then a class size of one won't be effective. This is why class size, as it pertains to policy and money, is partially a diversionary issue. There are other, more practical concerns.

Instructional Aides, Coaches, and Mentors

Another way to look at class size is through instructional aides, coaches, and mentors.

Some teachers have an aide, particularly in schools that qualify for Title I funds or Learning Assistance Program funds. Other teachers have a coach or mentor, student teacher, volunteer, or partner teacher. Classes with twenty-eight students and one full-time teacher have a ratio of 28:1, while classes with twenty-eight students and two full-time adults have a ratio of 14:1.

If these adults work with students, then classrooms probably are helped by their presence. But if smaller class sizes aren't a panacea, aides aren't either.

These extra adults often aren't there to help students. They frequently aren't even in the classroom for the entire day or for most of the day. The Square of Effective Learning rests on four corners. If there are problems with the curriculum and/or the learning environment, then a ratio of 14:1 is unlikely to fix a problem classroom. And if aides aren't working with students but are instead evaluating, judging, or "coaching" teachers, developing new systems, or handling paperwork, then their presence might actually be detrimental, draining precious time, energy, and attention from the classroom.

Teachers must decide if class size is a legitimate corner of the Square of Effective Learning or if it's a diversionary issue that allows administrators to avoid taking care of the real problems. If teachers had an effective learning environment without distractions, students who were at about the same place in learning and willing to learn, a solid curriculum, and the freedom to teach as they saw fit, would it be a problem if they had twenty-six students instead of twenty-two?

It's likely that, for most of them, it wouldn't be a problem.

DIVERT OUR ATTENTION TO STANDARDIZED TESTING

"As I like to say, what gets measured gets done."

—Former U.S. secretary of education
Margaret Spellings, speech at a national summit
titled "America's Silent Epidemic," May 9, 2007

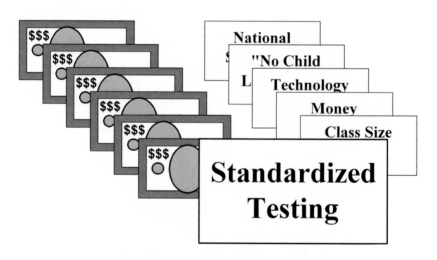

Standardized testing has been controversial since its inception. Parents fret over the cost; teachers fret over the impact on learning. Every year, test scores are scrutinized by all and criticized by most. State standardized tests are joined at the hip to NCLB, which calls for states to assess students with tests that are aligned with state learning standards.

Standardized testing has become a huge part of the education land-scape. It's a big, yet nearly pointless thing, when it should be a small, very important thing. It sucks the life and money out of the public school system, and that's why it's a diversionary issue.

Testing should be about Accountability. It's supposed to measure progress over time, whether students have stored information in their long-term memories well enough to be able to pull it out in response to prompts. The real benefit to testing is to tell us whether the educa-tion system is working for the students. Testing is where the education establishment could be held accountable to the public, but the public is not receiving the whole truth.

What many parents and teachers don't know is that standardized testing—as it's currently structured—means little in terms of academic knowledge.

What Was the Point Again?

Spokane superintendent Brian Benzel and administrator Karin Short said in January 2007 that Washington's standardized tests—the Wash-ington Assessment of Student Learning (WASL)—were "just the floor" of expectations: "We want our kids to exceed that," Short said.

Students who were able to pass the math, reading, and writing sections of the WASL, according to a 2007 Office of Superintendent of Public Instruction (OSPI) press release, were "eligible to earn the Certificate of Academic Achievement [CAA] in addition to their high school diploma" (Class 2007). (Logically, then, the CAA was an award for being able to reach the floor.)

In May 2010, Dr. Benzel said the tests originally were designed to test the students, but that over time, they also came to test the system. They were never intended to be a college-readiness or work-readiness indicator, he said, but were designed to test reading, writing, and math "at a basic level."

It's depressing. In 2009, the tenth-grade math WASL required a 56.9 percent score to pass, yet just 42.3 percent of Spokane's tenth-grade students were able to pass this "floor" of expectations. Just 41.4 percent passed science.

See figure 9.1 for a sample question from the seventh-grade math WASLs from years 2002 to 2004. OSPI sent out this question on a promotional flyer as a guide for parents.

Look at the equation below.
$$72 + 58 = 130$$

Chris added 70 and 60 to find the sum instead of using the number sentence above. Clearly explain or show why Chris's method results in the same answer.

Figure 9.1.   WASL Test Question for 7th Graders
Source: "State testing 2007: What You Need To Know" (n.d.), Office of Superintendent of Public Instruction Informational flyer.

A ten-year-old called this question "insulting." She said if this was the caliber of question they expect her to know in seventh grade, something clearly is wrong.

Meanwhile, Washington's tenth-grade students had five separate opportunities to pass the tenth-grade WASL. Those who couldn't do it could apply to show their competency through alternative "testing," including something called a WASL/grades comparison. That option worked like this (see if you can read it with a straight face): A student who had at least a 3.2 GPA could compare class grades against a group of fellow students who passed the WASL, and if the student's grades were above the mean of the grades of the rest of the group, then that could count as an alternative to the WASL ("WASL/Grades Comparison" n.d.). In 2009/10, this became a "GPA Comparison."

It's absurd. Alternatives to testing were rightly designed to help some students meet a reasonable standard, but they were usurped to help tell a lie. They pretend-prove that "disadvantaged" children are succeeding, that achievement gaps are narrowing, and that districts are marching toward 100 percent proficiency. It's a sickening betrayal of our children. Faced with this, it's easy to see testing as the problem. But tests are tools. The problem is how the tool is used.

The Costs

By any measure, standardized testing is "spendy." Its true cost is tricky to figure because many expenses aren't included in published figures.

There are initial development costs and ongoing costs in management, printing, salaries, shipping, scoring, and reporting. There are costs at the district, state, and federal levels. There are costs in lost time for instruction and learning. As students prepare for and take the tests, they tend not to focus on new learning. Students who have already passed might be left to themselves to study, work on other projects, or sleep late.

In 2006, Dr. Donald Orlich, professor emeritus of the Science Mathematics Engineering Education Center at Washington State University, Pullman, estimated total direct costs of the WASL at about $207 million, plus $100 million spent annually on costs related to salaries and lost instruction and learning time.

($100 million here, $100 million there—pretty soon you're talking real money.)

In April 2008, this author submitted a request to OSPI asking for the costs of state testing. On June 11, some of the data came back. It took several more requests to get data on alternative tests and contracts. Nothing ever arrived on district costs or indirect costs. For district costs, this author used a figure estimated by a district employee, extrapolating it across the state.

It's a truckload of taxpayer dollars, and there is no guarantee this is all of it. Figures are for tests, alternatives to the tests, and publishing contracts. Using just these figures, for the years from 1995 to 2012 (in state, federal, and estimated local money), the total for testing in Washington comes to $685,016,046. That's about $40.3 million per year, or about $38.72 per student (at 2009 enrollment). In 2008, OSPI was calculating a cost of just $17 per booklet.

This is just one state. Multiply the figure by fifty to get a very rough estimate of the taxpayer money spent annually on state standardized testing. Money availability is not the problem. How it is spent—and how expenditures are reported—are definitely problems.

What Do Standardized Tests Tell Parents and Teachers?

Standardized tests should tell teachers and parents whether students know what they need to know in order to progress to the next class, the next grade, and the next stage of their lives. However, Washington's tests apparently represent "the floor" of expectations, our high school graduation requirements have been so minimal as to be embarrassing, and no administrator speaks frankly about college remediation rates.

Here are some other concerns about the testing.

In Washington, no one could see the finished tests. Tests were thus an evaluation tool for the state, not an informative tool for teachers and parents. OSPI said in its undated flyer "Education Reform Is about the Skills, Not the Test," "The WASL is not a diagnostic test—that is, its purpose isn't to pinpoint where an individual student is struggling and what kind of help is needed. Teachers use a variety of diagnostic, classroom-based assessments to tailor instruction to students' needs. To keep student learning on track, no test can substitute for parent conferences, report cards and other regular communication between families and schools throughout the year."

This statement is disingenuous. A lot is at stake with these tests: taxpayer money, district autonomy, lost instruction time, on-time graduation, and students' sense of their abilities. Yet, students who failed repeatedly were never allowed to see the tests. (Even criminal suspects get to face their accuser.) Some of the little ones were even harassed with a chart on school walls—their progress (or lack of prog-ress) graphically represented and displayed for all to see.

In a January 2007 interview, then Spokane superintendent Brian Benzel said that several elementary schools had created these "assess-ment walls," where progress toward meeting the standards was marked on the wall. "It's very personalized," he said.

Personalized, yes. But respectful? Children could see the chart every day, as could their friends and family members, but they had little abil-ity to affect it. What they knew was that they were not measuring up. Instead of being a golden opportunity to learn, therefore, the WASL was an annual sucker punch—from grade three forward.

State standardized tests like the WASL should be open to public scrutiny. Scrap the "assessment walls," and give the tests to the people. Put that taxpayer money to better use, and allow students to learn from the tests. Teachers and parents need to figure out how to help their students. Students need to see what they didn't understand. In

2007, a high school teacher wrote, "There is no useful information communicated back to the teacher from the WASL that will assist that teacher in teaching the student who is labeled incompetent in mathematics. With virtually no feedback and no opportunity to remediate specific problems, the test does nothing to help the test taker improve his or her math skills."

Washington had a process for parents to view their children's tests, but it must have been easier to visit someone in a jail. Parents applied to the state (with a maximum ninety-day turnaround time). The tests were located and sent to the district. Parents were called to set up an appointment at the district office. There, parents signed a form saying they knew they couldn't write anything down, divulge test specifics, or have a copy of the tests.

How would this system work if everyone did it? If every parent asked to see the tests, and every test had to be pulled and delivered to districts, and appointments had to be set up for every parent to sit individually with district employees . . . how could it work? It only worked if almost no one did it. In 2010, Washington's new standardized tests weren't available to parents for viewing until September 2010. Thus, the results were of almost no use at all.

It isn't helpful to remove parents and teachers from the accountability process. It's quieter and easier, but not helpful. If tutoring or supplementing is necessary, parents and teachers need to know in time to make it happen before the student begins the next grade or tries to graduate. It's ironic that we all have to fight to be informed. Every time we turn around, some administrator type is blaming parents and teachers for the problems in public education.

Standardized tests are supposed to measure whether students are meeting the standards, which are allegedly encapsulated in the approved curricula. But the curricula keep changing. Every few years, there's another experiment.

The parade of curricula in Spokane Public Schools is phenomenal—an ongoing stream. In April 2009, Spokane had a list of curricular material that was forty typed pages long. Just the list of math materials was eleven typed pages long. Additionally, as curricula are flipped in and out, at huge cost in time, resources, and money, change is usually complete and district-wide. With no control group to use as a comparison, how do administrators calculate effectiveness or compare test results from one year to another?

If scores go down, they can say, "We just made this change; give us time to adjust." If scores go up, they can say, "See? We're having great success." But instead of assessing students' learning—as they're intended to do—or system effectiveness—as they should do—tests are assessing the new curricula, or teachers' understanding of the new curricula, or the school's ability to implement the new curricula. Perhaps in math, the tests are assessing the effectiveness of the entire reform math philosophy. (Hey, now, there's a thought.)

Trends in scores also can't be trusted due to problems in reliability and validity. J. Brickell and D. Lyon's 2003 study "Reliability, Validity, and Related Issues Pertaining to the WASL" analyzed seventeen technical reports and studies on the WASL. Noting concerns with reliability and validity, they urged caution in depending on the tests alone to determine student achievement.

In 2010, the WASL was ushered out in favor of the Measurements of Student Progress (MSP) (grades three to eight) and the High School Proficiency Exam (grades nine to twelve). Several young sources in Spokane who took the new MSP said test takers received lists of basic mathematical formulas and word definitions before writing the test. Anecdotal feedback also indicated that test questions were highly subjective. The answers, the students agreed, could have been anything.

If so, the MSP would lack reliability (and quite possibly validity).

Statistical reliability and validity are related. Both are necessary for any test to be an accurate measure of a student's abilities and/or progress. A test can be reliable (repeatable), yet accurately measure the wrong thing over and over. A test also can be valid (testing the right thing), yet not with any degree of consistency. Good tests are both reliable and valid.

The following discussion of statistical reliability and validity is brief, designed solely to articulate specific concerns with state testing. It's supported by personal experience and knowledge, along with general support from J. D. Brown's online resource Statistics Corner.

Statistical Reliability

Reliability is an estimate of the degree of consistency and repeatability of a measure. Every change in procedure or the testing environment (every variable) can affect reliability.

Reliability concern 1: Tests evolve. Every year, state standardized tests change—the questions, emphases, scorers, and techniques. Sometimes the tests are replaced, as they were in Washington State in 2010. With every change, the tests are less useful in measuring change or progress over time.

Reliability concern 2: Passing scores are lowered. In 2004, cut scores (the level at which a score is a passing grade) were lowered for the WASL for fourth and seventh grades, allowing more students to pass. In 2005, cut scores for the tenth-grade WASL also were lowered.

OSPI was asked in April 2008 about these drops in cut scores. Employees kept sending information on scaled scores (these are ranges, which didn't change). In July 2008, after repeated requests and finally after a request for public information, OSPI finally confirmed that several raw cut scores had been lowered. And so, the pass rates were a whole new ball game.

In August 2010, Washington's Board of Education approved cut scores for the new math tests for grades 3–8—three months after students took the tests. Committees determining these cut scores were given select information on testing results. The board approved cut scores of less than 60 percent for all but grade 3 (which was just more than 60 percent). In grades 7 and 8, students needed just 55 percent to pass. Tenth-graders needed just 56.9 percent to pass. According to OSPI, these cut scores also set the point at which students are considered to be "proficient" in math.

Reliability concern 3: Scoring templates change. Templates help the scorers of tests know how to grade the questions. Sometimes, an answer will cause rethinking of the template. OSPI said that any changes to rubrics were made during "pilot testing" using twelve hundred student responses and again during "operational testing" using eighty thousand student responses. Templates were therefore not necessarily the same from year to year.

Reliability concern 4: Scoring is subjective. Traditional math is an inherently black-and-white subject, simple to test and grade. Reform math, on the other hand, is more subjective. Parents and teachers have said they found questionable grading in the math tests. On questions requiring a written answer, the math was correct, the spelling and grammar were correct, the writing was legible, and the entire answer was there. Yet, points were docked. In some cases, queries were made of the district personnel; they had no explanation.

Statistical Validity

Validity is the degree to which a test measures what it's designed to measure. It should be possible to draw accurate and meaningful conclusions or inferences from test results. Two measures of validity are criterion validity and content validity.

Criterion (or concurrent) validity indicates (1) whether the test correlates well with a similar outside measure, and (2) whether test scores predict how well students will do on some other, similar measure. If a test were designed to predict how well students would do on SAT tests, for example, and it failed to do so, it would lack predictive validity.

Content validity indicates (1) whether test questions are a representative sample of all testing objectives, and (2) whether test questions match up well with testing objectives. If a test were to measure arithmetic, for example, but contained questions on language skills, it would not match up well with testing objectives.

Validity concern 1: In many states, as in Washington State, there are no publicly released comparisons of test scores against comparable outside measures of the entire student body. Perhaps scores went up because the tests became easier. Perhaps students are actually going backward with higher scores and less knowledge.

Validity concern 2: The math portion of many standardized tests has called for short and long answers using little math and lots of words. Literacy thus takes up time and space that should be used for mathematics. Perhaps administrators decided that reading and writing should be a big part of math. If they didn't, there is an obvious problem with content validity (the objective is math, yet they're also testing for literacy).

But when students get answers wrong on a word-heavy math test, how do we know if they didn't understand the math, didn't read the question properly, didn't understand the question, didn't write legibly, were unable to put together a coherent answer, or ran out of time?

On Washington's math WASL, no grading marks were made on tests. No "literacy" score was provided. No explanations were given. Local teachers have said that correct math answers using standard algorithms could receive fewer points than wrong answers including expected written words. Thus, points were deducted from answers that were mathematically correct.

Tests like this aren't good indicators of the quality of the math instruction. A math teacher can be brilliant—the best math teacher ever—but if the test is in literacy and not math, the math teacher must bow to the English teacher.

When state standardized tests are excessively expensive, secretive, unreliable, and not valid, this effort to be publicly Accountable becomes pretense—a diversionary issue.

It's terrible to know that a great deal of student testing is wasted time and money. This is *not* an argument to adopt national tests. Nearly every teacher in every classroom in every state in this country could do this high-stakes testing faster, better, and most likely at little extra cost to the taxpayer. They are unlikely to get that chance, however. National standardized tests are coming soon to a district near you.

In 2010, the Department of Education began pushing states to develop national tests. In June 2010, a "thirty-one-state consortium," including Washington State, applied for a federal grant of up to $160 million to develop national assessments based on the Common Core Standards (the national standards). A few months later, this consortium won its $160 million grant.

It's all rather odd, since Washington State has not shown much ability to develop strong standardized tests and also because Washington State had not, as of June 2010, adopted the national standards.

DIVERT OUR ATTENTION TO MONEY

"We have area coordinators now strolling through our class-rooms with what in mind? There is no feedback, and what could possibly be observed in a five-minute time frame? They sit in the principal's office and usually take up a half day in the building, to what means? If this is their purpose, then I suggest that we can do without them as a cost-cutting measure."

—Elementary school teacher

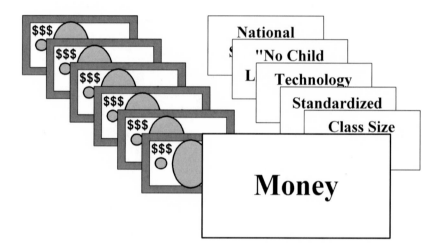

A favorite administrator word is "money." As in, "To fix the public-education system, we need a lot more money." But billions of taxpayer dollars are frittered away every year on things that will not help the children learn better.

If you want the public-education system the way it is—an unwieldy, complicated, test-driven, administrator-heavy behemoth—you have to pay for it. But effective education doesn't need to be expensive. What it needs is in the Square of Effective Learning—prepared teacher, prepared students, a solid curriculum, and an effective learning environment.

As federal education expenditures blast their way to scary new heights, we still have to listen to administrators panic over budget cuts. How is it possible? Where does the money go? Does someone have it in a sock drawer? Did it fall out of the truck? Is it buried in the back yard? The money gets spent, folks— there's no doubt about that.

Let's talk about the funding. Citizens pay taxes: federal, state, county, city, sales, property, and business. The government collects this money and redistributes it, based on department budgets and legislative priorities. One destination for your tax dollars is the U.S. Department of Education.

Federal Taxpayer Money

From 1965 to 2003, the federal government spent a total of $242 billion to improve education for disadvantaged children through the Elementary and Secondary Education Act (Paige and Gibbons 2003). In the last few years, the ED budget has grown (see figure 9.2).

Year	Dept. of Ed (ED) Outlay	Total Federal Outlay	% of Total Federal Outlay
1980	$ 14.6 billion	$ 591 billion	2.5
2001	$ 35.5 billion	$ 1.863 trillion	1.9
2008	$ 65.96 billion	$ 2.982 trillion	2.2
2010	$ 106.9 billion	$ 3.720 trillion	2.9

Figure 9.2.   Federal Taxpayer Support of Education.
Source: Data extracted from Office of Management and Budget, http://www.budget.gov

You might think the $106.9 billion for the ED in 2010 is an anomaly, perhaps because of the American Reinvestment and Recovery Act. But teetering around the $100 billion mark is the new norm. According to Table 4 of the U.S. Government Historical Tables, Fiscal Year 2011, outlay estimates for the ED for the next several years (2011 to 2015) are $94.3 billion, $85.2 billion, $88.7 billion, $93.8 billion, and $96.7 billion.

Compare that to the expense in 1980, when the ED became part of the cabinet (just $14.6 billion), or 2008, the year before Secretary of Education Arne Duncan took over ($65.96 billion). In 2015, school districts likely will say they still don't have enough.

On October 1, 2009, the ED promised another $21 billion in formula grants. This money was separate from the $100 billion in "stimulus" funding. The 2010 health care bill also helped pass a federal takeover of college loans—and so another $173 billion was budgeted for "loans, grants, tax credits and work-study programs to help students go to college" ("President's Education Budget" 2010).

Skim through the ED's press releases. Secretary Duncan is like Santa Claus, handing out billions of taxpayer dollars to good little states and territories: $805 million to eight states, $1.2 billion to ten states, $554 million for Florida, $607.6 million to New York, $415.4 million to Illinois, $1.2 billion to California, another $814 for New York, another $487 million for California, $1 billion for Texas, $514 million to Pennsylvania . . . and this is from just a few press releases from August and September 2010. The largesse has been nonstop almost from the moment the man took office, early in 2009.

It sounds like a lot of money. Ha. It's a pittance. Read on.

These numbers represent federal taxpayer money. There also is state and local taxpayer money and funding from other sources. As noted previously, the ED's "FY 2011 Budget Summary" said the total projected to be spent in 2008–2009 on elementary and secondary education (from all sources) was $658 billion. For 2009–2010, it was projected to be $664 billion. In May 2010, Secretary Duncan petitioned Congress for another $23 billion in "emergency" funding to "save" teachers' jobs, plus $3 billion for other jobs. In August 2010, Congress provided $10 billion more for the ED, supposedly to save education jobs.

To put this in context, as noted briefly in chapter 3, the total outlays for the entire U.S. Department of Defense in 2009 were $636.5 billion—for every plane, ship, tank, lease, boot, bullet, rocket, and MRE, for every soldier, for soldiers' education and health care, for the health care and housing of their dependents, and for two ongoing wars ("Department of Defense Funding Highlights" n.d.)—all for less than what was spent from all sources on a failing K–12 education system. It's hard to believe. One stares at the numbers, thinking, That can't be right. Yet, there it is.

Public education is like Audrey II of the classic rock musical *Little Shop of Horrors*. It booms, "Feed me!" as it greedily sucks in the nation's economic lifeblood. In return, it spits out hapless graduates who are not proficient in arithmetic or grammar, much less able to compete on an international level. The money could be $664 trillion—it won't get students where they need to go because money isn't the problem. Try to convince administrators of that.

Superintendents Say Billions More Are the Answer

The 1889 Washington State Constitution says the state has a "paramount" duty "to make ample provision for the education of all children residing within its borders." But what does "ample" mean? The authors of the document should have specified actual dollars, because "ample" is the word that ate Washington State.

Terry Bergeson, Washington State's former superintendent, said more dollars were key to improving education. She said so—at least ten times—in her 2007 State of Education speech and at various times in newspapers around the state. With a new administration, the money obsession continues. In November 2008, Superintendent Randy Dorn called for a $100 billion education "bailout" from Congress. In a *Spokesman-Review* article, Superintendent Dorn said the federal government didn't know how to spend the money, but he did (Hansen 2008).

Superintendent Dorn got his wish: $100 billion additional federal dollars. But states continue to cut budgets. Districts continue to say they're strapped. What was solved?

In 2008–2009, Seattle Public Schools spent $11,062 per student, almost $1,800 more per student than the state average, and the district had a tenth-grade math pass rate of 48.9 percent.

The District Says More Money Is the Answer

Administrators in Washington State say education is underfunded, meaning that the state doesn't pay 100 percent of the cost of programs that districts must, by law, provide. Mandated items local administrators have said are underfunded include transportation, special education, programs for non-English-speaking students, and substitute teachers. This is not a complete list.

Districts also have suffered enrollment drops, leading to a drop in state revenue without a commensurate drop in cost per student. In Spokane, the enrollment drop in 2006 of 350 students was said to cost the district $1.6 million in revenue ("Funding Forecast 2007–2008" n.d.).

In 2007, several districts joined a lawsuit against the legislature, attempting to force a change in the funding formula for basic education and pressing for full funding for mandated items. They meanwhile balanced their budgets by cutting nonmandated items or dipping into rainy-day funds. Some districts diverted voter-approved levies intended for enrichment programs. To voters, these levy diversions can feel like a sleight of hand. "Vote for kids!" we hear each time a levy is up for renewal. Teachers and parents don't find out where the money went, but we can see where it didn't go. Apparently, these diversions are legal.

In 2010, Washington districts won their lawsuit. The Quality Education Council was created by the legislature to redefine "basic education" and recommend how to finance that new definition. Meanwhile, the governor continues to complain of financial shortfalls, and her budget proposal entailed deep cuts to public education ("2010 Budget Highlights" n.d.; "Governor Chris Gregoire" n.d.).

This money obsession makes administrators easy pushovers for mistakes like the federal Race to the Top (RTTT) grant initiative. In May 2010, Spokane superintendent Nancy Stowell listened to a board director express concerns that accepting RTTT money would spell the end of local control over education policy. It was "punitive for no reason," another director said.

Dr. Stowell told the school board that the money situation is "desperate" and that she would go after every dollar she could. She had ninety days after getting the money, she said, to come up with a plan for spending it. She also said RTTT was coming anyway, so the district might as well get some money for it. (Ponder that lovely sentiment for a moment.)

The RTTT money could be trillions. If it doesn't positively affect the Square of Effective Learning, it won't do the children any good.

What Happened to the Previous Billions?

Washington's teachers union has claimed that Washington ranks near the bottom for per-student spending, but perhaps everyone else is spending too much on the wrong things. A more telling statistic is that in 2006, according to a Washington Policy Center report, the state ranked thirty-eighth nationally for how much of its education money actually went to classroom instruction.

Liv Finne, director of the organization's Center for Education, found that just 59.5 percent of state education expenditures were spent on classroom instruction (including teacher salaries). The rest went for things like administration, transportation, and buildings and maintenance.

In Spokane Public Schools, 77.7 percent of the 2009–2010 budget supposedly went to instruction, but the "instruction" category includes items not directly related to the classroom, such as principals, counselors, health, extracurricular, and the entire Department of Teaching and Learning. (These categories are set by the state.) Actual expenditures for just classroom instruction were less than 60 percent of the total. There was another 1.95 percent for the libraries and roughly 0.5 percent for curricula.

Washington State isn't alone. In 2006, an initiative called "First Class Education" would have set a minimum of 65 percent for how much education money had to be spent on instruction. Yet, states could stuff anything into their definition of "instruction," including administrator salaries, professional development, technology, and extracurricular activities.

In 2007, the National Academy of Sciences report "Is America Falling Off the Flat Earth?" said, "The United States spends more per student on secondary education than any other nations except Switzerland and Luxemburg and more on primary education than any nation except Luxemburg. The problem appears to be not *what* we are spending but rather *how* we are spending it. States, on the average, spend only 61 percent of their education budget on classroom instruction" (Augustine 2007).

In fiscal year 2009, Arizona spent 56.9 percent of its education money in the classroom. The website for the Arizona Office of the

Auditor General said that figure was "the lowest that it has been in the 9 years the Auditor General's Office has been monitoring classroom dollars."

> While the classroom dollar percentage should not be the sole criterion for evaluating school districts' financial performance, it is a useful measure in several respects. First, its decline indicates that many districts are likely using CSF [Classroom Site Fund] monies to shift their non-CSF monies away from the classroom, which violates state law. Second, available data indicates that, in Arizona, higher classroom dollar percentages appear to be associated to some extent with higher student achievement. Further, high spending outside the classroom is a potential sign of inefficient operations. (Office of the Auditor General 2010)

In May 2010, Spokane's superintendent told board directors that 50 percent of any money awarded to Washington State for the federal Race to the Top grant competition would stay at the state level. In public documents, the state superintendent and governor promoted the 50 percent cut of the take for districts that signed on to RTTT, but neither mentioned the remainder of the money or specified where it would go ("2010 Session Summary" 2010; Dorn 2009).

Administration

Budgets get bigger, belts get tighter and programs are cut, but the salaries of top administrators tend to be stable or increasing. A February 2010 *Spokesman-Review* report said three area school districts employed 133 administrators and staff who were paid at least $100,000 per year. In September 2010, the newspaper noted how many of Spokane's $100,000+ administrators had received raises in 2010 of 3 percent or more.

Spokane superintendent Nancy Stowell's pay increase brought her total compensation to $222,576.48 annually—about $55,000 more than the state governor's published salary; about $100,000 more than the state superintendent's published salary; and just $4,700 less than the 2009 salary of the vice president of the United States (Washington Citizens' 2009; Bureau 2010; Lawrence-Turner 2010a, 2010e).

People tend to make the following arguments to justify higher salaries:

"We have to keep pace with other districts." (No, we don't.)

"These costs are not unreasonable, compared to other districts." (Irrelevant.)

"We aren't top-heavy when you compare us to other districts." (Irrelevant.)

"We have to pay this money in order to get the very best people."

Ah. The flaw in the last argument is the assumption that the money does obtain the very best people. And how would they know that? By student achievement? In Spokane, would that be the 38.9 percent pass rate on the 2010 state math test, the 28.7 percent cohort dropout rate, the net drop of about twenty-five hundred students since 2002, or the 87 percent remediation rate in math at two local community colleges?

Staci Vesneske, a Spokane administrator who now makes nearly $125,000 per year, discussed the district's staffing and salaries in the February newspaper article, saying that it "takes people" to deal with issues of curriculum, adherence to learning standards, graduation, and NCLB requirements. "The fact that we've been able to address that with fewer people is impressive," she added. How does she define "address"? Obviously, it doesn't mean "to improve." Spokane's curricula have been weak for a decade, teachers aren't allowed to teach to the new state standards, the on-time graduation rate is 62 percent, and increasing numbers of schools fail to meet their adequately yearly progress, as defined by NCLB.

Spokane has several area directors (administrators who oversee district schools). Many parents aren't sure what they do. In 2007, Spokane cut more than $10 million from its budget, and one item cut was a school, at a savings of about $450,000. That's about what four area directors cost in base salary. Can it be that administrators are critical to student learning, whereas an elementary school isn't? If what they do is essential to student learning, and no one else can do it as well for less, then they're worth the money.

In 2010, this author queried one of the area directors about a middle school study she was supposedly doing. It took several e-mails, phone calls, a telephone appointment, and seventy-five days just to find out that she wasn't doing a special study.

Teacher Contracts

Dr. Marguerite Roza wrote in her 2007 Educator Sector report "Frozen Assets" that eight common provisions of teacher contracts have a tenuous connection to better student learning: (1) seniority pay, (2) pay based on credentials and experience, (3) professional-development days, (4) paid sick and personal days, (5) class-size limitations, (6) teachers' aides, (7) health and insurance benefits, and (8) retirement benefits.

Dr. Roza said these provisions tie up "an average of 19 percent of every school district's budget." Of that, more than half is in seniority pay. Dr. Roza noted that teacher experience has an initial effect on student learning, but it seems to level out after about five years. Therefore, she said, if the intent of seniority pay is to reward teachers for their hard work and years of service, then fine. But if it's to reward them for getting better results with longevity, the data doesn't support it. Dr. Roza wondered if the money for the eight provisions could be spent "differently, and with greater effect."

(A Spokane teacher said she gets a $200-per-year longevity stipend, which doesn't seem like a lot, considering the challenges.)

It's easy to support higher teacher salaries or benefits. Teachers have a tough and important job, and it isn't made any easier by administrators who continually muck around in their classrooms. They should be paid well. But, let's not kid ourselves. Teacher benefits—like administrator benefits—are not intrinsically linked to better educational outcomes.

Better student outcomes have to come through the Square of Effective Learning. Improving teachers' ability to teach will largely come through more content knowledge, better classroom-management skills, and fewer district-initiated absences from the classroom.

Where Would Additional Billions Go?

What would administrators do with more billions? They tend to press legislators and taxpayers for some combination of the following: full-day kindergarten, smaller classes, more and better-qualified teachers, summer school, mentoring, abuse prevention, transportation, early childhood, building improvements, English as a second language, "enrichment" activities, professional development, special education, technology, counselors, outreach, finance systems and data collection, collective bargaining, and security.

A very long list of budget items in a 2007 OSPI press release for school years 2007 to 2009 included these items:

- $25 million for more classified staff such as security and technology employees
- a $25 million down payment on enhanced transportation funding
- $12 million for technology upgrades
- $19 million for classified and administrator pay
- an increase in the National Board Certification bonus from $3,500 to $5,000 per year and extra $5,000 certification bonuses for teachers working in high-poverty areas ("Education Was Legislature's Focus" 2007)

It's rare to hear any of them specifically call for better curricula or anything else that directly affects the Square of Effective Learning.

Economic Times Are Tough; Overhead Is High; Accountability Is Critical

An August 2008 *New York Times* article reported that higher prices, foreclosures, and an economic downturn left schools struggling (Dillon 2008). School officials were raising lunch prices, shortening the school week to four days, cutting or eliminating bus services, restricting field trips, and laying off teachers, administrators, and other staff. In Mount Vernon, New York, the entire athletics program was cut, prompting donations from the community (Hu 2008b). In 2009, after the ED announced its $100 billion education "stimulus," school districts were still cutting. To save money, some snipped off minutes, hours, or even full days from the schedule.

During the 2008 governor's race in Washington State, a budget shortfall was projected to be about $3 billion, but by early 2009—a few months after the incumbent was reelected—it magically climbed to almost $9 billion, precipitating cuts to education. Another $2 billion deficit was predicted for 2010–2011 and more cuts to education proposed: "Many non-basic education programs are scaled back or eliminated. This will affect students throughout the state by increasing class sizes and reducing supports for teachers. The elimination of levy equalization and state-funded all-day kindergarten will affect students in our poorest districts. The suspension of state funding for gifted programs, career and technical education, and many other programs will reduce the breadth of offerings available to students" ("2010 Budget Highlights" n.d.; "Governor Chris Gregoire" n.d.).

The American taxpayer has been betrayed. Hundreds of billions of dollars are spent every year in this country on a failing education system. And everyone in public education wants more.

Title I, Free and Reduced Lunch, and Social Services Programs

It feels miserly and mean to question funding for Title I and other aid programs, but, especially in times of economic mishandling, accountability is critical to developing and maintaining a strong and healthy system. Some people argue that most parents won't scam the system, so it's better to feed everyone's kids rather than allow one child to go hungry.

All children should be properly fed. Families shouldn't be scared away from asking for help when they need it. The nation shouldn't balance education budgets on the backs of the disadvantaged. However, financially supporting families that don't qualify for the programs burdens the system and takes away resources from those who do. Programs must be distributed (and funded) properly.

Let's bite the bullet and ask. How many of the Title I billions belong there? How many students qualify for aid programs? It might be most, it might be all, but we don't know for sure. In some districts, just a minute percentage of families are checked to see if they qualify.

In 2008, income limits for Washington State's Basic Food Program increased to 200 percent of federal poverty guidelines, upping the number of qualifying families. Spokane Public Schools encouraged families to "take advantage of this simple way to help stretch the family budget." The district e-mail said, "The more students who take advantage of the school meals program, the more federal money will come into our schools." (You knew that was coming.)

In 2008 and 2009, Washington State subsidized meals for 40.4 percent of its students. Larger districts reflected a similar trend: Seattle, 41.3 percent; Tacoma, 58.8 percent; Spokane, 53.5 percent; Kent, 41.9 percent; Federal Way, 46.7 percent; Vancouver, 47.3 percent. Then there's Yakima at 77.6 percent.

A parent said he's dismayed that districts increasingly cover or make room for social services programs: child care for children of teenage students; food and clothing banks; dental care; teaching English as a second language; one-on-one tutoring for English-language learners.

"Is it the school's job to financially support families?" the parent wondered. "Isn't that what Social Services is for? Perhaps we've saddled schools with financial burdens that aren't theirs to carry." Social services are designed to help families in need. When schools host and pay for those services, it drains time and resources away from the primary mission: academics.

It's sacrilege to say it, but public education doesn't need more money. The money it gets needs to be spent differently. Examine automatic assumptions. A lesson plan can be developed on a piece of paper. Students can learn algebra with a $100 textbook, a pencil, and a notebook. They can do research at the library, and they can be tested with teacher-developed problems.

Central-office administrators want, but don't need, TI-84 calculators, SMART Boards, document cameras, instructional coaches, area directors, layers of assistants, and travel budgets. Public education would benefit from having fewer central-office administrators altogether.

Extras should be paid for with extra money. Instead, they've become pretend needs, and the Square of Effective Learning has become the extra.

This is why money is a diversionary issue. The constant clamoring for more of it serves mostly to feather nests, pay for cool toys and ever-widening social services, and divert, money, resources, and attention away from the two most pressing education problems we have:

- Students aren't learning what they need to learn academically.
- Students aren't learning what they could learn academically.

The solution to those two problems entails relatively inexpensive things that directly affect what happens in the classroom (in the Square of Effective Learning). If adults have extra money in the budget and they want other things like conferences and neat technology, then fine, but let's not pretend any of it will solve the two most important problems we have.

DIVERT OUR ATTENTION TO TECHNOLOGY

"A 19- or 20-year-old ticket seller couldn't make change for $20 after someone had purchased two $6 tickets from him. Explaining his difficulty, he said, 'Where I work, they have a computer to figure it.'"

—Paul Turner, in a *Spokesman-Review* column 2008

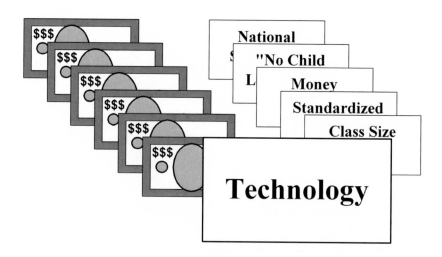

Reform mathematics has long carried the message that calculators belong in K–12 classrooms. But the debate continues, with arguments like the following:

- "It's unnecessary for students to learn how to do arithmetic because they'll always have calculators and computers to do that for them. Calculators free children from spending time doing things they know how to do."
- "We live in a technology-driven society. Students need to learn to use available technology, or they won't be competitive in the international marketplace."
- "Calculators and computers should be limited in the younger grades, but they're helpful for older students who do more complicated projects."
- "Constant use of calculators inhibits learning. Children become dependent and don't develop the number sense they need to determine whether an answer makes sense."

The debate has been left in the dust, however, as technology swamps the classrooms. Calculators are used in grades as early as kindergarten and allowed on some standardized tests. Children learn how to do PowerPoint before they can spell it. The need for hardware and software is incorporated into textbooks and project requirements. An elementary school teacher in Spokane said calculators are handed out as part of the *Connected Mathematics* curriculum.

Taxpayer money has filled schools with technology. It's happened partly because technology is a big, lucrative business. But there are other reasons.

Students should eventually learn to use technology. We don't want students graduating not knowing how to use a computer or calculator. That would have a negative impact on their prospects in college, trades, or the job market. That's reasonable.

Not all students have home access to technology. Not all students have a computer at home. Families that can't afford a basic calculator surely can't afford a graphing calculator. Computer use typically is free at libraries, but access might be limited. That's reasonable too.

Calculators and computers are useful and cool. Next to a computer program of bright visuals, a page of math problems seems uninteresting. With computers, it's easy to do a lot of research in one sitting. Practicing arithmetic and writing skills with quality software might be helpful if managed in the right way. In more advanced math, calculators can limit arithmetic errors that cloud understanding.

A side benefit: The computer, like the television before it, can always occupy a few restless children.

Some manufacturers helpfully produce or finance studies showing how their product assists in the learning process. A cursory search of the National Science Foundation (NSF) awards page produces several of these.

The National Council of Teachers of Mathematics (NCTM) promotes technology in all classrooms for all grades. According to a 2002 NSF report titled "Elementary and Secondary Education IT in Schools," the NCTM's 1989 document "Curriculum and Evaluation Standards for School Mathematics" urged "the use of calculators to reduce the time spent on paper and pencil methods of calculating."

Former NCTM president Dr. Lee V. Stiff's 2001 article "Making Calculator Use Add Up" cites studies from the 1990s supporting calculators and computers in the classroom. His article concludes with this: "Calculators can and should be used to promote higher-order thinking. . . . The depth of problem solving that students can pursue with proper use of calculators is astounding—and it's something for which every teacher should strive from the time students enter school until they graduate."

In 2000, Daniel Golden, then a *Wall Street Journal* reporter, wrote that Texas Instruments was marketing its calculators with teachers and textbook publishers and had provided substantial funding to the NCTM. In the article, Golden, now editor at large with *Bloomberg News*, also provided anecdotal evidence of a negative impact of heavy calculator use on students' procedural fluency and ability to memorize.

The federal government also has promoted technology in classrooms. In 2002, then U.S. secretary of education Rod Paige announced an education initiative called the "Enhancing Education through Technology (Ed Tech) Program." Its "primary" goal was to "improve student achievement through the use of technology." The website talked about improving achievement and engaging "students in solid academic curriculum like never before."

But the Ed Tech website was short on facts, and it assumed without proof that the use of technology improves learning. The entire page read like a sales pitch. Why would the ED try so hard to sell the public on technology in the classroom? Shall we just follow the money?

The hype has yet to be borne out. A research arm of the ED issued a 2007 report on the effectiveness of reading and mathematics software. The study, mandated by Congress as part of NCLB, examined thirty-three districts, 132 schools, 439 teachers, and sixteen software products. The study found the software's effects on test scores to be statistically insignificant from zero (Dynarski et al. 2007). This report came out long after math and reading software became commonplace in classrooms. It's doubtful the report changed a thing.

In April 2008, OSPI said ninety-seven Washington teachers would receive a total of $873,000 for training as "technology integrators and peer coaches" ("Federal Grants to Help Teachers" 2008). Each would receive $9,000 to cover the training, technology, and "related costs, such as substitute teachers."

(Geez. Doesn't OSPI want anybody to teach any more?)

Read the following excerpt from OSPI's press release. See if this isn't more of the standard education mantra "Buy it first, and then figure out how to make it useful": "Peer coaches work with colleagues . . . to incorporate digital technologies into teaching and learning—software, graphing calculators, interactive whiteboards, digital cameras and more. . . . Together they identify ways to use this technology to strengthen curricula and improve academic achievement."

The grants were funded through Title II, Part D, of the federal Elementary and Secondary Education Act, also known as the "Enhancing Education through Technology" initiative. And there it is: the Ed Tech program.

Hearing a rumor that calculators were being introduced into the first and second grades, this author called over to an area school to ask. The principal at that elementary school said calculators were available for any teacher who wanted to use them, even in kindergarten.

Well, sure, why shouldn't kindergarteners learn how to use calculators? Why should we expect K–6 students to learn arithmetic? Why should anyone do research by going to libraries and pulling out dusty books, when it's all on the Internet? Why should we memorize facts, dates, names, or places when we can just Google them? Why go to school at all? In fact, why should any of us ever get out of bed?

(No, that's silly. We have to get out of bed. Somebody has to feed the dog.)

It's ironic that proponents of reform feel so positive toward calculators, considering their stance against rote, passive types of learning. A calculator is as rote and as passive as you can get. If you plug in numbers, you'll get an answer. If you don't understand what goes in and why, you won't have any basis for understanding what comes back out. Garbage in, garbage out.

A high school math teacher articulated the calculator problem. He was to teach high school math to foreign students who barely spoke English and who had (the equivalent of) a first-grade education. He gave them a test of arithmetic, and they all received a score of zero. They didn't understand the numbers or the operations. So he gave them calculators. He said, "See this button with the "×" on it? That's this symbol. See this "2"? That's this button right here. See the match? Now, take the test." All passed the test with 100 percent, even though none had a clue of what they were doing.

The teacher said an administrator had complained to him about teacher resistance to calculators. The administrator said she was tired of math teachers talking about how students couldn't do arithmetic. She told him, "You just give them a calculator and get on with teaching them higher mathematics."

The teacher shook his head incredulously. "You can't teach someone higher mathematics if they don't know lower mathematics," he said. "There are teachers who believe that you can. . . . A constructivist believes that you really don't need skills that much to understand the broad concepts of mathematics, and they're right. You don't need skills that much to understand the broad concepts, but to actually do calculus or to do trigonometry . . . you'd better have some skills. You can't just have a broad concept."

Dr. Shannon Overbay, associate professor at Gonzaga University, said she first became concerned about reform math while teaching in Oregon. Most of her students had gone through high school with a reform curriculum. "Their lack of basic skills in arithmetic and algebra was alarming to me," she said. "Students were extremely dependent on their TI graphing calculators and could not graph even basic functions, solve equations, or do simple computations without their calculators." She said she stopped allowing students to use calculators in some classes.

One student stood out from the others, Dr. Overbay said, with outstanding skills. The student came from a poor village in Mexico and had never owned a calculator. "She had done all of her work with pencil and paper. She was clearly outperforming students who had 'honors' integrated math at the local high school."

At Gonzaga, however, Dr. Overbay continues to see a dependency on calculators: "My students often complain that they never learned their times tables and say that they should not have been allowed to use calculators in grade school. They do see the damage that has been done. . . . Yet many math educators say that we need to give the calculator and other such technology an even bigger role in math classes."

A worry about calculators is their tendency to bump aside fractions. In mathematics, exact answers are important. Fractions always give exact answers, whereas decimals often don't. Also, if rounding is done through several steps of a problem, then with each rounding, the answer gets farther away from what is "exact."

Advanced calculators can handle fractions, but they don't give students practice in handling fractions. The brain benefits from the processes of thinking it through and writing it down. Yet, the norm in reform classes is to use calculators. Many students now have a weak understanding of fractions or of how to convert between decimals, fractions, and percentages.

A professional in the trades discussed the theory that people will always have calculators and computers and so learning basic skills is a waste of time. He said he wouldn't want to rule out calculators. They're a big help, he said, especially with more complex numbers. However, he reiterated, people in the trades need to have math skills. They need to have some sense of whether the answer is accurate.

The 2008 National Mathematics Advisory Panel (NMAP) said that "high-quality computer-assisted instruction" should be considered as a "useful"—or "potentially useful"—tool for learning, but stopped short of advocating for the use of calculators throughout K–12 instruction. In fact, the final report warns, "The Panel cautions that to the degree that calculators impede the development of automaticity, fluency in computation will be adversely affected" (NMAP 2008).

Strategic Teaching's 2007 report on Washington State's math standards said that calculators have value but shouldn't replace computational fluency: "Students need to add, subtract, multiply, and divide whole numbers, fractions, and decimals without a calculator," the report said. "At the secondary level, again, the use of technology should not circumvent student fluency with hand calculations" (Plattner 2007).

Computers and calculators are relatively new inventions. Many people over forty-five went their entire K–12 experience without either—and most have respectable typing, writing, and math skills. Somehow we picked up computer and calculator skills even though we lived through the dog years of punch cards, COBOL, and DOS.

The current reliance on technology in K–8 is a distraction, a crutch, and a hindrance. Students will sit at classroom computers playing games, arguing over whose turn it is, or creating sheets of WordArt for no useful purpose. They want to work out the simplest calculations using their calculators. They know how to work document cameras and SMART Boards, yet many cannot reliably subtract twenty-six from fifty.

In 2008, a sixth grader said computers helped her learn to type and made research easier, but other than that, she didn't think they're necessary in the classroom. She has no choice. Fighting the proliferation of technology is like trying to hold back the tide with a fork.

New York Times articles have discussed using video games as "bait to hook" young students and to "vanquish an archfiend: algebra" (Hu 2008a; Rich 2008).

This is emblematic of current thinking. In times gone past, teachers taught, and students learned. Now, many teachers feel they have to sweeten the pot by "hooking," cajoling, and entertaining. An elementary school teacher expressed frustration that "parents and administrators expect kids to have fun at school every day and in every subject." Learning isn't always "fun," she said, but it's necessary, and it can be enjoyable. "I often feel like I have to 'sing and dance' to get or keep kids' attention," she said.

It's unfortunate. Things that help students enjoy the learning process are structural: Efficiency, logic, organization, and reassurance (the "Don't worry, I'm here, and we'll do it together. I'll show you, you'll practice, and then you'll have it").

Instead, students are thrown to the wolves every day with pretend fun things like games, group projects, "discovery," and calculators for every little thing. They become used to it. Fed a constant refrain of "Maybe math isn't your best subject," they don't realize that their weak skills are due to poor curricula and inefficient delivery.

Just because administrators spend our tax dollars chasing after calculators and every stray-dog piece of "fun" software, it doesn't mean we have to accept it. Parents can insist on no calculators in K–8. Teachers can tell students to do all reasonable calculations by hand. If students go through pre-algebra with a good textbook and without a calculator—and it isn't that difficult to do—they'll gain a good sense for numbers.

Question everything that diverts money, time, and resources away from academic learning.

DIVERT OUR ATTENTION TO NO CHILD LEFT BEHIND

"Even when the experts all agree, they may well be mistaken."

—Bertrand Russell

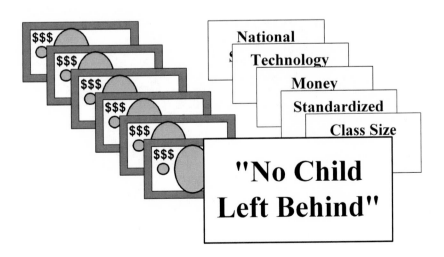

In 2001, the federal government passed legislation called the No Child Left Behind Act. President George W. Bush proposed the law shortly after his inauguration, and the act was signed into law in 2002. President Bush described NCLB as the "cornerstone" of his administration: "Too many of our neediest children are being left behind."

With the passage of NCLB, Congress effectively reauthorized the Elementary and Secondary Education Act, the principal federal law from 1965 affecting K–12 education. NCLB was a massive "overhaul" of elementary and secondary education.

A decade later, NCLB's clock ticks loudly in everyone's ear. NCLB stated that by 2014 all children must meet a standard set by the state in which they live. There are financial and practical consequences for districts that fail to meet predetermined learning targets and goals, so every eligible student must do well on state tests or on an acceptable alternative. Designed to be a helpful aspect of public Accountability, NCLB quickly became an expensive bureaucratic nightmare . . . and thus, a diversionary issue.

When NCLB became law, the Department of Education said success in education would come through high standards, annual assessments, accountability for results, highly qualified teachers in every classroom, information and options for parents, and all children on grade level by 2014. The act was built on four "common-sense pillars":

- accountability for results
- an emphasis on doing what works based on scientific research
- expanded parental options
- expanded local control and flexibility

(Sadly, look at where we are now: manipulated data, "research" that supports pet social theories, few parent options, and almost no local control or flexibility.)

The problem with NCLB was that, rather than mandating equity of opportunity, as it should have done, it mandated results—an impossible thing to do. People aren't vending machines, where we plug in $658 billion and out pops a college student. Americans seize opportunities and decide how much effort they're willing to expend. NCLB told students, "You will succeed, and you'll do it in the time frame we choose. The decision to succeed or fail is no longer open to you." Not only is it impossible to mandate success, it's un-American.

About Title I

Title I was designed to funnel extra money to schools that have high numbers of low-income families. The thinking is that student academic performance is connected to family income level. Examine any assessment of a broad group of students, and you'll often (although not always) find a correlation between family income and student achievement. This doesn't mean children from rich families are smarter. It means other factors are at play in student learning.

Most standardized test scores do show significant gaps between students from higher- and lower-income families and between students whose parents had the most and least education. The 2006 Organization for Economic Cooperation and Development (OECD) Program for International Student Assessment also notes the effect of a disadvantaged home: "Poor performance in school does not automatically follow from a disadvantaged home background. However, home background . . . remains one of the most powerful factors influencing performance. On average across the OECD countries, it explained 14 percent of the student performance variation in science."

By 2007, more than half of all American public and charter schools used Title I funds. In 2010, President Barack Obama proposed reauthorizing and renaming the now $14.5 billion program, placing a new emphasis on college and career readiness.

NCLB's Strong Points (the "Good")

Achievement for all: The goal of NCLB is to bring all students to a standard of learning. Inherent in that goal is the need to close "achievement gaps" between groups of students.

Choice: If a Title I school fails to meet adequate yearly progress (AYP) targets for two consecutive years, students can change schools (a program called Choice).

Tutoring: If a Title I school fails to meet AYP targets for three years in a row, students can receive free tutoring or other remediation (Supplemental Education Services). In 2008, eleven states were approved to offer this tutoring in the first year of school improvement status.

Transparency: Standardized tests were to provide "independent information about each child's strengths and weaknesses." (Teachers and principals were supposed to be able to use that data to determine student progress, craft individualized lessons, and make decisions.)

Accountability: Parents were to have access to "easy-to-read, detailed report cards on schools and districts" that include data broken out by every conceivable human category, including English-language proficiency, migrant status, and disability status.

Teacher quality: States had five years to mandate certain teacher and aide qualifications.

Money: Originally, NCLB was not designed to run public education; it was designed to support and help fund improvements in public education.

Achievement, assistance, accountability, teacher quality, and money—it's all good. Now, we must talk about the problems with NCLB.

NCLB's Weak Points (the "Bad")

"In exchange for the strong accountability," the NCLB parents' guide says, states and agencies would have "more flexibility in the use of their federal education funding": "As a result, principals and administrators spend less time filling out forms and dealing with federal red tape. They have more time to devote to students' needs. They have more freedom to implement innovations and allocate resources as policymakers at the state and local levels see fit, thereby giving local people a greater opportunity to affect decisions regarding their schools' programs" (Paige and Gibbons 2003).

It didn't work out like that. Administrators spend their days splitting statistical hairs, desperately trying to show they're meeting NCLB requirements. Certain exceptions are available to districts, but nearly all children must pass the tests with proficiency. That's every child—the smart ones, the average ones, the ones who refuse to learn, the ones who can't learn at this moment, and the ones who will drop out and start robbing their neighbors at the first opportunity.

Any failures in meeting the targets—whether one failure or twenty—were viewed the same under NCLB. Districts and states were limited in their ability to prioritize. The goal of "flexibility" fell out of reach. Administrators had to prove success. Subjects were narrowed, standards were lowered, statistics were parsed, teachers were forced into curriculum boxes, and the definition of proficiency came to mean the passing score. All of this desperation was because of the punitive consequences.

The Consequences of Failing to Progress (the "Punitive")

The fifty thousand schools in America that qualify for and accept Title I funds face serious ramifications for failing to meet AYP targets.

As noted, Title I schools that don't meet all AYP targets for two years in a row are identified as "needing improvement." They must develop a two-year plan for turning things around and accept help in developing and implementing this plan. Students are given the opportunity (the "choice") to transfer to another school that doesn't "need improvement."

Title I schools not meeting all AYP targets for three years in a row also must offer free tutoring, remedial classes, or Supplemental Educational Services.

Title I schools not meeting all targets for four years in a row also are subject to "certain corrective actions" from the state, such as replacing staff and changing curricula.

If a Title I school fails to meet all targets for a fifth straight year, the district must initiate plans to restructure the school, such as reopening the school as a charter school, replacing all or most of the staff, or turning over operations to the state or to a private company "with a demonstrated record of effectiveness."

Every school in the district must meet predetermined levels of AYP, or the district as a whole can eventually be ruled as "needing improvement." The same helpful law that offers choice and free tutoring, therefore, also plays havoc with enrollments, planning, and budgets.

Students can go elsewhere, administrators can be fired, and schools can be closed down.

By 2008, tens of thousands of schools nationwide were failing to make AYP. Administrators were frantic. In response, Secretary of Education Margaret Spellings proposed changes to "strengthen" NCLB, including allowing states to distinguish between schools requiring intervention and those that were close to meeting targets. However, she also moved to force "more rigorous" restructuring and to create AYP targets for graduation, including for minorities and students with disabilities (U.S. Department of Education 2008b, 2008c, 2008d).

The federal government isn't supposed to have this level of control over public education. According to 20 USC 3403, education is a state responsibility. Additionally, you can't have "excellence" and everybody or "proficient" and everybody—not unless the terms "excellence" and "proficient" are redefined so as to lose all meaning.

In January 2010, the Obama administration announced plans to fix NCLB. A *New York Times* article said part of the fix could entail allotting federal taxpayer money based on academic achievement rather than as an entitlement. States would have to show certain improvements in order to get the money (Dillon 2010a, 2010b). The new federal goal would be that all students be college or career ready by 2020. The administration's "hope," the article said, is to eventually tie all federal money to the same requirements as those for Race to the Top.

(RTTT gives points for allowing charter schools, using student-achievement data to evaluate teachers, and adopting common standards.)

This is not better.

You'd think that after their negative experiences with NCLB, states would be resistant to any new federal agendas and mandates. Led by Texas and Alaska, a small number of states and school districts did take a step back from RTTT and/or the Common Core Standards, but most just climbed on board (see the next section for more on this).

Education administrators are in a box of their own making. You can see why they're focused—almost to the exclusion of all else—on infinitesimal upticks and downticks in pass rates, and you can see the potential for myriad problems as states scramble to drag every parent and child into compliance with a federal vision. Eventually, the system should collapse under its own weight, but before it goes down, it will sacrifice truckloads of dollars, the bright futures of millions of children, and the economic and practical stability of the nation.

Education advocates love the concept of no child being left behind. It's our fondest dream for the world. But dreams must be rooted in reality. Some students will be left behind to some degree. Some will find a way to succeed, and others will give up. That's the nature of children, of people, of families in a free society. Some children aren't capable of succeeding on a basic level, much less to anyone's definition of proficiency. Ironically, as a consequence of this law, some children who are capable of succeeding and excelling won't have the opportunity.

"No child denied the opportunity" is the more realistic and truly American goal. As a local parent noted, "The pursuit of an education is a right not to be denied, but the attainment, like happiness, is not guaranteed." If achievement gaps are to be narrowed, the nation's time and money is better spent on providing all students with the same opportunities, access, and quality of schools. These are worthwhile goals.

Americans have the right to choose to fail. We also have the right to choose to excel. It's that flexibility that made America strong. We must allow for the most basic right Americans have: the freedom to choose the process. But flexibility has been legislated and mandated right out of the public-education system. Everyone is supposed to gather happily and contentedly at the Babbling Brook of Mediocrity, where we can clasp hands, sing "Kumbaya," and hand out plaques of appreciation and certificates of merit to everyone.

Talk to principals, superintendents, boards of education, state administrators, legislators, and the secretary of education. The quieter you are, the more they'll think you don't care or you agree with what's being done.

Make your voice heard. We get to do that in America, and we must.

DIVERT OUR ATTENTION TO NATIONAL STANDARDS, TESTS, AND CURRICULA

"The proper role of the Education Department is in helping states, districts and schools collect data to drive good decision making."

—Former U.S. secretary of education Margaret Spellings, in a 2007 *Washington Post* op-ed

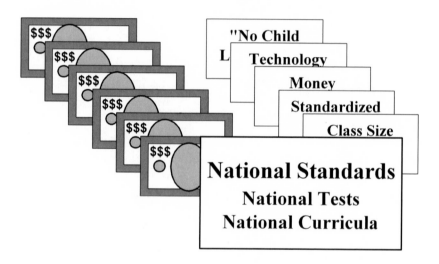

After a 2007 ED report indicated differences among the states as to what constitutes academic "proficiency," Secretary of Education Margaret Spellings (2007c) expressed her concerns in a *Washington Post* editorial that some people might be tempted to press for national standards and a national test.

That would be "unprecedented and unwise," Secretary Spellings wrote. Not only are national standards not necessarily "synonymous" with high standards, they might actually lower learning standards while doing little "to address the persistent achievement gap."

Additionally, she noted, forcing (untested) standards and tests on the states would contradict both tradition and the U.S. Constitution, which places most responsibilities for education in the hands of state and local governments and administrators. "They design the curriculum and pay 90 percent of the bills," Secretary Spellings said. "Neighborhood schools deserve neighborhood leadership, not dictates from bureaucrats thousands of miles away."

Ah, the irony. Secretary Spellings worked under President George W. Bush. His No Child Left Behind Act could be seen as a dictate from bureaucrats thousands of miles away. However, in light of the federal push for the Common Core Standards, Secretary Spellings's comment was prescient. Are national standards constitutional? Will they be good for students? For the country? They'll be good for a few businesses. It's also likely they'll suck up administrative time and billions of taxpayer dollars without having a direct, positive effect on the classroom.

That's why they're a diversionary issue.

In June 2009, the National Governors Association (NGA) Center for Best Practices and the Council of Chief State School Officers (CCSSO)—in partnership with Achieve Inc., ACT, and the College Board—announced an initiative to develop national learning standards (or their preferred term, "Common Core Standards"). The CCSSO is a supposedly "nonpartisan" group of people who run departments of elementary and secondary education: Administrators.

Before the standards were even written, Washington was one of forty-eight states to sign a memorandum of agreement (MOA) saying it would participate in their development—despite the $1.6 million the state just spent revising its own math standards.

The federal government isn't supposed to write education standards, so the standards movement is purportedly grassroots, driven by the states. However, Secretary of Education Arne Duncan has pushed hard for states to sign on to the federal Race to the Top grant initiative. States are more likely to successfully compete for RTTT grants if they agree to make certain permanent changes to public education (such as adopting the national standards, allowing charter schools, and tying teacher assessment to student test scores).

Where is the research to support this new federal agenda? Where are the data and controlled studies showing that these national standards will result in improved student learning? There is nothing. Texas and Alaska demurred from signing on to RTTT, and a few other states are having second thoughts, but the stated federal plan is to tie Title I money to the same requirements as RTTT (Dillon 2010a, 2010b). How long will the rebels be able to hold out?

Washington State signed on quietly, with nary a peep to the public. Concerns were met with variations on this: "Signing the MOA doesn't mean we're signing on to the standards. We're just agreeing to look at them." Six months later, Washington was poised to adopt the unfinished standards—sight unseen—with Senate Bill 6696 (SB6696).

Under the heading "Common Core Adoption," the original SB6696 said the state "shall" adopt "a common set of standards"—not "might" adopt them. Math advocates fought the language, and revisions were made, replacing "shall" with "may" and including a legislative review.

Why would legislators even consider giving away constitutionally protected state autonomy for a few coins they might not get? Why would they adopt nationally directed education standards sight unseen? Why would anyone support a bill like this?

A revised SB6696 easily passed through Washington's Democrat-controlled Senate on February 11, with just five nay votes. A final version became law on March 11. Cosponsor Senator Chris Marr (D) told this author in a taped interview on February 12 that he didn't know much about the bill he was cosponsoring, but he was motivated by the RTTT money and had "faith" in the process. He shouldn't. Secretary Duncan is going way beyond his mandate. It's all there in 20 USC 3403:

> The establishment of the Department of Education shall not increase the authority of the Federal Government over education or diminish the responsibility for education which is reserved to the States and the local school systems and other instrumentalities of the States. . . . No provision of a program administered by the Secretary or by any other officer of the Department shall be construed to authorize the Secretary or any such officer to exercise any direction, supervision, or control over the curriculum, program of instruction, administration, or personnel of any educational institution, school, or school system, over any accrediting agency or association, or over the selection or content of library resources, textbooks, or other instructional materials by any educational institution or school system, except to the extent authorized by law.

That's so 1980s. As of February 2010, the ED's "High Priority Performance Goals" include a "cradle-to-career" federal "education strategy," mandated "intensive" reform for struggling schools, ensuring "teacher evaluation systems" that are connected to student achievement, and fostering—some say demanding—state collaboration ("Overview: Department of Education" 2010).

What right does the federal government have to press any sort of education agenda on the "cradle"? Or on preschool? Additionally, in a world where teachers have some measure of academic freedom, tying teacher assessments to student outcomes might be reasonable. But in districts like Spokane, where the leadership has a death grip on classroom instruction and a habit of blaming teachers for weak outcomes, teachers are in the crosshairs.

Secretary Duncan claims the federal role in education is limited. Don't believe it. Read through his speech to the 2009 Governors Education Symposium ("States Will Lead the Way" 2009). Despite the constant refrain of "This effort is state-led, state-led, state-led," the federal agenda is loud and obvious throughout. Money is dangled in front of the governors' eyes, promised to states that are "absolutely pushing reform in real and measurable ways." You'll note that student achievement is not required for RTTT money—just policy changes that Secretary Duncan advocates.

This is not about the students.

The lack of transparency was a problem from the beginning. The national standards initiative was formally announced June 1, 2009—along with plans to release "college- and career-ready standards" just one month later. That's either really fast work, or they were at it for a while—in secret. The NGA declined until July 2009 to even give out names of people involved in writing the standards—a perplexing stance that appeared to faze few in the media.

In July 2009, this author began querying the ED, the CCSSO, the NGA, Achieve, the Washington State governor's office, and OSPI about the national standards initiative.

U.S. Department of Education: The ED tried several times to pass off questions to the CCSSO. Following a Freedom of Information Act (FOIA) request, there was one clarifying phone call and then nothing.

After a threat to make a federal case of it, still nothing. In 2010, an e-mail was sent to the ED's new feature "AskArne." This resulted in a carefully phrased reply that didn't answer the questions. On the FOIA request—despite continuing requests—still nothing.

The ED appears to be ignoring an FOIA request.

CCSSO, NGA, and Achieve: From the CCSSO—nothing. From the NGA—nothing. From Achieve—there was one return phone call that referred all questions to the CCSSO.

Governor: The governor's office provided internal documents indicating early agreement from the governor, state superintendent, and the State Board of Education (SBE) on supporting the standards initiative. Executive Policy Advisor Judy Hartmann said in an October 2009 taped interview that, before they were adopted, the national standards would have to go through the same vetting process as the state standards (this would include advisory committees and professional reviews).

In January 2010, however, before the national standards were completed, SB6696 stated under the heading "Common Core Adoption" that "By August 2, 2010, the superintendent of public instruction shall revise the essential academic learning requirements and standards . . . by adopting a common set of standards for students in kindergarten through grade twelve."

(SB6696 was "by request of Governor [Chris] Gregoire.")

State Board of Education: In a May 2009 letter to the governor, the chair of the SBE wrote, "Our potential adoption of these new standards hinges on the rigor, relevance, and value of what's developed; we will not sign on to standards that fail to meet the proven effectiveness of our current standards."

An SBE presentation dated October 2009, however, laid out how Washington would sign on to RTTT, adopt the standards, develop committees, and notify the public ("Washington's 'Race to the Top' Proposal" 2009).

Deputy superintendent: Deputy Superintendent Alan Burke responded to an FOIA request by e-mail in August 2009, saying that answers to certain questions about cost and process were "unknown at this time." However, if more than 15 percent of the national standards were unacceptable, he said, the standards would not be adopted in Washington State.

The language in SB6696, however, is that the state may not add more than 15 percent to each content area of the national standards. This effectively places a limit on how rigorous the national standards can be, once adopted in Washington State.

State superintendent: In a September 2009 press release, Superintendent Randy Dorn said the national standards would be "examined thoroughly and transparently. Any changes to the state's standards would not occur for at least two years, and then only after an ample opportunity for public review and comment" ("Common Core Standards Draft Released" 2009). The public had thirty days to respond, Dorn's release said. However, he added, with no apparent trace of irony, the feedback "must be supported by research and evidence."

On January 25, 2010, however, Superintendent Dorn said he supported SB6696—which still included the word "shall"—and even said it doesn't go far enough.

By April 2010, still before the national standards were completed, Governor Gregoire and Superintendent Dorn were pressuring school districts to sign a memorandum in support of the state's RTTT application.

In June 2010, Superintendent Dorn announced that Washington would lead a thirty-one-state consortium to develop national assessments based on the (national) Common Core Standards. His press release said, "By the end of 2011, states in the consortium must agree to adopt the Common Core State Standards in English language arts and math."

In July 2010, Superintendent Dorn "provisionally" adopted the national standards.

All of this is before the legislative reviews mandated by SB6696.

District school board: In May 2010, as Superintendent Dorn coincidentally visited the city, Spokane's school board voted 3–2 to support Washington's RTTT application. Without addressing concerns raised that day—about the punitive nature and questionable constitutionality of the national plan, the probable loss of local control and lowering of standards, the lack of transparency, and the pittance of money in-volved—three board directors voted in favor.

No one has ever articulated how RTTT will help the children learn better.

How will other philosophies and commercial products survive—competing as they'll be on a not-so-level playing field with well-con-nected organizations and companies, savvy marketers, and the U.S. Department of Education? How will teachers and parents advocate for the children when decision makers are all shadowy faces and strangers in Washington, D.C., and when decision makers appear to care little for transparency or proper process?

The ED website says, "Please note that in the U.S., the federal role in education is limited. Because of the Tenth Amendment, most edu-cation policy is decided at the state and local levels. So, if you have a question about a policy or issue, you may want to check with the relevant organization in your state or school district."

That's hilarious. The feds are now in charge of policy. Just don't plan to ask them any questions about it.

National Curriculum

In May 2009, Secretary Duncan reportedly told a reporter that not hav-ing national curricula is "crazy." Writing in May 2009 for what is now *Bloomberg Businessweek*, Steven Levine said, "Both Duncan and the Tough Choices members steer carefully around the phrase 'national education.' . . . Yet that's clearly where the Administration is headed. Duncan wants to nudge the winning states toward agreeing on rigor-ous, shared curricula that could spread across the country. 'The idea of 50 states doing their own thing I think is crazy,' Duncan says. Race to the Top is a way 'to say to a set of states, "You lead the national conversation. You do this."'"

And that's why Secretary Duncan's "You lead" is really "You do this," which is really "Do it my way," which is really "Do it my way or else."

People who sell education-related products—such as calculators, textbooks and software—and people who run associations and organizations all must be monitoring these developments closely, perhaps already tailoring their products and language to "align" with this new federal push. No doubt some are involved behind the scenes, working with allies and partners to sway things to their best advantage. Partnerships are good for business.

The national initiatives were supposedly "voluntary," supposedly "grassroots," supposedly "state led." And yet, it's been alarming to watch as—one after another—states, districts, school boards, unions, organizations, and associations fell to this untested initiative.

- It wasn't because it was a lot of money. RTTT is a pittance, comparatively speaking.
- It wasn't because the national standards are so great. They weren't even written when people began signing on. Early reviews of the math standards indicated serious weaknesses. The final draft of the math standards was dramatically different—weaker many say—than the March draft.
- It wasn't because states or districts have great plans for using RTTT money in the classroom. The use of that money is mandated by the federal government.

It was disturbing to file an FOIA request with the ED and get nothing, to be told one thing by state officials and see something else happen, to see governors and superintendents circle the districts, pressuring school boards to support state involvement.

This doesn't feel voluntary at all.

Will this "national"-izing of public education drive companies out of business? Are parents' homeschooling rights in jeopardy? Already the parent voice is weak; how strong can it be at a national level? How will teachers and parents be heard over the clamor of well-heeled interests such as the Bill & Melinda Gates Foundation, the NGA, Achieve, Texas Instruments, Pearson, and the College Board?

Any time doors close and shades are drawn, it's time to worry. Even if these shadowy faces had managed to create perfect national standards, they won't last. What happens then? Once we have national standards, tests, and curricula, we will never, ever get rid of them.

As students continue to choke on reform math, it's tempting to wish that districts would be forced by law to adopt better curricula. But it's a bad precedent, bad for the country.

State, district, teacher, and parent rights must be preserved—for the people. Districts must always be able to choose alternatives. We must always be able to compare procedures and results against something from the outside. Teachers must always have a say in the curriculum—that all-important corner of the Square of Effective Learning. Parents must always have multiple options for their children's education, and when all else fails, they must be able to "vote with their feet." Taxpayers must always have recourse when their money is spent unwisely. Dissent is necessary to keeping any system honest and strong.

When dissent is disallowed, there are consequences for all of us.

10

CONSEQUENCES TO THE STUDENTS AND THE NATION

"Two of the essential elements for economic growth, easy access to cheap capital, and easy access to a world-class workforce, have moved elsewhere in the world. Building a world-class workforce falls squarely in the domain of our K–12 public education system. Reclaiming our standard of living starts by rebuilding our education system. It is not optional any more. It is a required assignment for every citizen of this country."

—Retired high-tech executive

There are two things to mention before we talk about consequences.
   1. A nondecision is a decision.

Nondecisions are decisions because the decision was to not decide. If you're trying to decide whether or not to quit your job, then for as long as you don't quit, you're deciding to still be there. As long as the education establishment is undecided about how to fix education, the decision has been to leave things that way. It's a decision to not listen, to not take action, to not stand up for what's right, to be too afraid to speak up when counterproductive things happen, and to not say, "Wait a minute—is this working for the students?"

District administrators, principals, and, yes, many teachers and parents are complicit in things being the way they are—if only for the fact that they didn't speak up.

2. For every action, there is an equal and opposite reaction (Newton's third law of motion).

Sometimes, things happen in response to an action. Other times, they happen in response to a lack of an action. There will be consequences to the students

- as long as the bureaucracy refuses to do what needs to be done to fix education;
- every time districts make changes on the basis of weak information;
- when teachers are unwilling to stand up for right things or to speak up when they feel bullied or are pressured into doing wrong things (even if teachers have very good reasons—"I could lose my job," for example);
- when money is spent on inefficient, ineffective things that don't have a positive impact on the Square of Effective Learning;
- when the public can't go to administrators or teachers for truth.

Administrative indecision, inaction, poor decision making, and ennui carry dramatic and often permanent consequences for the students and for this nation. The children's future is being compromised, and their future is the country's future. Here are a few of the consequences.

Students waste their time: Students waste much of their youth failing to learn what they need to know. Can they learn it later, after they finally get to leave high school? Some can. Most won't. And why should they have to? Isn't that what thirteen plus years of school are for? If a K–12 education doesn't prepare students to begin college, start a trade, begin an apprenticeship, join the service, run a business, enter the workforce, or operate a household . . . what was the point?

Students think they're incapable: They see math, grammar, science, and other subjects as "too hard," or that they aren't "good at them." Students lose confidence and begin to resist. They view themselves as failures. This wrong belief will affect everything they will ever do—or not do. Math isn't too hard. Phonics works. Science is fun. School is a good place to be. Truly, it's immoral—sinful, really—to stand by and allow this to happen.

No one learns efficiently, effectively, or sufficiently: Few can excel. Many never have the opportunity to do the very best they can do. This consequence affects the community and the country in myriad destructive ways.

Nothing improves: If administrators aren't willing to look at what they're doing wrong, then they don't have to do anything but shake their head in dismay. Publicly, they can say everything is fine and that all they need to do is tweak this or that. Privately, they can have fits every now and again and throw the whole thing out, and it will be déjà vu all over again. And taxpayers will pay hideous amounts for it, all over again.

Students can't fulfill dreams or take over the process of building, repairing, saving, or running their country: After thirteen plus years of school, the students should be able to begin reaching for the stars. It's like watching a completely preventable traffic accident take place, right there before your eyes. It's such a waste of talent and ability—of limitless potential cut short.

Institutional memory is lost: The long-term success of a country depends on the handing down of culture, experience, and knowledge to the next generation. American public administrators, legislators, government types, and policy setters are purposefully reforming and transforming this country's institutional memory right out of it. There is little continuity, and ever-less academic knowledge being passed on. Everything is new and innovative; nothing is tested, tried, and found to be worthy. Students learn to admire innovation rather than wisdom, and to appreciate excitement and activity rather than accuracy and effectiveness.

This country is at a critical turning point with respect to mathematics and science. The generations that grew up in the 1960s and 1970s were generally taught with more-traditional approaches and can clearly see the problems with reform instruction. The next generation, however, will not have this knowledge. Who will fight for mathematics then?

Generational respect is lost: The arrogance and disrespect given to the wisdom, experience and authority of teachers and parents have a deathly impact on the critical and delicate bonds between generations. Children are taught to challenge knowledge before they understand it, and to see wisdom as "old-school" and not useful in the twenty-first century. They learn to not go to their parents or teachers for help.

Many education decision makers have no problem with standing between students and parents. They see no issue with taking over, re-directing, and deliberately dismantling parent authority—then turning around and blaming parents for the problems. Remember who is the ultimate boss of public education. You are. You don't have to explain or persuade. Do you want your twins in the same class, or your child to be held back? Do you expect to be called if your child skips? Do you expect your children to be taught grammar and arithmetic? You're the boss. You decide. Don't let administrators convince you that you don't know anything.

Beware the Tree Syndrome

Firmly rooted in the heavily fertilized soil of research,
The sapling sends no buds aloft.
Its destiny lies in the stunted undergrowth,
Its only acquaintances—scrub of similar nature.
Pity the life not knowing the forest of towering oaks
To which it ought to aspire.

—Fred Strine, poet and former teacher, North Bend, Washington

WHY PARENTS DON'T SPEAK UP

"Education is unique among consumer products; when it comes time to work as advertised, it's the customer that gets labeled as defective."

—Kevin Killion, on the Illinois Loop website

On February 10, 2010, more than a dozen parents pushed the Spokane school board to retain a special bus route just for them. The process was amazing—they talked; board directors listened; questions were asked and answered. On March 24, the board meeting again was packed as community members argued over the location of one of the schools.

When math is discussed at board meetings, however, the chairs are mostly empty, and Spokane's board directors generally meet public commentary with brief comments or silence. Clearly, math would benefit from being attached to a bus route or a building.

It is easier to talk about buses than academics. Public education is now a complicated affair. It's difficult to know where to begin. It's easy to get tripped up, and administrators are skilled at redirecting things.

There's the language: Acronyms abound in education: NCLB, NCTM, NAEP, ESEA . . . Who knows what they mean? Then there are the learning standards, which typically are written in clunky language and generalities. And there's the "edu-speak," an irritating in-house jargon that employs words and phrases like "incentivize," "scaffolding," "curriculum compacting," "functionalities," "metacognition," and "vertically articulate."

The way to deal with this is to stop them cold. Ask administrators to explain. Get out the dictionary, and don't be embarrassed. No sane person uses the term "incentivize." Use humor: "I would like to incentivize you to be more vertically articulate with me so I can improve the functionality of our meeting and thereby scaffold my understanding about what it means to compact curriculum . . . metacognitively speaking."

There's the math: For many people, math is intimidating. Logarithms, calculus, slopes, quadratic equations . . . how many of us can use these terms with any confidence? Many parents feel they have nothing helpful to contribute, especially since administrators keep telling them they don't get it.

The way to deal with this is to know what your children are supposed to learn and to be sure they do. For as long as you can, try to know the material yourself. Read the textbook, if you have one. If you don't, find one secondhand. (Make sure it contains real content.) Read through the homework. If you need to, take a college class to brush up. Don't be afraid to ask for explanations and examples from the teacher.

What really is the problem: Is it the curricula? The tests? Learning standards? The No Child Left Behind Act? Students? Us? Where should we focus our attention? Administrators keep talking about money, but will more money automatically translate into better test scores? (I'll take "no" for $664 billion, Bob.)

The way to deal with this is to become informed. Do Internet searches with terms like "education advocacy" or "math advocacy." Read books and blogs such as the Betrayed blog. Hit libraries and bookstores. Join an advocacy group such as Where's the Math? Talk to teachers, administrators, and board directors. When you're brushed off, persist politely.

There's the bureaucracy: It's hard to get a straight answer. It's hard to understand the answers we get. The problem seems too big for us. How do we prove anything? Everybody talks circles around us, and they have scatter plots showing how great everything is. We can't debate with the school board, and the board defers to administrators. Administrators blame problems that can't be solved. Legislators are too busy. Teachers won't speak frankly. Principals sound like politicians. We can vote, but elections come and go, and the problem remains.

The way to deal with this is to not let them get away with it. Get answers in writing rather than over the phone. When they divert the conversation, wait them out and ask your question again. Develop allies in the district—most non-decision makers are friendly—and file formal requests for public information. Calmly ask questions until you understand.

They keep changing things: Try to pin down the situation, and the next thing you know, it's different. Administrators can then say, "We're working on it. We think we've got it now. Just give us another year, and we'll show you." To which teachers and parents might reasonably respond, "Well, okay. I guess I can't complain about it now."

Don't fall for this. It's your right to know. Ask for the research that supports their decision making. You shouldn't have to wait for it. It should already be there.

Changing city hall is slow, laborious work: Parents have lives, children, activities, work. Who has the time and patience to sit and dig through myriad smoke screens to figure out what to say and to whom?

The way to deal with this is to put your life on hold, say goodbye to your family, and live next to the computer for a few years. Just kidding. Understanding the problem requires a massive effort if you try to figure it out on your own. It doesn't have to be that hard. Read books like this one, and push for change while living in your home.

They don't appear to listen: Few administrators give indications of really wanting to know what you think. It isn't enough to be reasonably intelligent, educated, well informed, and consistently polite. Even professionals with extensive backgrounds in subject matter and teaching have been dismissed when their concerns were oppositional to the agenda.

In Spokane, administrators have said parents have nothing to tell them about teaching or the curriculum. It often takes a formal request to get information from our state education agency. In 2009, a contact in our governor's office didn't respond to three requests for an interview. The U.S. Department of Education has an outstanding Freedom of Information Act request from July 2009 concerning its role in the national standards.

Administrators talk about "partnerships" with parents and teachers, but many don't want that. Parents are annoying if they're truly involved. Teachers are problems if they dare to disagree. But parents and teachers must be involved—enough to know what the children should be learning versus what they are learning, enough to help choose curricula, enough to step in when things aren't working, enough to oppose unhelpful policy.

Blind trust in the establishment has gotten us where we are now, with a generation of students who are functionally illiterate in subject matter and who are forced to give up their seats in colleges and in the workforce to better-prepared people from other countries.

There's the emotional investment: Parents volunteer. We get to know the teachers, principals, and office staff. We might complain privately to our friends, but it's a different matter to complain publicly to administrators.

The way to deal with this is to advocate quietly, go up the chain of command, follow the rules, know what you're talking about, and be polite but persistent. The children's futures are at stake. It's our responsibility to hold administrators accountable.

People get angry: It's true. When you force people to publicly address issues they don't want to address in public, they become angry or defensive. Remember that anger often masks fear. If administrators are masking fear with anger, they know they have a weaker position.

You can step into that weaker position and push it over. And often, anger is just a manipulative tool, used as a controlling or bullying tactic.

The way to deal with administrative anger is to remember your goal. You're there to advocate for yourself, for the children, for your class, your business, the community, and the country. If your good intentions are met with anger, ask yourself if it's actually fear. Is it being used as a means of putting you off? Can you politely persist? Can you speak with someone else, file a formal request for public information, or come up with a different approach? You have options, and you can make a difference. It's a challenge, but it's doable. It depends on how far you're willing to go.

Alas, there are the bullying tactics: Teachers have a tenuous security, but even those outside of the K–12 system can find their livelihood in jeopardy. Dr. David Klein, a mathematics professor at California State University, Northridge, offered this disturbing story as an example of how good intentions can lead to a threat to one's livelihood.

Invited to Washington State in 2006 by advocacy organization Where's the Math?, Dr. Klein gave a talk to "several hundred parents, teachers and a handful of state legislators" concerning K–12 math standards and math textbooks. Shortly after he returned to California, a Washington administrator sent a letter directly to his campus president, wrongly attributing remarks to Dr. Klein and accusing him (falsely) of inciting violence. The administrator also sent copies to Dr. Klein and to his department chair.

Fortunately for Dr. Klein, his talk had been taped. Effusive apologies followed from Washington's state superintendent. Dr. Klein says now, "You can imagine what could happen to classroom teachers or untenured professors who don't toe the party line."

The way to deal with the potential for bullying is to prepare in advance. Bullies often attack the vulnerable, so try to be perceived as a person who is pleasant and reasonable but who will push back. Keep records of conversations, witnesses, events, and timelines. Bring a tape recorder to meetings. Take notes. Save interviews, documents, e-mails, and Web pages. Remember that computers break, websites change, information is removed from Web pages, people leave the district, and memories fade, so keep everything saved on the computer, with more than one backup.

When all else fails, you can hire a lawyer.

Retired teacher Martha McLaren, professor of atmospheric sciences Clifford Mass, and parent Da-Zanne Porter decided to hire a lawyer to fight a curriculum adoption in Seattle Public Schools. They filed a lawsuit in May 2009 after the board voted to adopt the *Discovering* math series for high school after months of public testimony by parents and math advocates who had detailed what they saw as critical shortcomings in the curriculum.

In a momentous decision, Judge Julie Spector ruled on February 4, 2010, that the school board's decision was "arbitrary" and "capricious." After reviewing the administrative record, she found that the school district had presented "insufficient evidence for any reasonable Board member to approve the selection of the Discovering Series."

Although Seattle Public Schools was not ordered to cease and desist in its adoption, the board was required to revisit the adoption process. Seattle Public Schools is appealing the decision.

Parents and teachers have been betrayed, but they have options. Never forget that.

WHY TEACHERS DON'T SPEAK UP

Some teachers might see the title *Betrayed* and (without reading the book) feel offended or criticized. It's bound to happen—most teachers are well used to being criticized. But that would be an unfortunate mischaracterization both of the content of this book and the author's intent.

It's one thing to wish that more teachers would go public about what they see in their classrooms; it's another entirely to blame them. Administrative types do that. The Betrayed blog and this book do not.

Most teachers work much harder than what the public sees, and they care deeply about the children. Their job is difficult, and they do the best they can. It's hard to be a whistle-blower.

It's difficult for the rest of us to imagine suffering every day with an administrative boot on the neck when one really wants to fight for curricula that are designed to get students to college; to argue for better policy, accountability, solid research, and proof of success; and to advocate for academics over social engineering. Teachers who do that can be undermined and marginalized, given less advanced classes, disciplined, or even fired—tossed out for "insubordination." Or they can burn out and wind up somewhere with a tutoring business.

But some teachers blame the students, and they must stop doing that. The problem is no more the children's fault than it is the teachers' fault. Children know why they're in school. They want to learn. Some teachers will say, "Ha! You don't know the kids in my class!" But children are the same everywhere. Even when they've lost hope, when they're afraid, when their lives are complicated, when they're worried, distracted, and stressed out, when they're putting up as many barriers as they can, they still want to learn. They want to feel capable and cared about. They want to understand and be understood. They want to succeed.

It's the adults' job to connect the curriculum to the students' needs and desires, as much as it can be done. Many public schools (and many parents) fall short in these areas, but big destroyers of child curiosity and teacher motivation are the burdens administrators place on teachers and students. The education bureaucracy imposes a never-ending stream of new policies, procedures, curricula, training, substitutes, rules, testing, budget cuts, "Why aren't they passing?" and, finally, "What we really need are quality teachers."

How great would it be if bureaucrats lost their iron grip on the classroom? What if public school teachers had the freedom to teach, motivate, tutor, challenge, and engage? No one else in education knows the students better than the teachers do. But no one knows the children better than the parents do. Teachers should be in charge of classrooms, and parents should be in charge of their children. Instead, a constant stream of loopy education theory is forced on all of us by people who don't know the classes, families, or children.

In some districts, teachers are given strict timetables or written scripts to follow. They might see their favorite textbooks removed from their classrooms or their colleagues punished or fired for speaking up. In other districts, teachers are saddled with "mentors" or "instructional coaches" who tag alongside them, supposedly helping them learn how to teach. Years after reform curricula are implemented, these mentors continue to "professionally develop" teachers in how to use the curricula.

In Spokane, Washington, as of October 2008, there were 93.5 (full-time-equivalent) instructional coaches, each making a salary from $35,861 to $70,338, for a total cost of $6,083,944.

(According to the district, federal and state tax dollars paid for about 75 percent of this cost. To the taxpayer, however, it's all our money.)

Some teachers say coaches create busywork and they would rather have more teachers, but it's too late. Coaches are now part of the bureaucracy, and for several reasons. Their presence calls for more taxpayer money. They can be counted as teachers when class size is calculated. They can check on teachers and indoctrinate in preferred philosophy. Since their job is to train teachers, they also can serve to divert criticism from administrators (who can then shrug their shoulders and say it isn't their fault: "We have a real problem with quality teaching").

When districts implement a new curriculum, problems elsewhere are often excused away with a promise to professionally develop the teachers in how to use the new curriculum. ("It didn't work there," the argument seems to go, "but that's because they didn't do it right.")

Some teachers in Spokane, however, have said they found the professional development to be condescending and unhelpful. They were happy when it was over. Meanwhile, they were forced to follow the district's reform curricula, and they were not allowed to teach basic arithmetic skills to students.

In August 2010, the What Works Clearinghouse issued a "quick study" on professional development (PD) given to 7th-grade math teachers on the teaching of rational numbers (2010c). The study, which encompassed data on 200 teachers and 4500 students in 80 schools, found no discernable improvement in students' understanding of rational numbers as a result of the PD. In addition, the study found that the PD "had no impact on teacher knowledge of rational number topics and on how to teach them." The PD was "administered by either America's Choice or Pearson Achievement Solutions."

Nevertheless, taxpayers are forced to pay for ongoing PD, plus conferences, travel, substitute teachers, and coaches. Snake oil salesman should be so lucky to have a product that—having failed in so many places—still inspires blind faith from administrators who obediently follow it around, certain that they have the magical key to making it work.

At the end of the indoctrination, and after dedicated use of the prescribed curriculum, teachers are still thrown to the wolves.

In a 2008 interview, Spokane superintendent Nancy Stowell said teachers who say they've been disciplined for speaking up about weak curricula might have other "issues" or not be very "successful" as teachers. That wasn't the last time Dr. Stowell delivered this message. In 2010, as the school board adopted *Holt Mathematics*, she reminded everyone that "it is less about the book and more about the quality of the teacher in the classroom" ("Minutes" 2010).

Federal and state administrators also talk about the need for "effective" or quality teachers (as if we don't have them now) and about removing "ineffective" teachers. It's a cornerstone of the new federal "transformational" thinking. Meanwhile, no administrator ever talks about the need for better central-office administrators.

(Removing all of the ineffective ones would definitely leave a hole.)

There's another, sneakier way to blame teachers: performance pay. Employee effectiveness *should* help determine teacher pay and employment, just as it does in any other career, but standardized tests aren't necessarily the best way to gauge teacher effectiveness. Tests vary greatly in quality, and many factors bear on test scores.

Nevertheless, a 2008 *New York Times* article reported that New York City had begun assessing some of its teachers based on student test results. The assessments weren't intended to affect tenure determinations or annual ratings, administrators said; they were just guides for teachers to better understand their "shortcomings" (Medina 2008).

Hey, here's a thought: Perhaps some of the teacher shortcomings are actually curricula shortcomings, policy shortcomings, or administrator shortcomings.

Some districts pay teachers extra for better student grades. The sly message is that teachers aren't trying hard enough. If they get an incentive, however, they'll try harder, and then everything will be fine. It's devious and underhanded, but it will persuade many.

In some districts, teachers can earn anywhere from a few thousand dollars to tens of thousands of dollars in bonuses for student progress on achievement tests or on report cards. It would be great if teachers could resist this siren call to accept blame, but it's difficult for anyone to turn down a $25,000 bonus on principle. Besides, most teachers will assume they're being rewarded for good work. It won't occur to them that administrators are willing to pay big money for scapegoats. One has to wonder if these policies will encourage grade inflation, with inappropriately high scores.

In 2008, the federal government waded into performance pay and incentive programs with the $200 million Teacher Incentive Fund (TIF), which rewarded teachers (and principals, oddly) for increases in student achievement. In 2010, the TIF budget was $437 million.

If teachers did teach better in response to bonuses and incentives, that would mean they are part of the problem. They could have taught better before and just didn't. They were mercenary—responding to money. But experience suggests that teachers like that are uncommon.

No single curriculum will serve all children, particularly in today's "inclusive" classrooms. Most teachers can't choose the curriculum, yet they're blamed for the results. They're expected to teach all students to a predetermined standard, with the same flawed curriculum, and when the results are poor, they're criticized. If they speak up about the unfairness of it all, they can be disciplined, demoted, or fired for "insubordination."

(Perhaps teachers should file a class-action lawsuit against school districts.)

Why won't teachers speak up publicly or even just sit down privately with their principals, area directors, curriculum coordinators, superintendents or commissioners, union reps, and lawyers—and explain why the system is broken? One can't imagine.

But teachers are the ones who know what's going on in their classrooms. Their voice is critical to changing anything for the better.

11

WHAT CAN BE DONE?

"The quality of the thinking that got us into this mess is not sufficient for getting us out."

—Attributed to Albert Einstein

In early 2007, Washington State superintendent Terry Bergeson seemed put out that the state's education system was being criticized. She was quoted in a *Spokesman-Review* article: "No matter where you look, people across the country are saying 'What is Washington doing?' We have a revolution happening in our schools, but you don't hear the positive stuff. The yammerers out there complaining about what's not happening rule the day" (Roesler 2007).

In her November 2007 State of Education speech, Dr. Bergeson had more to say. "Critics abound and they have an important role," she said, "but they don't motivate people to continue the hard and passionate work of transforming education and thus the lives of our children."

In 2008, the people of Washington decided someone else should "continue the hard and passionate work," and Dr. Bergeson was not reelected. Locally, it would be so much easier to fix education if certain central-office administrators also would get out of the way. Perhaps more key administrative positions should be elected.

Let's imagine a productive education system:

- capable and dedicated teachers with strong core subject knowledge and the freedom to teach in the most efficient, most effective way
- administrators and governments that support but don't obstruct or interfere
- curricula that are objective-oriented, rigorous, and clearly written
- special classes for students who need something different
- a disciplined, respectful learning environment that's focused on academics
- an ethic of discipline, self-restraint, and hard work (from students, teachers, principals, and administrators)
- real consequences (for everyone) for failures to do the job
- teacher and parental involvement in curricular and policy decision making

If a person were queen or king for a day, one could make good things happen relative to public education. But this is probably the philosophy behind the dramatic expansion of the federal role in American education, so perhaps it's best to leave the kings and queens in Europe.

The following wish list is structured around the Square of Effective Learning.

LAURIE ROGERS'S WISH LIST

Corner 1: The Teacher's Ability to Teach

Eliminate "professional development" that indoctrinates in discovery or is designed to sell a product. Bring the teachers up to speed in academic content—the ones in the job now and the ones who are in the pipeline.

Improve the rigor and content of teacher education. Get rid of education degrees. Require degrees in

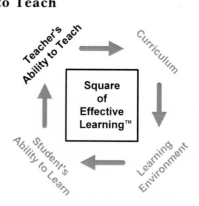

academic content with teaching endorsements. In elementary school (where content knowledge must be more broadly based), teachers also can "team teach" so as to effectively share content knowledge.

For all teachers, require minors in math, along with courses in English grammar. For middle school teachers, require majors in the subject they're teaching. For high school teachers, require majors or degrees in the subject they're teaching. Reward teachers for master's degrees in core academic subjects, not for master's degrees in education.

Require teachers to use the most efficient and most effective methods of teaching as the primary methods. Allow them to adapt their instruction to fit students' needs, but shift the teaching methodology to teacher-directed instruction. Refer to John Hattie's *Visible Learning* for an analysis of the research of the effectiveness of direct instruction versus the effectiveness of other methods. Move discovery learning and group work to their proper places—in smaller doses and after children have a core basis of knowledge. Reintroduce and reemphasize the importance of academic content, standard algorithms, phonics, efficiency, effectiveness, accuracy, and proficiency (teaching to mastery).

Limit the amount of time classes are taught by substitutes. Principals in training should not also try to juggle classrooms. Monitor classes taught by student teachers. Work with teachers to develop partner classes so that teacher absences are not so disruptive. Eliminate most district-initiated teacher absences.

Corner 2: The Curriculum

Allow parents to participate in curriculum discussions and vote on curriculum decisions.

Adopt the clearest, most rigorous standards. Teach to those standards.

Work with college professors to determine the skills necessary for success in college, and work backward to adopting K–12 curricula (with textbooks) that will cover the standards and develop those skills.

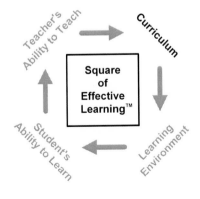

Require curriculum departments to have on hand sufficient peer-reviewed, scientifically based research to support their recommendations. Require that they welcome, examine, and discuss contrary views.

Add back the academic subjects that have been neglected, such as arithmetic, algebra, trigonometry, English grammar, history, civics, foreign languages, science, communication, and debate.

Corner 3: The Learning Environment

Refocus schools on academics. Remove from the class day all but very occasional nonacademic distractions. Remove test preparation from the schedule. If students can't pass the tests, modify the instruction on the content and allow more time to practice the content.

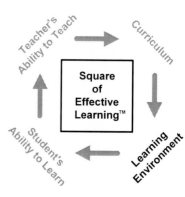

Eliminate the focus on self-esteem and social issues. Reinforce (by expecting it, not by teaching it) hard work, respect, and honesty. Implement and enforce consistent rules for behavior with consequences for all.

Remove calculators from elementary classrooms. Limit time on computers. Beef up libraries, and hire more librarians.

Make gifted education part of basic education and fund it accordingly. Provide opportunities for academically capable children to excel.

Acknowledge that achievement gaps are a part of life. Change the focus from closing achievement gaps to helping children achieve their own levels of excellence. Offer alternatives. Give students the time and attention they need to learn the required material.

Offer courses that cater to job and career tracks. Work with trades and businesses to develop in-school and after-school programs for middle school and high school students that give them a chance to develop job skills not available in the classroom.

Corner 4: The Student's Ability to Learn

When students haven't gained mastery of the skills for their grade level, provide them with mandated tutoring and/or remedial work before they move to the next grade.

If students aren't ready for the next course or grade, don't move them there—not without applicable remedial help.

Reintroduce the notions of discipline and suspension for bad behavior, along with the idea of parents being held accountable for the behavior of their children.

Provide regular opportunities for parents, teachers, and students to have two-way conversations with school boards and all state and district policy makers.

Expect parents to participate in decision making and to vote on policy changes that are dramatic shifts in policy or expensive. Open the process to all parents, not just to a few like-minded individuals.

Develop multiple, concerted ways to listen to the students. Encourage dialogue between administrators and professionals such as mathematicians, businesspeople, scientists, and people in the trades.

Other Items That Are Necessary, but Not in the Square of Effective Learning

Post the district check register online so that expenditures are transparent to all.

Videotape all board meetings and work sessions, and post them online so that community members who can't attend can still see what happened and hear what was said.

Make all board memberships and superintendencies elected positions.

Superintendents and principals should have at least five years of classroom experience (not pretend experience where their name is on the door but they're doing something else).

Decision makers—superintendents, curriculum coordinators, and board members—should head into classrooms every year to be classroom aides, not just to observe or do a photo op. Principals should teach one class per semester or year (not pretend teach). In this way, the leadership will be better equipped to make informed decisions.

Cut down dramatically on the number of administrative positions. Hire efficiency experts to examine the district and cut out wasteful spending. Use the savings to hire more classroom teachers. Start by cutting all $100,000 plus administrators and replace most of them with hungry people who have teaching experience and content knowledge and who can prove their value. See what happens.

Fire nonperformers. Fire those who refuse to recognize that there is a problem, are unwilling to research ways to fix the problem, or are unwilling to engage in fixing the problem. Fire those who don't know their subject area and are unwilling to seek additional core-subject education. Fire those who can't properly support their decisions with legitimate, scientifically conducted research.

Audit curriculum departments. Fire anyone who has inappropriately "padded" a budget or worked inappropriately with publishers.

Fire superfluous administrative personnel. Retrain instructional coaches and put them back in the classroom.

Make data and reports straightforward, truthful, honest in intent, comprehensive, transparent, and easily accessible.

Keep standardized testing, but make sure tests are timely so that they inform instruction. Tests should be valid and reliable, as well as transparent and easily accessible to students, teachers, and parents. Avoid cushy contracts with friendly publishers.

Stay within budget. Define classroom instruction narrowly, and then set a maximum that can be spent on things that aren't directly related to classroom instruction.

Make it illegal to divert taxpayer money to pay for items not specified at the time that voters approved the levies.

Fully fund all legislatively mandated activities, but evaluate all "mandated" classroom activities for their worth in terms of student academic learning. Don't waste money and time on things that won't directly and positively affect the Square of Effective Learning.

Do not adopt national standards or curricula. Reject Race to the Top as unconstitutional (or at least constitutionally questionable), heavy-handed, inefficient, and expensive.

Eliminate the U.S. Department of Education. Return control of public education to where it belongs—the states. (Expect to need just a small fraction of the taxpayer money that is currently spent on public education.)

What You Can Do Right Now

Well, that was a nice little dream. It would be great if we could make all of the changes we want for our children, but most of us are average folks, trying to make a living, teach our classes, raise our children, and do the best we can. As individuals, what can we do to make positive changes in public education? Here are a few things you can do right now.

1. Vote.

   Before you vote, find out more about the people who are running for election. Consider the long-term consequences of their policies, and determine where you stand. Ask questions. Demand answers. Then vote. Teach the children to vote.

2. Stay informed about the children.

   Keep on top of how your children are doing. Go to parent-teacher conferences, and listen carefully with an open mind. Don't trust the district to adequately prepare the children for postsecondary life. Look up your district's curricula on the Internet, and find out what other people are saying. Look at the homework, help your children learn, keep on top of assignments, and teach the children to be curious, lifelong learners.

3. Become informed about the issues.

   Learn more about the issues in education. The Internet and library can be helpful tools in your quest for knowledge. Education advocates are generous with information.

4. Be involved in the classroom and school.

   Volunteer if you can. Talk with other teachers, parents, and advocates. Ask questions. Go to conferences. Parents can help grade homework. (Teachers should grade the homework, but parents can learn a lot from helping out.) Review the curricula. Find out how things really are. If people try to dissuade you by calling you a helicopter parent or a problem teacher, say thank you.

5. Be involved in the school district.

Attend board meetings. Read meeting minutes. Don't allow board members and administrators to brush you off or intimidate you with edu-speak. If you don't understand what they're saying, ask them to rephrase it. Send questions by letter or by e-mail—or set up meetings, and ask questions in person. Take a tape recorder with you to meetings. (Be sure to follow the laws in your state about recording meetings and interviews.)

6. Stand up for yourself and the children.

Be vocal. Ask questions. It's your job as the public version of the judiciary. Don't allow administrators to divert the conversation. Don't accept platitudes and pats on the head. Be certain you have specific answers to your questions. You can be polite and assertive at the same time. (Others might say that being assertive is impolite, but they probably don't want to answer your questions.) Please see table 11.1 for a list of typical comments administrators use to minimize questions from parents and teachers. Also included are suggestions for responses that will help keep the focus of the conversation on the issue at hand.

7. Form alliances.

Get to know the school board members if you can. Often, they don't listen to parent advocates very well, but when a group of teachers stands up to talk, they do. So, get together with other activists. Talk to other teachers and parents. Form groups, and network. Seek out the quiet people, the ones who are thinking. Schmooze. Everyone knows someone on the school board. Invite them for tea or have them over for dinner. Build a relationship on a personal level, and work on it. Many voices together get more attention than one voice.

8. Be involved in the process of change.

Set up an organization. Build a website. Send out newsletters. Write a book or blog. Run for the school board. Write letters to the editor. Join a site council. Meet with administrators. Contact legislators. Become a teacher. Conduct research. Host a debate. Get on a curriculum adoption committee. Support other advocates. If you write something down, attribute properly.

9. Say no to stupid things.

   Opt out of standardized tests that waste your tax money and don't properly test the children. Opt out of math curricula or math classes that don't teach proper mathematics. Opt out of science classes that are full of games and fuzzy concepts. Opt out of schools and districts that aren't concerned with accuracy, facts, and achievement. If you don't like how the money is spent, say no when they ask you for more.

10. Know what the children know.

    Find out what the children should know at their age, and fill in the gaps. Assess them with tests that give a clear idea of the skills they're missing. Some, like *Singapore Math* and *Saxon Math* provide free assessments online. Some options are listed in figure 11.1.

```
* Singapore Math
      * MAP
   * Kumon Math
   * Saxon Math
 * Indian Math Online
     * ITBS/ITED
* Diagnostic Online Math
   Assessment (DOMA)
* Sylvan Learning Center
   * College Tests
```

Figure 11.1.   Some options for evaluation and/or testing your student

It's up to teachers and parents to keep track, ask questions, demand answers, and find a way to make the system work for the children. The criticism in these pages is well intended; it's how a system becomes and remains great, and it's about Accountability. Answering that criticism is how the system remains Accountable to the public.

When All Else Fails, Leave the System

More and more teachers and parents are choosing alternatives to public education. According to the 2009 federal "Digest of Education Statistics," nearly 11 percent of all K–12 students were being taught in private schools or at home. Added to that, however, are charter schools, magnets, online classes or virtual schools, cooperatives, and options within school districts. Teachers and parents choose these alternatives for their appealing characteristics:

- Parent choice: They provide a better fit for the students and winnow out unmotivated families, teachers, and administrators.
- School safety: They offer safer environments that are less likely to suffer incidents of violence, bullying, vandalism, and general misbehavior.
- Teacher choice: They provide a better fit for the teachers and winnow out unmotivated families and colleagues.
- Curriculum choice: They offer exemptions from certain state and federal laws that regulate public schools, and they allow for more flexibility in policy, in choice of curriculum, and in money management.
- Small populations: They offer smaller populations where students don't feel invisible, and they allow for more attention from teachers.
- Education: Statistics indicate that many private schools do provide a better education, with higher SAT scores, higher rates of college admission, and lower remediation rates.

You can say no to the madness. Your tax money might be spent on inadequate curricula and on tests that no one has to pass, but you have the right to vote with your feet. Don't blindly trust administrators to do what's best for the children.

Even if the system were magically perfect tomorrow, that perfect system would last only as long as it took to gain a new round of people to run it. It's the nature of people, and it's the history of education. People want to be seen as relevant, they believe in reform, and they want to think all children can succeed equally. Additionally, the entire system—

school, district, state, federal government, legislators, and colleges—won't change at once; nor will it all change in the same way. Mostly, a perfect system wouldn't last because the constant experimentation and change are great ways for people to avoid capital *A* Accountability, to create a name for themselves, and to make a lot of money.

Say no to it. You can. If we all say no, then no is what it will be.

Please join the fight for a better education for our children. We don't have to take this lying down. Intimidating, self-interested, and deceitful behavior does not have to remain the status quo. Public education has been called the great equalizer, and it still is. It's just not an equalizer in a good way. Teachers, parents, and the students themselves can work for it to be the way it should be.

Join me on my blog at http://betrayed-whyeducationisfailing.blogspot.com, join a different group, or start your own group. Check out table 11.1 before you close this book. It's a primer on the frustrating things administrators say when you ask them questions, and it offers suggestions for things you can say in reply to keep conversations on track.

Together, we can rise up and take back the classroom from those who have stolen it. Together we can save our children and our country.

ASKING QUESTIONS OF ADMINISTRATORS

It's best to view education advocacy as a series of engagements rather than as one battle you want to win. It takes time. Plant a seed, and nourish it until it grows. When asking questions of administrators, always be polite, but challenge the automatic assumptions. Determine if your question was answered (they're very good at diverting). Take notes. Use a tape recorder (with notification, if it's state law). Ask questions by e-mail (so you have an electronic paper trail). Back up your computer every day and rotate backups. Keep a record. Don't throw anything out.

Attribute properly. Don't quote anything you can't prove.

(Note: This author has heard variations of every one of the establishment responses.)

Table 11.1.

Parents (and Teachers) Say	The Establishment Replies	Suggested Follow-Up
This approach to mathematics is illogical and counterproductive.	Research shows this approach is best. Math might not be the child's (or your) best subject. The problem is the money, standards, teachers, and students.	I'd like to see the research that supports this approach. If you'll tell me when it's ready, I'll pick it up.
Only 60 percent of students pass the math tests. No one seems able to pass the science tests.	We were successful in raising reading scores. We're working on math. We'll get to science. Sixty percent might be good depending on where the group began.	The children in the system need better math and science instruction. What are you doing to improve the instruction?
A lot of parents are frustrated.	You're the only one who's ever complained.	*I'm* frustrated. Let's discuss *my* frustration.
These children need a more direct teaching style.	The district is committed to a student-centered approach. Research shows that it builds enthusiasm, cooperation, and deeper understanding.	My children need a more direct teaching style. How do we get that for them?
Why are all types of learners taught together? It doesn't seem to work.	"Inclusion" is good for students. Children learn from each other. We don't want to track students. Gifted programs are elitist.	My children need a different learning environment. How do we get that for them?
We want more traditional math.	That's only because it's what you had. Not all children can learn it. Learning alternative methods gives them something to fall back on. They need math for the twenty-first century.	My children learn best with a traditional approach to traditional mathematics. They don't need anything to fall back on. How do we get that for them?
The math curricula aren't teaching algebra.	Not everyone needs algebra. Students can pick it up in high school or college.	How do we get my children instruction in algebra?

Engineers, mathematicians, math professors, and advocates say these reform programs won't get the children to college.	People who complain "don't get it." Parents aren't math smart. They're stuck in the past. Teachers might not be all that talented. Students have bad upbringings, raging hormones, short attention spans, and poor priorities. Engineers don't know how to communicate. Math professors don't know how to teach to children. Advocates are extremist and negative. They have a hidden agenda. Besides, not everyone will go to college.	In order to be admitted to college, these children will need to be proficient in reading, grammar, algebra, geometry, trigonometry, and precalculus (or calculus). How do we get these children these skills?
We want more phonics.	Not all students need phonics.	How do we get more phonics?
The children need a textbook so they have continuity.	Our programs align with the standards. Students have the materials they need.	How do I get a copy of the materials?
I want the children to have a textbook so I can help them.	Today's curricula use a hands-on, exploratory approach. Textbooks are boring, expensive, and unnecessary.	How do I get a copy of whichever textbook materials there are?
We don't want our young children using calculators or computers in the classroom. The technology interferes with learning basic skills.	Research shows that technology is helpful. Technology prepares students for jobs in the twenty-first century. Calculators and computers help them learn and can take the place of arithmetic.	I do not want these children using calculators in the classroom. How do I make my wishes clear to the administrators?
Teachers are reluctant to speak frankly about the curricula.	They might have issues or be adverse to change. They might not be successful teachers. They might be insubordinate.	I'll mention your concerns to all of the teachers I know.

(continued)

Table 11.1.

Parents (and Teachers) Say	The Establishment Replies	Suggested Follow-Up
Teachers seem to be away a lot for district-mandated activities.	Teachers need professional training in order to be truly excellent.	The absences negatively affect the classroom.
The constant rotation of substitutes and student teachers confuses students.	We work hard to choose the best teaching personnel. They do a fine job, and we're proud of them.	The problem of teacher absences hasn't been addressed.
My child knows this material because we taught him. He's bored and resists school.	Your child's teacher works hard to find ways to challenge your child. We love our teachers, and we appreciate them.	My child's teacher is great but very busy. How do we help my child excel?
My child can't concentrate in these big, noisy classrooms.	Has your child ever been tested for ADHD?	None of the children can concentrate. Are you suggesting they all have ADHD? How do we get a quieter environment?
The class is constantly being distracted by nonacademic events.	We want to enrich the environment and teach the whole child. Our activities add to the learning experience.	How do we remove the distraction so the class can focus on academics?
The children are frustrated. They're beginning to act out a bit.	Have you spoken with their teachers? Perhaps they need an IEP (individualized education program).	How do we get them more challenging material and a more focused classroom?
My child is quite bright. She finds the program boring. Can she move ahead?	Your child can learn by helping the teacher—not to "teach" but just to "show" others how to do things.	My child is not a teacher. I do not want her to teach other students. How do we help her excel?
Fewer than half pass math, and almost no one passes science.	Those scores might be good, depending on where those groups began.	What does the district do specifically to help the students who didn't pass?
Since 1999, the number of students in Advanced Placement (AP) classes has tripled, but only half pass the exams.	We continue to increase AP enrollment and statistically perform well on the AP exams. Students must have learned something while they were there.	The goal of AP classes is college credit. Students who don't pass won't receive college credit.

The SAT scores dropped.	They didn't drop as much as elsewhere. Overall trends show we're doing well.	The fact that the scores dropped hasn't been addressed.
Large numbers of students are dropping out or requiring remedial help before beginning their postsecondary life.	It's a national problem. Students who need remedial help can get it. Statistics show things are getting better. We're doing so well, other states look to us for guidance.	The problem of the high dropout rate and high remediation rate hasn't been addressed.
My neighbors have all left the district. They're suggesting we leave too.	We haven't heard that. People who leave us tend to leave because of jobs, lower-cost housing, or a normal demographic ebb and flow.	Have you conducted a survey of families who left? I would like to see that report.
I think public education is broken.	We hope you'll talk to legislators about fully funding education and that you'll vote for the levy.	How does that money translate into a better curriculum and a more focused learning environment?
We want regular public conversations with policy makers.	You can call or write or set up a private meeting. You can come to board meetings or talk with your child's teacher or with the principal.	These are not two-way, open, and public conversations. How do we get regular, public conversations with policy makers?
I'm worried about my children's future in (middle school, high school, college).	Your children will be fine because they have you for a parent.	I'm not worried about their well-being. I'm worried about their education. Let's stay focused on that.

APPENDIX: ACRONYMS AND TERMS

Acronym	What It Stands for	What It Is
ACT	American College Testing	A national college entrance exam
AP	Advanced Placement	A College Board program that offers college-level courses at schools in the United States and Canada
AYP	Adequate yearly progress	NCLB's benchmark of student progress
CCSSO	Council of Chief State School Officers	Administrators who head departments in elementary and secondary education
ED	U.S. Department of Education	The federal department that oversees education
FY	Fiscal year	The period of time used to delineate the start and end points of financial statements
ITBS	Iowa Test of Basic Skills	A standard test of skills
ITED	Iowa Test of Educational Development	A standard test of skills

Acronym	What It Stands for	What It Is
NAEP	National Assessment of Educational Progress ("the Nation's Report Card")	A national exam that assesses a "representative" sample of test takers
NCLB	No Child Left Behind Act	A federal law, a feature of which is that, by 2014, all students must meet state standards
NCTM	National Council of Teachers of Mathematics	An organization that works for certain goals relative to K–12 mathematics instruction
NEA	National Education Association	A teachers union
NGA	National Governors Association	A lobbying organization for governors
NMAP	National Mathematics Advisory Panel	A panel commissioned in 2008 by the president to advise the president and secretary of education
NSF	National Science Foundation	A government agency that promotes science and engineering through funding, research, and education
OSPI	Office of Superintendent of Public Instruction	The office that oversees education in Washington State
PD	Professional development	Teacher training, frequently in teaching methodology or curricula rather than academic content
RTTT	Race to the Top	A federally constructed grant competition
SAT	Scholastic Aptitude Test	A national college-entrance exam

SBE	State Board of Education	A sixteen-member board that keeps tabs on education in Washington State
SES	Supplemental Educational Services	Tutoring for children in Title I schools, as outlined in NCLB
SPS	Spokane Public Schools	The school system in the city of Spokane, Washington
TI	Texas Instruments	A corporation
Title I	Part of the Elementary and Secondary Education Act of 1965	Legislation providing extra funding to schools with many low-income families
WASL	Washington Assessment of Student Learning	Washington State's standardized tests
WEA	Washington Education Association	A teachers union
WWC	What Works Clearinghouse	A federal government initiative to evaluate education research

REFERENCES

31-state consortium submits RTTT assessment application. June 23, 2010. Retrieved July 26, 2010, from the Office of Superintendent of Public Instruction Web site: http://www.k12.wa.us/Communications/PressReleases2010/ConsortiumRTTT Application.aspx.

$350 million now available to help consortia of states create next generation of assessments. April 6, 2010. Retrieved May 24, 2010, from the U.S. Department of Education website: www2.ed.gov/news/pressreleases/2010/04/04062010c.html.

2007 report to families. June 8, 2007. Retrieved April 30, 2008, from the Office of Superintendent of Public Instruction website: http://www.k12.wa.us/resources/pubdocs/2007ReporttoFamilies6-8-07.pdf (site discontinued)

2008 average ACT scores by state. 2008. Retrieved September 5, 2008, from the ACT Inc. website: www.act.org/news/data/08/states.html.

2010 budget highlights. n.d. Retrieved June 17, 2010, from the Office of Financial Management, State of Washington website: www.ofm.wa.gov/budget10/highlights/education.pdf.

2010 session summary, office of Governor Chris Gregoire: Education to meet the challenges of the 21st century. April 2010. Retrieved June 21, 2010, from the Governor Chris Gregoire website: www.governor.wa.gov/priorities/budget/education.pdf.

A forty year analysis of STEM degrees: The devil is in the details. September 12, 2006. Press release. Retrieved April 29, 2008, from the Commission on Professionals in Science and Technology website: www.cpst.org/STEM/STEM6_Press.doc.

ACT high school profile report: The graduating class of 2008: Washington. 2008. Retrieved September 5, 2008, from the ACT Inc. website: www.act.org/news/data/08/pdf/states/Washington.pdf.

Adelman, C. June 1999. Answers in the tool box: Academic intensity, attendance patterns, and bachelor's degree attainment. Retrieved March 24, 2008, from the U.S. Department of Education website: www2.ed.gov/pubs/Toolbox/index.html.

Advanced Placement report: Washington State earns two national distinctions. February 8, 2007. Press release. Retrieved December 5, 2007, from the Office of Superintendent of Public Instruction website: www.k12.wa.us/Communications/pressreleases2007/AdvancedPlacement.aspx.

Advanced Placement report to the nation, 2007. 2007. Retrieved May 4, 2008, from the College Board website: www.collegeboard.com/prod_downloads/about/news_info/ap/2007/2007_ap-report-nation.pdf.

American students show steady progress in math, rank high in international education comparison TIMSS. December 9, 2008. Press release. Retrieved December 18, 2008, from the U.S. Department of Education website: www2.ed.gov/news/pressreleases/2008/12/12092008.html.

Aos, S., M. Miller, and A. Pennucci. December 2007. Report to the Joint Task Force on basic education finance: School employee compensation and student outcomes. Retrieved May 14, 2008, from the Washington State Institute for Public Policy website: www.wsipp.wa.gov/rptfiles/07-12-2201.pdf.

Archer, R. December 29, 2007. A solid education goes beyond curriculum. *Spokesman-Review*, 5B.

———. March 14, 2008. District 81 retention policy needs attention. *Spokesman-Review*, 6B.

Augustine, N. R. 2007. Is America falling off the flat Earth? Rising above the gathering storm committee. National Academy of Sciences, National Academy of Engineering, and Institute of Medicine of the National Academies. Retrieved June 6, 2010, from the National Academies Press website: www.nap.edu/catalog.php?record_id=12021#orgs.

Babcock, J., P. Babcock, J. Buhler, J. Cady, L. Cogan, R. Houang, N. Kher, et al. 2010. Breaking the cycle: An international comparison of U.S. mathematics teacher preparation. The Center for Research in Math and Science Education, Michigan State University. Retrieved May 12, 2010, from the Michigan State University website: www.educ.msu.edu/content/sites/usteds/documents/Breaking-the-Cycle.pdf.

Balfanz, R. June 2009. Putting middle grades students on the graduation path: A policy and practice brief. Everyone Graduates Center and Talent Development Middle Grades Program. National Middle School Association. Retrieved May 19, 2010, from the Johns Hopkins University website: www.nmsa.org/portals/0/pdf/research/Research_from_the_Field/Policy_Brief_Balfanz.pdf.

Balfanz, R., and N. Legters. September 2004. Locating the dropout crisis: Which high schools produce the nation's dropouts? Where are they located? Who attends them? Retrieved May 13, 2010, from the Johns Hopkins University website: http://web.jhu.edu/bin/c/s/report70.pdf.

Bergeson, T. March 4, 2007. Not letting kids off the hook in math. Retrieved March 15, 2008, from the *Seattle Post-Intelligencer* website: www.seattlepi.com/opinion/305910_mathbergeson04.html.

———. November 16, 2007. A state of distinction: Educating for a sustainable democracy and a sustainable world. Retrieved March 10, 2008, from the Office of Superintendent of Public Instruction website: http://www.k12.wa.us/Communications/stateofed/2007stateofeducation.pdf (site discontinued)

Borasi, R., and J. Fonzi. n.d. *Professional development that supports school mathematics reform.* Vol. 3 of *Foundations: A monograph for professionals in science, mathematics, and technology education.* Retrieved April 9, 2008, from the National Science Foundation website: www.nsf.gov/pubs/2002/nsf02084/NSF02084.pdf.

Brickell, J., and D. Lyon. January 2003. Reliability, validity, and related issues pertaining to the WASL. Retrieved March 5, 2008, from the Washington Education Association website: http://cms.washingtonea.org/wea/member/prof-dev/Accountability/Rel_Validity_WASL2.pdf (site discontinued)

Brown, J. D. September 1997. Reliability of surveys. *Shiken: JALT Testing & Evaluation SIG Newsletter* 1, no. 2: 17–19. Retrieved September 8, 2010, from the Statistics Corner website: www.jalt.org/test/bro_2.htm.

Brown, P. May 16, 2005. Best, brightest pushed into private schools. Originally printed in the *Orlando Sentinel.* Retrieved October 21, 2010, from the *Spokesman-Review* website: www.spokesmanreview.com/breaking/story.asp?ID=3994.

Brunell, D., S. Malarkey, B. Phillips, C. F. Adrian, S. Leahy, K. T. Johnson, M. Straub, et al. November 10, 2006. Personal communication to legislators. Retrieved March 15, 2008, from the College & Work Ready Agenda website: www.collegeworkready.org/downloads/coalition_letter.doc.

Building on a legacy. 2004. Annual report of the RAND Corporation. Retrieved October 21, 2010, from the RAND Corporation website: www.rand.org/.

Bureau of Labor Statistics. March 19, 2010. Politicians. Retrieved September 20, 2010, from the Bureau of Labor Statistics website: www.salaries.wa.gov/default.htm.

Burrill, G. October 1997. NCTM standards: Eight years later. *School Science and Mathematics* 97, no. 6: 335–39. Retrieved April 30, 2008, from the CNET Networks Inc. website: http://findarticles.com/p/articles/mi_qa3667/is_199710/ai_n8759766.

CCS Institutional Research. May 27, 2010a. Community Colleges of Spokane, Remediation Rates for Students by Recency Since High School Graduation, for Academic Years 2004–05 through 2008–09, with a Five-Year Average. Data source: SBCTC Data Warehouse.

———. May 27, 2010b. Community Colleges of Spokane, Remediation Rates for Students by Recency Since High School Graduation, for Academic Years 2004–05 through 2008–09, with a Five-Year Average. Students from Spokane-area high schools only. Data source: SBCTC Data Warehouse.

Center for the Study of Mathematics Curriculum (CSMC). 2004a. An agenda for action: Recommendations for school mathematics for the 1980s. Retrieved May 5, 2008, from the CSMC website: www.mathcurriculumcenter.org/PDFS/CCM/summaries/agenda4action_summary.pdf.

———. 2004b. Curriculum and evaluation standards for school mathematics. Retrieved May 11, 2008, from the CSMC website: www.mathcurriculumcenter.org/PDFS/CCM/summaries/standards_summary.pdf.

Certification of enrollment: Second substitute House Bill 1906. April 17, 2007. Retrieved March 10, 2008, from the Washington State Legislature website: http://apps.leg.wa.gov/documents/billdocs/2007-08/Pdf/Bills/Session%20Law%202007/1906-S2.SL.pdf.

Certification of enrollment: Senate Bill 6313. March 26, 2008. Retrieved April 11, 2008, from the Washington State Legislature website: http://apps.leg.wa.gov/documents/billdocs/2007-08/Pdf/Bills/Session%20Law%202008/6313.SL.pdf.

Charles A. Dana Center professional development for teachers (The). Spring–summer 2010. Retrieved April 15, 2010, from the Charles A. Dana Center website: www.utdanacenter.org/pd/downloads/pdbrochure.pdf. (site discontinued)

Chat with the superintendent: An on-going opportunity to ask the superintendent questions. May 7, 2008. Retrieved May 22, 2008, from the Spokane Public Schools website: http://www.spokaneschools.org/Interview/transcript.asp?iid=39 (site discontinued)

Chat with the superintendent: Curriculum. March 5, 2008. Retrieved April 30, 2008, from the Spokane Public Schools website: http://www.spokaneschools.org/Interview/faq.asp?id=32 (site discontinued)

Class of 2008 on track on WASL requirements. June 8, 2007. Retrieved January 26, 2008, from the Office of Superintendent of Public Instruction website: www.k12.wa.us/Communications/pressreleases2007/JuneWASLrelease.aspx

Class of 2010 maintains 90 percent passing rate: 12th graders solid in reading and writing, but math scores remain a concern. June 16, 2010. Retrieved June 16, 2010, from the Office of Superintendent of Public Instruction website: www.k12.wa.us/Communications/PressReleases2010/HSPErelease.aspx.

Class size. n.d. Retrieved March 5, 2008, from the National Education Association website: www.nea.org/home/12584.htm.

Classes of 2009 and '10 on track with WASL graduation requirement. August 26, 2008. Retrieved May 16, 2010, from the Office of Superintendent of Public Instruction website: www.k12.wa.us/Communications/pressreleases2008/WASL2008Score Release.aspx.

Classes of 2009 and 2010 on track with WASL requirements. June 16, 2008. Retrieved June 16, 2008, from the Office of Superintendent of Public Instruction website: www.k12.wa.us/Communications/pressreleases2008/WASLRelease.aspx.

Common core standards draft released: New standards developed to help U.S. students compete internationally. September 21, 2009. Retrieved June 21, 2010, from the Office of Superintendent of Public Instruction website: www.k12.wa.us/Communications/PressReleases2009/CommonCoreStandards.aspx.

Common core state standards joint statement: Mathematics education organizations unite to support implementation of Common Core State Standards. June 2, 2010. Retrieved June 2, 2010, from the National Council of Teachers of Mathematics website: www.nctm.org/standards/content.aspx?id=26088.

Confrey, Jere, and Vicki Stohl, eds. 2004. On evaluating curricular effectiveness: Judging the quality of K–12 mathematics evaluations. Washington, DC: National Academies Press. Retrieved May 20, 2008, from the National Academies Press website: http://books.nap.edu/openbook.php?record_id=11025&page=R1.

Connected Mathematics: Authors and staff. n.d. Retrieved April 12, 2008, from the *Connected Mathematics Project* website: www.connectedmath.msu.edu/pnd/authors.shtml.

Cook, T. M., D. K. Leedom, J. O. Grynovicki, and M. G. Golden. February 2000. *Cognitive representations of battlespace complexity: Six fundamental variables of combat.* Aberdeen Proving Ground, MD: Army Research Laboratory.

Coram, R. 2004. *Boyd: The fighter pilot who changed the art of war.* Boston: Back Bay Books, Hachette Book Group.

Core-Plus Mathematics. n.d.a. Retrieved May 11, 2008, from the Western Michigan University website: www.wmich.edu/cpmp/developers.html.

——. n.d.b. Second Edition. Retrieved May 22, 2008, from the Western Michigan University website: www.wmich.edu/cpmp/2ndEdition.html.

Crabb, R. April 11, 2008. Lawmakers budget school time on deficit. *Spokesman-Review,* 7B.

Cribb, T. K., Jr., and Lt. Gen. J. Bunting III. November 20, 2008. Our fading heritage: Americans fail a basic test on their history and institutions. Retrieved December 20, 2008, from the Intercollegiate Studies Institute's National Civic Literacy Board website: www.americancivicliteracy.org/report/pdf/11-20-08/civic_literacy_report_08-09 .pdf.

Cuniff, M. May 17, 2008. Teachers union votes no confidence in Bergeson. Retrieved May 18, 2010, from the *Spokesman-Review* website: www.spokesman.com/stories/2008/ may/17/teachers-union-votes-no-confidence-in-bergeson.

Department begins competition for $437 million in teacher incentive fund grants: Program targeted to assist high needs schools & subject areas. May 20, 2010. Retrieved May 20, 2010, from the U.S. Department of Education website: www2.ed.gov/news/ pressreleases/2010/05/05202010.html.

Department of Defense funding highlights. n.d. Retrieved May 24, 2010, from the Government Printing Office website: www.gpoaccess.gov/usbudget/fy11/pdf/budget/ defense.pdf.

Digest of education statistics: 2009. n.d. Retrieved May 18, 2010, from the U.S. Department of Education Institute of Education Sciences, National Center for Education Statistics website: http://nces.ed.gov/programs/digest/d09.

Dillon, S. August 31, 2008. Hard times hitting students and schools. Retrieved September 1, 2008, from the *New York Times* website: www.nytimes.com/2008/09/01/ education/01school.html.

——. January 31, 2010a. Obama to seek sweeping change in "No Child" law. Retrieved March 27, 2010, from the *New York Times* website: www.nytimes.com/2010/02/01/ education/01child.html.

——. February 21, 2010b. Obama to propose new reading and math standards. Retrieved May 21, 2010, from *the New York Times* website: www.nytimes.com/2010/02/22/education/22educ.html.

Director. n.d. Retrieved May 5, 2008, from the University of Mississippi website: www.olemiss.edu/depts/cetl/director.html (site discontinued).

Dorn, R. October 22, 2009. Personal communication. WA State plans for a phase 1 Race to the Top grant application. Retrieved June 21, 2010, from the Office of Superintendent of Public Instruction website: www.k12.wa.us/Communications/StimulusPackage/Phase1AppCommunication10-22-09.doc.

Dynarski, M., R. Agodini, S. Heaviside, T. Novak, N. Carey, L. Campuzano, B. Means, et al. March 2007. Effectiveness of reading and mathematics software products: Findings from the first student cohort. Retrieved March 24, 2008, from the National Center for Education Evaluation and Regional Assistance website: http://ies.ed.gov/ncee/pdf/20074005.pdf.

Education: Lessons about learning. n.d. Retrieved April 11, 2008, from the National Science Foundation website: www.nsf.gov/about/history/nsf0050/pdf/education.pdf.

Education reform is about the skills, not the test. n.d. Informational sheet. Retrieved March 9, 2008, from the Office of Superintendent of Public Instruction website: http://www.k12.wa.us/assessment/WASL/whyWASL3letterhead.pdf (site discontinued)

Education was legislature's focus. April 23, 2007. Press release. Retrieved April 21, 2008, from the Office of Superintendent of Public Instruction website: www.k12.wa.us/Communications/pressreleases2007/2007Session.aspx.

Elementary and secondary education IT in schools. April 2002. Retrieved March 19, 2008, from the National Science Foundation website: www.nsf.gov/statistics/seind02/c1/c1s8.htm.

Expert panel selects exemplary, promising mathematics programs. October 6, 1999. Retrieved April 10, 2008, from the U.S. Department of Education website: www.ed.gov/PressReleases/10-1999/mathpanel.html.

Facts about . . . 21st-century technology (The). n.d. Retrieved March 24, 2008, from the U.S. Department of Education website: www.ed.gov/nclb/methods/whatworks/21centtech.html.

Federal grants to help teachers integrate new technologies into instruction. April 22, 2008. Press release. Retrieved April 28, 2008, from the Office of Superintendent of Public Instruction website: www.k12.wa.us/Communications/pressreleases2008/PeerCoachingGrant.aspx.

Ferrini-Mundy, J. 2001. Introduction: Perspectives on Principles and Standards for School Mathematics. *School Science and Mathematics* 101. Retrieved June 20, 2010, from the Questia.com website: www.questia.com/googleScholar.qst?docId=5002423382.

Finne, L. August 2006. An overview of public school funding in Washington. Retrieved October 21, 2010, from the Washington Policy Center website: www.washingtonpolicy.org/publications/brief/overview-public-school-funding-washington.

Flores, A. October–November 2007. Examining disparities in mathematics education: Achievement gap or opportunity gap? *The High School Journal* 91, no. 1: 29–42.

Forty-nine states and territories join Common Core Standards Initiative. June 1, 2009. Retrieved June 7, 2009, from the National Governors Association website: www.nga .org/portal/site/nga/menuitem.6c9a8a9ebc6ae07eee28aca9501010a0/?vgnextoid =263a584a61c91210VgnVCM1000005e00100aRCRD&vgnextchannel=759b8f20053 61010VgnVCM1000001a01010aRCRD.

Four SPS schools earn academic achievement awards. January 16, 2007. Press release. Retrieved April 7, 2008, from the Spokane Public Schools website: http://www.spokan-eschools.org/DistrictNews/NewsReleases/newrelease.asp?id=911 (site discontinued)

Funding forecast 2007–2008. n.d. Informational material, Spokane Public Schools.

FY 2010 budget request. n.d. Retrieved June 20, 2010, from the National Science Foundation website: www.nsf.gov/about/budget/fy2010/index.jsp.

Gardella, A. January 20, 2010. Looking to expand, but fearing it, too. Retrieved May 13, 2010, from the *New York Times* website: www.nytimes.com/2010/01/21/business/ smallbusiness/21sbiz.html.

Garelick, B. Fall 2006. Miracle math. *Education Next* 6, no. 4: 38–45. Retrieved April 13, 2010, from the Education Next website: http://educationnext.org/files/ednext20064 _38.pdf.

Gates, R. October 30, 2008. Speech by Defense Secretary Gates on nuclear deterrence: Gates says U.S. needs a "hedge" strategy as long as nuclear weapons exist. Retrieved May 6, 2010, from the America.gov website: www.america.gov/st/texttrans-english/ 2008/October/20081030151217eaifas0.2037317.html.

Ginsburg, A., S. Leinwand, T. Anstrom, E. Pollock, and E. Witt. January 28, 2005. What the United States can learn from Singapore's world-class mathematics system (and what Singapore can learn from the United States): An exploratory study. Retrieved April 30, 2008, from the American Institutes of Research website: www.air.org/files/ Singapore_Report_Bookmark_Version1.pdf.

Glod, M. March 14, 2008. Panel urges schools to emphasize core math skills. Retrieved March 14, 2008, from the *Washington Post* website: www.washingtonpost.com/ wp-dyn/content/article/2008/03/13/AR2008031301492.html.

Golden, D. December 15, 2000. Calculators may be the wrong answer as a "digital divide" widens in schools. Retrieved May 18, 2010, from the *Wall Street Journal* website: http://online.wsj.com/article/SB976838326811281152.html.

Gonzales, P., T. Williams, L. Jocelyn, S. Roey, D. Kastberg, and S. Brenwald. Originally published December 2008. Highlights from TIMSS 2007: Mathematics and science achievement of U.S. fourth- and eighth-grade students in an international context. Retrieved December 12, 2008, from the National Center for Education Statistics website: http://nces.ed.gov/pubs2009/2009001.pdf.

Gootman, E. August 19, 2008. Mixed results on paying city students to pass tests. Retrieved August 20, 2008, from the *New York Times* website: www.nytimes .com/2008/08/20/education/20cash.html.

Governor Chris Gregoire: Frequently asked budget questions. n.d. Retrieved June 2010, from the Governor Chris Gregoire website: www.governor.wa.gov/priorities/ budget/faq.asp.

Gray, L. January 25, 2001. Modified version of testimony to members of the Higher Education and Education Policy Joint Committee of the Minnesota State Legislature. Retrieved March 6, 2008, from the University of Minnesota website: www.math .umn.edu/~gray/testimony.html.

Greenberg, J., and K. Walsh. June 2008. No common denominator: The preparation of elementary teachers in mathematics by America's education schools. Retrieved April 3, 2010, from the National Council on Teacher Quality website: www.nctq .org/p/publications/docs/nctq_ttmath_fullreport_20090603062928.pdf.

Greene, J. P., and M. A. Winters. September 2006. Getting farther ahead by staying behind: A second-year evaluation of Florida's policy to end social promotion. Civic Report 49. Retrieved April 1, 2008, from the Manhattan Institute website: www .manhattan-institute.org/html/cr_49.htm.

Grigg, W., P. Donahue, and G. Dion. 2007. The Nation's Report Card: 12th-grade reading and mathematics 2005 (NCES 2007-468). Retrieved April 30, 2008, from the National Center for Education Statistics website: http://nces.ed.gov/nationsreportcard/ pdf/main2005/2007468.pdf.

Guidance on the Enhancing Education through Technology (Ed Tech) program. March 11, 2002. Retrieved March 24, 2008, from the U.S. Department of Education website: www.ed.gov/programs/edtech/guidance.doc.

Guidelines and materials for submitting mathematics programs for review. n.d. U.S. Department of Education, archived information. Retrieved April 8, 2008, from the U.S. Department of Education website: www.ed.gov/offices/OERI/ORAD/KAD/ expert_panel/mathguid.pdf.

Guiding principles for mathematics curriculum and assessment. June 2009. Retrieved June 7, 2009, from the National Council of Teachers of Mathematics website: www .nctm.org/uploadedFiles/Math_Standards/NCTM%20Guiding%20Principles%20 6209.pdf.

Habash, A. October 2008. Counting on graduation: An agenda for state leadership. Retrieved April 13, 2010, from the Education Trust website: www.edtrust.org/sites/ edtrust.org/files/publications/files/CountingOnGraduationOct2008.pdf.

Hansen, D. November 22, 2008. Departing Bergeson cites schools' progress. *Spokesman-Review*, 1B.

Hartocollis, A. April 27, 2000. The new, flexible math meets parental rebellion. Retrieved May 5, 2008, from the *New York Times* website: http://query.nytimes.com/ gst/fullpage.html?res=9F04EFD61130F934A15757C0A9669C8B63.

Hattie, J. 2009. *Visible learning: A synthesis of over 800 meta-analyses relating to achievement*. New York: Routledge.

Heavin, J. February 18, 2007. Critics contend math doesn't add up. Retrieved May 3, 2010, from the *Columbia Daily Tribune* website: http://archive.columbiatribune .com/2007/feb/20070218news003.asp.

Hill, R., and T. Parker. December 2006. A study of *Core-Plus* students attending Michigan State University. *The Mathematical Association of America* 113: 905–21.

Retrieved March 6, 2008, from the Michigan State University website: www.math .msu.edu/~hill/HillParker5.pdf.

Hirsch, C. R., M. Bell, A. Isaacs, S. J. Russell, et al. June 14, 2007. *Perspectives on design and development of school mathematics curricula.* Reston, VA: National Council of Teachers of Mathematics. Summary of book retrieved May 8, 2010, from the NCTM website: www.nctm.org/Catalog/product.aspx?id=13233.

Historical tables, budget of the U.S. government, fiscal year 2011. n.d. Retrieved April 21, 2010, from the Office of Management and Budget website: www.budget.gov.

Hook, W., W. Bishop, and J. Hook. June 2007. A quality math curriculum in support of effective teaching for elementary schools. *Educational Studies in Mathematics* (Springer Netherlands) 65, no. 2: 125–48.

Hu, W. October 7, 2008a. Video game helps math students vanquish an archfiend: Algebra. Retrieved October 8, 2008, from the *New York Times* website: www.nytimes .com/2008/10/08/nyregion/08video.html.

———. October 16, 2008b. To keep Mount Vernon's high school sports alive, even rivals contribute money. Retrieved October 17, 2008, from the *New York Times* website: www.nytimes.com/2008/10/17/education/17sports.html.

Implementing the Common Core Standards. May 2010. Retrieved May 13, 2010, from the Pearson Education website: http://assets.pearsonschool.com/asset_mgr/current/ 201018/CCS_booklet.pdf.

In brief: Lawmakers vote to change WASL. March 6, 2008. Retrieved May 18, 2010, from the *Spokesman-Review* website: www.spokesman.com/stories/2008/mar/06/in -brief-lawmakers-vote-to-change-wasl.

Inside IMP. n.d. Retrieved May 14, 2008, from the *Interactive Mathematics Program* Resource Center website: www.mathimp.org/general_info/inside_imp.html.

It's about time. n.d. Retrieved May 20, 2008, from the *MATH Connections* website: www.its-about-time.com/htmls/mc/mcacknow.html.

Jackson, A. January 1998. Interview with Gail Burrill. *Notices of the AMS* 45, no. 1: 87–90. Retrieved April 10, 2008, from the American Mathematical Society website: www.ams.org/notices/199801/comm-burrill.pdf.

John F. Kennedy, XXXV President of the United States, 1961–1963. February 26, 1962. Retrieved May 23, 2010, from the American Presidency Project website: www .presidency.ucsb.edu/ws/index.php?pid=9075&st=&st1=.

Johnson, J. March 2000. Teaching and learning mathematics. Retrieved March 24, 2008, from the Office of Superintendent of Public Instruction website: www.k12 .wa.us/research/pubdocs/pdf/MathBook.pdf.

Kaminski, J. A., V. M. Sloutsky, and A. F. Heckler. April 25, 2008. Learning theory: The advantage of abstract examples in learning math. *Science* 320, no. 5875: 454–55.

Kirschner, P. A., J. Sweller, and R. E. Clark. 2006. Why minimal guidance during instruction does not work: An analysis of the failure of constructivist, discovery, problem-based, experiential, and inquiry-based teaching. *Educational Psychologist*

41: 75–86. Retrieved from the Center for Cognitive Technology website: www .cogtech.usc.edu/publications/kirschner_Sweller_Clark.pdf.

Klein, D. April 2000. Math problems: Why the U.S. Department of Education's recommended math programs don't add up. Retrieved April 8, 2008, from the Mathematically Correct website: www.mathematicallycorrect.com/usnoadd.htm.

——. 2003. A brief history of American K–12 mathematics education in the 21st century. Preprint of a chapter in *Mathematical Cognition*, ed. James Royer. Charlotte, NC: Information Age Publishing. Retrieved April 30, 2008, from the California State University, Northridge, website: www.csun.edu/~vcmth00m/AHistory.html.

——. 2007. A quarter century of US "math wars" and political partisanship. Preprint of an article that appeared in the *BSHM Bulletin: Journal of the British Society for the History of Mathematics* 22, no. 1: 22–33. Retrieved April 18, 2008, from the California State University, Northridge, website: www.csun.edu/~vcmth00m/bshm.html.

——. Summer 2010. Book review of *The death and life of the great American school system: How testing and choice are undermining education*, by Diane Ravitch. *Educational Horizons* 88, no. 4: 1–4.

Klein, D., R. Askey, R. J. Milgram, H. Wu., M. Scharlemann, and B. Tsang. November 1999. An open letter to United States Secretary of Education, Richard Riley. Personal communication. Retrieved December 5, 2007, from the Mathematically Correct website: www.mathematicallycorrect.com/riley.htm.

Konstantopoulos, S. March 2008. Do small classes reduce the achievement gap between low and high achievers? Evidence from Project STAR. *The Elementary School Journal* 108, no. 4: 275–91. Retrieved April 15, 2010, from the Chicago Journals website: www.journals.uchicago.edu/doi/pdf/10.1086/528972.

Largest international study of student achievement ever undertaken: Countries' rankings for 3rd and 4th grades to be released. June 10, 1997. Press release. Retrieved March 28, 2008, from the TIMSS website: http://timss.bc.edu/timss1995i/Presspop1.html.

Lawrence-Turner, J. February 6, 2010a. School administrators' pay among highest in county. *Spokesman-Review*, A1.

——. February 17, 2010b. Beyond the classroom: Program helps high-schoolers after the bell rings. *Spokesman-Review*, A5.

——. February 25, 2010c. Research targets middle schools. *Spokesman-Review*, A5.

——. June 27, 2010d. Dropout rates battle disconnected. *Spokesman-Review*, B1.

——. September 19, 2010e. Administrators out of school budget woes' reach. *Spokesman-Review*, A1.

Leaders and laggards: A state-by-state report card on educational effectiveness. February 2007. Retrieved March 13, 2008, from the U.S. Chamber of Commerce website: www.uschamber.com/reportcard/2007/default.htm.

Leaming, S. September 20, 2007. Enrollment drop surprises schools. *Spokesman-Review*, 1A, 11A.

Leinberger, L. March 12, 2009. Middle school includes all students. *Spokesman-Review*, 1W, 6W.

Lemke, M., A. Sen, E. Pahlke, L. Partelow, D. Miller, T. Williams, D. Kastberg, and L. Jocelyn. 2004. International outcomes of learning in mathematics literacy and problem solving: PISA 2003, results from the U.S. Perspective (NCES 2005-003). Washington, DC: U.S. Department of Education, National Center for Education Statistics.

Levine, S. May 28, 2009. Moving beyond No Child Left Behind. Retrieved June 9, 2009, from the *Bloomberg Businessweek* website: www.businessweek.com/magazine/content/09_23/b4134052764159.htm.

Local systemic change projects. n.d. Retrieved June 20, 2010, from the National Science Foundation website: www.nsf.gov/pubs/1997/nsf97145/projects.htm.

Loveless, T., S. Farkas, and A. Duffett. 2008. High-achieving students in the era of NCLB. Retrieved June 28, 2008, from the Thomas B. Fordham Institute website: www.edexcellence.net/doc/20080618_high_achievers.pdf.

Lutkus, A., and A. Weiss. 2007. The Nation's Report Card: Civics 2006 (NCES 2007-476). Retrieved March 14, 2008, from the National Center for Education Statistics website: http://nces.ed.gov/nationsreportcard/pdf/main2006/2007476.pdf.

Mapping 2005 state proficiency standards onto the NAEP scales (NCES 2007-482). June 2007. Retrieved April 30, 2008, from the National Center for Education Statistics website: http://nces.ed.gov/nationsreportcard/pdf/studies/2007482.pdf.

Mapping Washington's educational progress 2008. n.d. Retrieved March 14, 2008, from the Department of Education website: www.ed.gov/nclb/accountability/results/progress/washington.pdf.

Mass, C., B. Alexander, E. G. Adelberger, J. M. Bardeen, B. Balick, G. Borriello, D. G. Boulware, et al. February 26, 2008. Public statement by University of Washington faculty on math preparedness of incoming students. Retrieved February 29, 2008, from the *Seattle Post-Intelligencer* website: http://seattlepi.nwsource.com/dayart/PDF/PublicMathStatementUWFaculty.doc.

Math & science matter: The world is waiting. n.d. Retrieved March 15, 2008, from the College & Work Ready Agenda website: www.collegeworkready.org/downloads/mathandsciencematterflier_06_2007.pdf.

Math Trailblazers. 2001. Retrieved May 14, 2008, from the Education Development Center website: www2.edc.org/mcc/PDF/persptrailblazers.pdf.

Mathematics & science education expert panels. January 9, 2001. Retrieved April 8, 2008, from the U.S. Department of Education website: www.ed.gov/offices/OERI/ORAD/KAD/expert_panel/mathmemb.html.

Mathematics (edition 2), K–12 grade level expectations: A new level of specificity. September 8, 2006. Working Copy. Retrieved January 11, 2009, from the Office of Superintendent of Public Instruction website (site discontinued).

Mathematics education trust: 2004 annual report. 2004. Retrieved May 4, 2008, from the National Council of Teachers of Mathematics website: http://204.255.166.12/uploadedFiles/Lessons_and_Resources/Grants_and_Awards/2004_metannual.pdf.

Mathematics in Context. 2001. Retrieved May 14, 2008, from the Education Development Center website: www2.edc.org/mcc/PDF/perspmathincontext.pdf.

Mayer, R. E. January 2004. Should there be a three-strikes rule against pure discovery learning? The case for guided methods of instruction. *American Psychologist* 59, no. 1: 14–19. Retrieved April 30, 2008, from the University of Southern California website: http://projects.ict.usc.edu/itw/gel/MayerThreeStrikesAP04.pdf.

Mayfield, K. H., and P. N. Chase. Summer 2002. The effects of cumulative practice on mathematics problem solving. *Journal of Applied Behavior Analysis* 35, no. 2: 105–23. Retrieved April 30, 2008, from the PubMed Central website: www.pubmedcentral .nih.gov/picrender.fcgi?artid=1284369&blobtype=pdf.

McKeown, M., D. Klein, and C. Patterson. June 1, 2000. National Science Foundation systemic initiatives: How a small amount of federal money promotes ill-designed mathematics and science programs in K–12 and undermines local control of education. In *What's at stake in the K–12 standards wars: A primer for educational policy makers.* New York: Peter Lang Publishing Group. Retrieved April 7, 2008, from the California State University Northridge website: www.csun.edu/~vcmth00m/chap13.pdf.

Medina, J. October 1, 2008. Teachers to be measured based on students' standardized test scores. Retrieved October 1, 2008, from the *New York Times* website: www .nytimes.com/2008/10/02/education/02teachers.html.

Minutes of regular school board meeting. February 22, 2006. Retrieved April 30, 2008, from the Spokane Public Schools Board website: http://www.spokaneschools.org/ Board/minutes/02-22-06.pdf (site discontinued)

——. April 23, 2008a. Retrieved May 3, 2010, from the Spokane Public Schools website: www.spokaneschools.org/17331092592211777/lib/17331092592211777/ _files/042308.pdf.

——. October 8, 2008b. Retrieved May 3, 2010, from the Spokane Public Schools website: www.spokaneschools.org/17331092592211777/lib/17331092592211777/ _files/10-08-08.pdf.

——. November 5, 2008c. Retrieved May 3, 2010, from the Spokane Public Schools Board website www.spokaneschools.org/17331092592211777/lib/17331092592211777/ _files/11-05-08.pdf.

——. February 11, 2009. Retrieved May 22, 2010, from the Spokane Public Schools Board website www.spokaneschools.org/17331092592211777/lib/17331092592211777/ _files/02-11-09.pdf.

——. March 24, 2010. Retrieved June 21, 2010, from the Spokane Public Schools Board website www.spokaneschools.org/17331092592211777/lib/17331092592211777/ _files/Bdmn032410.pdf.

More families will qualify for free meals. September 24, 2008. Spokane Public Schools press release sent by e-mail on September 30, 2008.

More than 90 percent of seniors meet key graduation requirement. June 3, 2008. Press release. Retrieved June 3, 2008, from the Office of Superintendent of Public Instruction website: www.k12.wa.us/Communications/pressreleases2008/Class 2008Update.aspx.

National Center for Education Statistics. 2005. The Nation's Report Card: Mathematics 2005 (NCES 2006-453). Retrieved May 5, 2008, from the National Center for Education Statistics website: http://nces.ed.gov/nationsreportcard/pdf/main2005/2006453.pdf.

———. 2009a. The Nation's Report Card: Mathematics 2009 (NCES 2010-451). Washington, DC: National Center for Education Statistics, Institute of Education Sciences, U.S. Department of Education.

———. 2009b. The Nation's Report Card: Reading 2009 (NCES 2010-458). Washington, DC: Institute of Education Sciences, U.S. Department of Education.

National Commission on Excellence in Education. 1983. *A Nation at Risk: The Imperative for Educational Reform.* Washington, DC: U.S. Department of Education.

National Mathematics Advisory Panel (NMAP). March 2008. Foundations for success: The final report of the National Mathematics Advisory Panel. Retrieved March 18, 2008, from the U.S. Department of Education website: www.ed.gov/about/bdscomm/list/mathpanel/report/final-report.pdf.

NCLB compliance report 2007: Washington schools in "improvement" status, final report. November 19, 2007. Retrieved April 4, 2008, from the Office of Superintendent of Public Instruction website: www.k12.wa.us/ESEA/pubdocs/Districtfinal report-11-16-2007.doc.

NCTM public comments on the Common Core Standards for mathematics. n.d. Retrieved June 2, 2010, from the National Council of Teachers of Mathematics website: www.nctm.org/about/content.aspx?id=25186.

NCTM supports teachers and administrators to implement Common Core Standards. June 2, 2010. Retrieved June 2, 2010, from the National Council of Teachers of Mathematics website: www.nctm.org/news/content.aspx?id=26083.

Nethercutt, G. December 13, 2007. Build a better life through civic literacy. *Spokesman-Review,* 7B. Retrieved April 30, 2008, from the *Spokesman-Review* website: www.spokesmanreview.com/tools/story_pf.asp?ID=223525.

———. 2010. *In tune with America: Our history in song.* Spokane, WA: Marquette Books.

New study shows the unintended consequences of moving more pupils into eighth grade algebra and other advanced math classes: Approximately 120,000 unprepared students are now struggling. September 22, 2008. Retrieved October 27, 2008, from the Brookings Institution website: www.brookings.edu/reports/2008/~/media/Files/rc/reports/2008/0922_education_loveless/0922_education_press_release.pdf.

Obama administration supports emergency funding to save teacher jobs. May 13, 2010. Retrieved May 14, 2010, from the U.S. Department of Education website: www.ed.gov/blog/2010/05/obama-administration-supports-emergency-funding-to -save-teacher-jobs.

Office of the Auditor General for the State of Arizona. February 2010. Arizona Public School Districts' dollars spent in the classroom, fiscal year 2009. Retrieved May 17, 2010, from the State of Arizona Office of the Auditor General website: www .azauditor.gov/Reports/School_Districts/Statewide/2010_February/2010_Classroom_Dollars_Spent_in_the_Classroom_Prop301.htm.

Organization for Economic Cooperation and Development (OECD) Program for International Student Assessment (PISA). n.d. Retrieved March 28, 2008, from the

Organization for Economic Cooperation and Development website: www.pisa.oecd.org/pages/0,2987,en_32252351_32235731_1_1_1_1_1,00.html.

———. 2006. December 4, 2007. Retrieved April 7, 2008, from the Organization for Economic Cooperation and Development website: www.pisa.oecd.org/pages/0,3417,en_32252351_32235731_1_1_1_1_1,00.html.

Orlich, D. March 24, 2006. WASL: A costly lesson in ineffective spending. Retrieved October 17, 2007, from the *Puget Sound Business Journal* website: www.bizjournals.com/seattle/stories/2006/03/27/editorial3.html.

———. January 31, 2008. Eliminating WASL first step to equality. *Spokesman-Review*, 7B.

Our fading heritage: Summary. 2008. Retrieved December 20, 2008, from the Intercollegiate Studies Institute website: www.americancivicliteracy.org/2008/summary_summary.html.

Overview. n.d. Retrieved May 14, 2010, from the U.S. Department of Education website: www2.ed.gov/policy/landing.jhtml.

Overview: Department of Education high priority performance goals. February 2010. Retrieved June 22, 2010, from the U.S. Department of Education website: www2.ed.gov/about/overview/focus/goals.html.

Overview: FY 2011 budget summary: Table of contents. February 1, 2010. Retrieved May 25, 2010, from the U.S. Department of Education website: www2.ed.gov/about/overview/budget/budget11/summary/index.html.

Paige, R., and J. Gibbons. June 2003. No Child Left Behind: A parents [sic] guide. Retrieved March 15, 2008, from the Department of Education website: www.ed.gov/parents/academic/involve/nclbguide/parentsguide.pdf.

Pan, R. December 29, 2008. United States high school mathematics tests for top 1–10% of students show surprises, 1. Advanced Placement calculus test registration rises though failing students increase. Retrieved January 6, 2009, from the EducationNews.org website: http://ednews.org/articles/32327/1/United-States-High-School-Mathematics-Tests-for-Top-1-10-of-Students-Show-Surprises-I-Advanced-Placement-Calculus-Test-Registration-Rises-Though-Failing-Students-Increase/Page1.html.

Parent's brochures: FAQs for math adoption. n.d. Retrieved April 7, 2008, from the Spokane Public Schools website: http://www.spokaneschools.org/SecondaryMath/mathcir.stm (site discontinued)

Patterson, C. January 1999. School district alert for mathematics textbook selection: Independent analysis of mathematics textbooks. Retrieved April 30, 2008, from the Texas Public Policy Foundation website: www.texaspolicy.com/pdf/1999-01-01-textbook-math.pdf.

Plattner, L. August 30, 2007. Washington State mathematics standards: Review and recommendations. Retrieved June 21, 2010, from the Strategic Teaching website: www.strategicteaching.com/review_wa_standards_8-30-07.pdf.

Policies and procedures, number 1000. May 26, 2010. Legal status and functions of the board. From *Spokane Public Schools Policies and Procedures Manual*. Retrieved

September 17, 2010, from the Spokane Public Schools website: http://www2
.spokaneschools.org/polpro/.

Policies and procedures, number 4423. September 2, 1982. Grouping students for
instruction. From *Spokane Public Schools Policies and Procedures Manual*. Retrieved
from the Spokane Public Schools website: www2.spokaneschools.org/polpro/.

Policies and procedures, number 4425. November 28, 1988. Placement, promotion,
advancement, and retention of students. From *Spokane Public Schools Policies and
Procedures Manual*. Retrieved March 7, 2007, from the Spokane Public Schools website: www2.spokaneschools.org/polpro/.

Policies and procedures, number 4426. September 7, 2005. Curriculum policy. From
Spokane Public Schools Policies and Procedures Manual. Retrieved from the Spokane
Public Schools website: www2.spokaneschools.org/polpro/.

Policymakers urged to take a closer look at the U.S. science and technology work-
force: New report addresses relevance of current public policy. October 17, 2007.
Retrieved April 29, 2008, from the Commission on Professionals in Science and
Technology website: www.cpst.org/STEM/STEM9_Press.doc.

President's education budget signals bold changes for ESEA. February 1, 2010. Retrieved March 27, 2010, from the U.S. Department of Education website: www2
.ed.gov/news/pressreleases/2010/02/02012010.html.

Principles and standards for school mathematics. April 12, 2000. Reston, VA: National
Council of Teachers of Mathematics.

Principles and techniques of instruction. April 1, 1974. Washington, DC: Air Training
Command, Department of the Air Force, Headquarters U.S. Air Force [Obsolete.
Currently in use: "Information for designers of instructional systems, application to
education," Air Force Handbook 36-2235, Volume 10, November 1, 2002].

Professors of education: It's how you learn, not what you learn that's most important.
October 22, 1997. Press release for *Different drummers: How teachers of teachers view
public education*. Retrieved May 2, 2010, from the Public Agenda website: www
.publicagenda.org/press-releases/professors-education-its-how-you-learn-not-what
-you-learn-thats-most-important.

Program developers—MiC. n.d. Philosophy of MiC. Retrieved May 5, 2008, from the
Mathematics in Context website: www.showmecenter.missouri.edu/showme/mic
.shtml.

Progress report: An internal study of CPM's impact on mathematics instruction. April
1997. 1997. Retrieved May 12, 2008, from the *College Preparatory Mathematics* website: www.cpm.org/parents/statisticsPR.htm.

Research base. n.d. Retrieved May 12, 2008, from the *Contemporary Mathematics in
Context (Core-Plus)* website: www.wmich.edu/cpmp/parentresource/research.html.

Rich, M. October 5, 2008. Using video games as bait to hook readers. Retrieved October 7, 2008, from the *New York Times* website: www.nytimes.com/2008/10/06/
books/06games.html.

Rimer, S. August 26, 2008. Class of 2008 matches '07 on the SAT. Retrieved August 27, 2008, from the *New York Times* website: www.nytimes.com/2008/08/27/education/27sat.html.

Ripley, A. April 19, 2010. Should schools bribe kids? *TIME*, 40–47.

Rizzo, M. February 23, 2007. Quakerktown returns to "old math." Scores rose under current system, but grads say it hurt them all. Abstract retrieved May 3, 2010, from the *Morning Call* website: www.mcall.com.

Roesler, R. March 17, 2007. School debate sounds familiar. *Spokesman-Review*, 1A, 7A. Retrieved September 12, 2008, from the *Spokesman-Review* website: www.spokesman review.com/tools/story_pf.asp?ID=179810.

Roza, M. January 2007. Frozen assets: Rethinking teacher contracts could free billions for school reform. Education Sector Reports. Retrieved March 22, 2008, from the Education Sector website: www.educationsector.org/usr_doc/FrozenAssets.pdf.

Schiesel, S. June 9, 2008. Former justice promotes Web-based civics lessons. Retrieved June 9, 2008, from the *New York Times* website: www.nytimes.com/2008/06/09/arts/09sand.html.

Sebastian, S. February 15, 2007. "Reform math" doesn't add up, Dublin critics say. Retrieved September 9, 2010, from the *Columbus Dispatch* website: www.dispatch.com/live/contentbe/dispatch/2007/02/15/20070215-D1-04.html.

Seeley, C. October 26, 2004. Hard arithmetic is not deep mathematics. Retrieved May 5, 2008, from the National Council of Teachers of Mathematics website: www.nctm.org/about/content.aspx?id=918.

Senate Bill 6696. (Original Bill – not adopted). Retrieved July 26, 2010, from the Washington State Legislature website: http://apps.leg.wa.gov/documents/billdocs/2009-10/Pdf/Bills/Senate%20Bills/6696.pdf.

Shettle, C., S. Roey, J. Mordica, R. Perkins, C. Nord, J. Teodorovic, J. Brown, M. Lyons, C. Averett, and D. Kastberg. 2007. The Nation's Report Card: America's high school graduates: Results from the 2005 NAEP High School Transcript Study (NCES 2007-467). Retrieved April 30, 2008, from the National Center for Education Statistics website: http://nces.ed.gov/nationsreportcard/pdf/studies/2007467_1.pdf.

Sousa, David. 2007. *How the Brain Learns Mathematics.* Thousand Oaks, CA: Corwin Press.

Spellings, M. May 9, 2007a. U.S. Secretary of Education Margaret Spellings delivers remarks at national summit on America's silent epidemic. Retrieved March 27, 2008, from the U.S. Department of Education website: www.ed.gov/news/pressreleases/2007/05/05092007.html.

——. June 7, 2007b. Statement by Secretary Spellings on report comparing state proficiency standards using NAEP. Press release. Retrieved March 29, 2008, from the U.S. Department of Education website: www.ed.gov/news/pressreleases/2007/06/06072007.html.

——. June 9, 2007c. A national test we don't need. Op-ed sent to the *Washington Post* on June 9, 2007. Retrieved March 29, 2008, from the U.S. Department of Education website: www.ed.gov/news/opeds/edit/2007/06112007.html.

Spokane Education Association. n.d. September 1, 2009 to August 31, 2012: Collective bargaining agreement between Spokane School District No. 81 Board of Directors and the Spokane Education Association, representing Certificated, Partners in Building Spokane's Future. Retrieved September 18, 2010, from the Spokane Public Schools website: www.spokaneschools.org/174420121684251340/ lib/174420121684251340/_files/Certificated.pdf.

Standards 2000 project. n.d. Retrieved April 4, 2008, from the National Council of Teachers of Mathematics website: http://standards.nctm.org/document/prepost/ project.htm.

Standards revision team biographies: Dana Center facilitators. n.d. Retrieved May 16, 2008, from the Office of Superintendent of Public Instruction website: www .k12.wa.us/assessment/WASL/Mathematics/pubdocs/StandardsTeam2.doc (site discontinued)

Standards revision team biographies: National consultants. n.d. Retrieved May 17, 2008, from the Office of Superintendent of Public Instruction website: www.k12.wa.us/ assessment/WASL/Mathematics/pubdocs/StandardsTeam3.doc (site discontinued)

State ACT scores among nation's best. August 13, 2008. Press release. Retrieved August 13, 2008, from the Office of Superintendent of Public Instruction website: www .k12.wa.us/Communications/pressreleases2008/ACTresults.aspx.

State comparisons: National assessment of educational progress (NAEP). n.d. Retrieved March 17, 2008, from the National Center for Education Statistics website: http://nces.ed.gov/nationsreportcard/nde/statecomp/index.asp.

State SAT scores among best in nation: Participation rates up in all ethnic groups. August 18, 2007. Press release. Retrieved December 5, 2007, from the Office of Superintendent of Public Instruction website: www.k12.wa.us/Communications/ pressreleases2007/SAT2007.aspx.

State testing 2007: What you need to know. n.d. Office of Superintendent of Public Instruction informational flyer. Retrieved March 30, 2008, from the Office of Superintendent of Public Instruction website: www.k12.wa.us/assessment/pubdocs/ WASL2007.pdf.

States will lead the way toward reform. June 14, 2009. Retrieved June 22, 2010, from the U.S. Department of Education website: www2.ed.gov/news/ speeches/2009/06/06142009.html.

Stecher, B., S. Barron, T. Chun, and K. Ross. August 2000. The effects of the Washington State education reform on schools and classrooms: Initial Findings. CSE Technical Report 525. Los Angeles, CA: UCLA Center for the Study of Evaluation. Retrieved April 30, 2008, from the RAND website: www.rand.org/pubs/documented_briefings/2005/RAND_DB309.pdf.

Stevens and Whitman honored as schools of distinction. October 10, 2007. Press release. Retrieved April 7, 2008, from the Spokane Public Schools website: www .spokaneschools.org/DistrictNews/NewsReleases/newrelease.asp?id=982 (site discontinued)

Stiff, L. January 2001. Multiple paths to success. Retrieved May 1, 2008, from the National Council of Teachers of Mathematics website: www.nctm.org/about/content .aspx?id=1246.

———. April 2001. Making calculator use add up. Retrieved April 2, 2008, from the National Council of Teachers of Mathematics website: www.nctm.org/about/content .aspx?id=1242.

———. July–August 2001. Constructivist mathematics and unicorns. Retrieved May 1, 2008, from the National Council of Teachers of Mathematics website: www.nctm .org/about/content.aspx?id=1238.

———. December 2001. Status and the status quo–the politics of education. Retrieved May 1, 2008, from the National Council of Teachers of Mathematics website: www .nctm.org/about/content.aspx?id=1230.

Stories from 2007 schools of distinction. 2007. Informational sheets. Retrieved April 6, 2008, from the Office of Superintendent of Public Instruction website: www.k12.wa.us/ Communications/pressreleases2007/Stories2007SchoolsDistinctionESD101.doc.

Stotsky, S. n.d. The right calculation: The power of rigorous teacher tests for math. Retrieved May 5, 2008, from the Association of American Educators website: www .aaeteachers.org/calculation.shtml (site discontinued)

———. Summer 2005. Ed schools: The real shame of the nation. *EducationNews* 18, no. 3: 44–53. Retrieved May 3, 2010, from the EducationNews.org website: www.ednews .org/articles/ed-schools-the-real-shame-of-the-nation.html.

Strategic Research Associates. September 18, 2008. Spokane Public Schools: Perceptions in 2008 among those requesting out-of-district transfers: Summary of results, graphic summary, and text of responses to open-ended questions. Survey.

Strine, F. A. August 28, 2007. WASL cuts learning by at least 25 percent. *Spokesman-Review*, 5B.

Structure of the U.S. education system: U.S. grading systems. February 2008. UNEI International Affairs Office, U.S. Department of Education. Retrieved May 18, 2010, from the U.S. Department of Education website: www2.ed.gov/about/offices/list/ ous/international/usnei/us/grading.doc.

Stumbo, C., and S. Follett Lusi. 2005a. Standards-based foundations for mathematics education: Standards, curriculum, instruction, and assessment in mathematics. Retrieved June 9, 2009, from the Texas Instruments website: http://education. ti.com/sites/US/downloads/pdf/mathpaper02.pdf.

———. 2005b. Why isn't the mathematics we learned good enough for today's students? The imperative of mathematical literacy. Retrieved June 9, 2009, from the Texas Instruments website: http://education.ti.com/sites/US/downloads/pdf/mathpaper01.pdf.

Sullivan, G. R., and M. V. Harper. 1996. *Hope is not a method.* New York: Broadway Books.

Table 3: Mean SAT Reasoning Test™ critical reading, mathematics, and writing scores by state, with changes for selected years. 2007. Retrieved March 17, 2008, from the College Board website: www.collegeboard.com/prod_downloads/about/news_info/ cbsenior/yr2007/tables/3.pdf.

Table 3: Mean SAT Reasoning Test™ verbal and math scores by state, with changes for selected years. 2005. Retrieved March 17, 2008, from the College Board website: www.collegeboard.com/prod_downloads/about/news_info/cbsenior/yr2005/table3 -mean-SAT-reasoning-test.pdf.

Teacher incentive fund: Frequently asked questions. 2008. Retrieved October 28, 2008, from the U.S. Department of Education website: www.ed.gov/programs/teacher incentive/faq.html.

Teacher to teacher: Teacher effectiveness and ESEA. 2010. Retrieved May 14, 2010, from the U.S. Department of Education website: www.ed.gov/blog/2010/05/teacher -to-teacher-teacher-effectiveness-and-esea.

TERC. n.d.a. *Investigations in Number, Data, and Space*: Authors and collaborators. Retrieved May 14, 2008, from the TERC website: http://investigations.terc.edu/ developing/authors-collab.

——. n.d.b. *Investigations in Number, Data, and Space*: First edition authors. Retrieved May 14, 2008, from the TERC website: http://investigations.terc.edu/developing/ authors-collab/1st_ed_authors.cfm.

Testimony of Jack Jennings, president of the center on education policy. June 7, 2007. Testimony to the Subcommittee on Early Childhood, Elementary and Secondary Education, Committee on Education and Labor, U.S. House of Representatives. Retrieved March 29, 2008, from the Center on Education Policy website: www.cep-dc.org/index .cfm?fuseaction=document.showDocumentByID&nodeID=1&DocumentID=225.

TIMSS & PIRLS International Study Center. n.d. Retrieved September 9, 2010, from the TIMSS & PIRLS International Study Center website: www.timss.org.

Total expenditures for elementary and secondary education in the U.S. n.d. Retrieved March 27, 2010, from the U.S. Department of Education website: www2.ed.gov/ about/overview/budget/budget11/summary/appendix3.pdf.

Trends in International Mathematics and Science Study: TIMSS. 2003. December 14, 2004. Retrieved March 11, 2008, from the National Center for Education Statistics website: http://nces.ed.gov/pubs2005/timss03/summary.asp.

Tuition. n.d. Retrieved June 21, 2010, from the University of Chicago Laboratory Schools website: www.ucls.uchicago.edu/admission/tuition/index.aspx.

Tuition and fees. 2010. Retrieved June 21, 2010, from the Sidwell Friends School website: www.sidwell.edu/admissions/tuition-and-fees/index.aspx.

Turner, P. May 1, 2008. Film pick crashed and burned. *Spokesman-Review*, 5D.

Two Spokane schools earn national Title I distinguished school awards. November 8, 2006. Press release. Retrieved April 7, 2008, from the Spokane Public Schools website: www.spokaneschools.org/DistrictNews/NewsReleases/newrelease.asp?id=896 (site discontinued)

U.S. Department of Education. March 13, 2008a. U.S. Secretary of Education Margaret Spellings highlights findings of the National Mathematics Advisory Panel. Press release. Retrieved March 13, 2008, from the U.S. Department of Education website: www.ed.gov/news/pressreleases/2008/03/03132008.html.

——. March 18, 2008b. U.S. Secretary of Education Margaret Spellings announces No Child Left Behind "differentiated accountability" pilot. Retrieved April 4, 2008, from the U.S. Department of Education website: www.ed.gov/news/pressreleases/2008/03/03182008.html.

——. April 1, 2008c. U.S. Secretary of Education Margaret Spellings announces department will move to a uniform graduation rate, require disaggregation of data. Press release. Retrieved April 4, 2008, from the U.S. Department of Education website: www.ed.gov/news/pressreleases/2008/04/04012008.html.

——. April 22, 2008d. U.S. Secretary of Education Margaret Spellings announces proposed regulations to strengthen No Child Left Behind. Press release. Retrieved April 23, 2008, from the U.S. Department of Education website: www.ed.gov/news/pressreleases/2008/04/04222008.html.

——. May 7, 2008e. U.S. Secretary of Education Margaret Spellings delivers remarks at the Council of the Americas Conference in Washington, DC. Retrieved May 8, 2008, from the U.S. Department of Education website: www.ed.gov/news/pressreleases/2008/05/05072008.html.

U.S. Department of Education, Institute of Education Sciences, National Center for Education Statistics, National Assessment of Educational Progress (NAEP). 2007. The Nation's Report Card: Mathematics 2007: National assessment of educational progress at grades 4 and 8. Retrieved June 9, 2010, from the National Center for Education Statistics website: http://nces.ed.gov/nationsreportcard/pdf/main2007/2007494.pdf.

Vanneman, A., L. Hamilton, J. Baldwin Anderson, and T. Rahman. 2009. Achievement gaps: How black and white students in public schools perform in mathematics and reading on the National Assessment of Educational Progress (NCES 2009-455). Washington, DC: National Center for Education Statistics, Institute of Education Sciences, U.S. Department of Education.

Washington 8th graders show significant 10-year writing gains. April 3, 2008. Press release. Retrieved April 14, 2008, from the Office of Superintendent of Public Instruction website: www.k12.wa.us/Communications/pressreleases2008/NAEP2007Results.aspx.

Washington Citizens' Commission on Salaries for Elected Officials. May 19, 2009. Retrieved September 20, 2010, from the WCCSEO website: www.salaries.wa.gov/documents/2009-10FINALSalarySchedule5-19-09withRationaleStatement.pdf.

Washington State constitution. 1889. Retrieved March 22, 2008, from the Washington State Legislature website: www.leg.wa.gov/LawsAndAgencyRules/constitution.htm.

Washington's "Race to the Top" proposal. October 2009. Retrieved May 14, 2010, from the Washington State Board of Education website: www.sbe.wa.gov/documents/091031%20WA%20RTT%20board%20presentation.pdf.

WASL/grades comparison. n.d. Retrieved April 3, 2008, from the Office of Superintendent of Public Instruction website: www.k12.wa.us/assessment/CAAoptions/Comparison.aspx.

Welcome to the Doing What Works website. n.d. Retrieved May 2, 2008, from the U.S. Department of Education Doing What Works website: http://dww.ed.gov/site/?c=1.

What is changing in math education? February 13, 1996. Retrieved March 9, 2008, from the Mathematically Correct website: http://mathematicallycorrect.com/what.htm.

What Works Clearinghouse (WWC). February 2009. WWC intervention report: *Investigations in Number, Data, and Space*. Retrieved June 17, 2010, from the Institute of Education Sciences What Works Clearinghouse website: http://ies.ed.gov/ncee/wwc/pdf/wwc_investigations_022409.pdf.

——. January 2010a. WWC intervention report: *Connected Mathematics Project*. Retrieved June 17, 2010, from the Institute of Education Sciences What Works Clearinghouse website: http://ies.ed.gov/ncee/wwc/pdf/wwc_cmp_012610.pdf.

——. April 2010b. WWC intervention report: *Saxon Math*. Retrieved April 20, 2010, from the Institute of Education Sciences What Works Clearinghouse website: http://ies.ed.gov/ncee/wwc/pdf/wwc_saxonmath_042010.pdf.

——. August 2010c. WWC quick review: Effects of teacher professional development on middle school math students. Retrieved September 19, 2010, from the Institute of Education Sciences What Works Clearinghouse website: http://ies.ed.gov/ncee/wwc/publications/quickreviews/QRReport.aspx?QRId=154

——. September 2010d. WWC intervention report: *Saxon Math*. Retrieved September 17, 2010, from the Institute of Education Sciences What Works Clearinghouse website: http://ies.ed.gov/ncee/wwc/reports/elementary_math/sesm/index.asp

Word, E., J. Johnston, H. P. Bain, B. D. Fulton, J. B. Zaharias, C. M. Achilles, M. N. Lintz, J. Folger, and C. Breda. 1990. Student/teacher achievement ratio (STAR), Tennessee's K–3 class size study: Final summary report, 1985–1990. Nashville: Tennessee State Department of Education. Retrieved September 9, 2010, from the Health and Education Research Operative Services website: www.heros-inc.org/summary.pdf.

Wößmann, L., and M. R. West. March 26, 2002. Class-size effects in school systems around the world: Evidence from between-grade variation in TIMSS. Retrieved March 5, 2008 from the Harvard University website: www.hks.harvard.edu/pepg/PDF/Papers/PEPG02-02.pdf.

ABOUT THE AUTHOR

Laurie Rogers has been a child advocate since 2001. She is the author of the Betrayed blog, located at http://betrayed-whyeducationisfailing. blogspot.com.

Laurie began her child-advocacy career by creating Safer Child Inc., a nonprofit, online, parent-information resource. In 2007, she narrowed her focus to K–12 public-education research, and in 2010, she founded Focus on the Square™, a nonprofit organization dedicated to improving American K–12 education.

Laurie has a bachelor's degree in mass communications and a master's degree in interpersonal communication, emphasizing the evaluation of argumentation and logic.

Having worked previously as a financial consultant, a journalist, and a public relations specialist, she now advocates on education issues and has volunteered in elementary schools, tutoring children in literacy and math, and teaching chess, argumentation and knitting.

Laurie lives in Spokane, Washington, with her husband, daughter, and two cats.

"In *Betrayed*, Rogers lays bare the fiction that is reform math. Until parents across this nation vest themselves with the information found in these pages, rise up against the edu-speak that keeps reform math in place, and insist that educators TEACH mathematics, the devastation of reform math will continue to shortcut the hopes and dreams of the nation's children."

—Dick Padrick, professional engineer, Washington State

"Laurie Rogers has aptly titled her book *Betrayed*. Millions of families in this country send their students off to school believing that their children will be carefully taught all they need to know to be successful in whichever future endeavor they choose to pursue. No one wants to believe that education decisions are often based more on failed ideology rather than scientifically proven, successful models of instruction. Yet, that is what is happening, and as a result, our graduates now lag the rest of the industrialized world in math and science achievement.

Read this book to find out how this has happened. You will feel betrayed by the public-education establishment."

—Laura Brandt, parent and cofounder of Where's the Math?

"*Betrayed* is one parent's firsthand account from the math wars at Spokane Public Schools in Washington State. This compelling portrayal reveals why public-education bureaucrats deliver such poor academic outcomes for students: (1) lack of school choices for parents, (2) lack of professional autonomy for teachers and school principals, (3) broken accountability systems, and (4) no lack of money."

—Liv Finne, director for education, Washington Policy Center

"*Betrayed* is a must read for every parent and citizen concerned about the quality of public education. Laurie Rogers informs the reader about key issues in public education, while she unmasks the methods used by school officials to marginalize any public criticism. Knowledge is power. Reading this book before you take on the local school board will save you a lot of time and pain, while empowering you to make a difference in the education of our children.

—Bob Dean, Math Department chairman, Evergreen High School; Washington State Board of Education Math Advisory Panel member; OSPI Standards Revision Team; Where's the Math? Executive Committee

"Laurie Rogers has written an important book—it has passion, it has direction, and it has hope. All ingredients of a good read, but the topic is too important for just emoting, and this book has evidence, defensible interpretations, and weaves together a story about the status and future of schooling in the United States.

There is much positive thinking throughout. Laurie Rogers recognizes a commitment to improvement, and she identifies four critical problems that should be the focus of our debates: teachers' ability to teach, curriculum, learning environment, and students' propensity to learn.

All is not doom and gloom, but a solid case is made for making what matters the topic of debate, for identifying a threshold of success to aim for, and for involving all in then seeing the effects."

—Dr. John Hattie, Faculty of Education, University of Auckland, New Zealand, and author of *Visible Learning*

"Laurie Rogers's thoroughly researched book *Betrayed: How the Education Establishment Has Betrayed America and What You Can Do about It* will open your eyes to a bewildering array of state and federal bureaucracies, tainted educational research, and government-influenced textbook publishing, which exert a controlling influence over local school districts. Local school officials, marching lockstep with state and federal politicians, are looking to a future of federally funded and federally controlled schools.

If you want local schools for your children and your community, you're going to have to fight for them. Laurie Rogers's book is loaded with information and insights, which you will find extremely useful in this fight."

—George Brown, teacher of mathematics, Spokane, Washington

"Through astonishing facts and statistics, Laurie paints a common-sense picture of why American public education is failing to produce a competitive population. Through her tireless research and commitment to unveiling the truth for our children and our future, she clearly delineates the strengths and weaknesses within the current system and how we got here, and she outlines what all of us need to do to begin making repairs.

This is a truth every parent and teacher must know for the sake of our kids and our nation."

—Breann Treffry, parent and school volunteer, Spokane, Washington

"We are taught to trust those in authority: the police on the corner, the doctor at the hospital, and the schools with our children's future. When one of these trusted entities makes a choice that is harmful to us or to our children, we feel angry, we feel cheated, and we feel betrayed.

Teachers and parents, prepare yourself to be amazed by the statistics showing that more than 90 percent of our high school graduates are unprepared for college entry-level math. You will be confused to find administrators and school boards continuing to support a curriculum that is failing our students. You will be angry when you read the responses to parent questions—responses of disdain, the runarounds and the lies from people entrusted with our children's education.

Laurie Rogers's *Betrayed* is a rare book with a message for any parent or teacher seeking to challenge or influence administrators and school boards. Rogers's words will inspire and empower all who read them to join her advocacy for a curriculum that truly provides students with the skills they need to be successful."

—Elementary school teacher (anonymous), Spokane, Washington

"Laurie's research leaves no stone unturned, no question unasked. Her documentation is meticulous and thorough and unique in its scope and depth. She writes eloquently in a clear and easily understandable style. Her conclusions are inescapable, surprising, and at times shocking.

Everyone should read this book to find out how desperately we need workable methods based on valid research for educating the children of our nation. We all have a great stake in this, for without a well-educated populace, democracy cannot survive. Our nation cannot prosper economically and globally without engineers, scientists, mathematicians, doctors, teachers, and knowledgeable parents.

One woman's desire to find answers has provided the rest of us with the knowledge to become wise and courageous champions of truly great and sound education for all."

—Burma P. Williams, retired mathematics teacher
and private tutor, Spokane, Washington

"Wow! If parents, grandparents, voters, teachers, and others concerned with American education read this book, maybe the realization that things aren't what they could be would hit home. This book points out in every way that we are losing ground. I fully endorse the book and applaud the author for the factual research and perseverance that went into the information that was compiled."

—Jim Harrison, forty-one-year teacher, Spokane, Washington

"Laurie sees administrators who know little about math making decisions on how to teach it; school board members voting merely to back up incompetent administrators; schools of education who indoctrinate future teachers in 'research-based' methodologies where the research meets no accepted standard of validity; school officials who support those methodologies even in the face of obvious evidence that they don't work. She notes the absurdity of 'differentiated instruction' and the nonsense of taking time away from instructing students and using it for 'professional development' that pushes ed schools' failed theories on teachers. She has an uncanny knack of highlighting the most fundamental causes of the failure of our public schools and their inability to prepare our children to compete on the world stage. It's critically important that people interested in reversing the decline in our educational system (and the corresponding decline in our country) read it and take heed!"

—Ted Nutting, High school math teacher, Seattle